W9-BNO-026

Advance Praise for
Kiss, Bow, or Shake Hands:
Sales and Marketing

"As today's global workplace becomes more competitive, *Kiss, Bow, or Shake Hands: Sales and Marketing* provides practical 'real world' examples on how to behave, interact, and communicate successfully while working internationally. A must have for all global marketers!"

—*Mary Ogle*
Head of Global Market Access, Sanofi Pharmaceuticals

"I'm a huge fan of *Kiss, Bow, or Shake Hands*. And now I can consult *Kiss, Bow, or Shake Hands: Sales and Marketing* before I head off to a new country—just to make sure I don't commit a faux pas, or make a fool of myself."

—*Johnny Jet*
Travel Personality and Founder of JohnnyJet.com

"With precise, down-to-earth, eye-opening comments, Terri Morrison builds—once again—the necessary bridges to understand different cultures . . . and avoid moves that can end up in embarrassment, if not disaster."

—*Marcelo Bombau, Partner, M. & M. Bomchil Abogados*
(The Law Firm of M. & M. Bomchil), Buenos Aires, Argentina

"In an increasingly globalized environment, the ability to understand how businesses work across cultures is vital for success. Most of the growth potential for U.S. companies lies in overseas markets, and *Kiss, Bow, or Shake Hands: Sales and Marketing* should be required reading for both students and practitioners of international business."

—*Kim Cahill*
Director, Institute of Global Management Studies
Fox School of Business, Temple University

"Terri Morrison does a consistently excellent job of making the cross-cultural jump understandable, interesting, and exciting. This newest *Kiss, Bow, or Shake Hands: Sales and Marketing* promises to be an excellent resource for anyone aspiring to do business abroad."

—*Brian Hirsch, Ed.D*
Director, Trinity Career Services, Trinity University

"The authors are able to look through their cultural lens and provide an in-depth and valuable overview of the entire spectrum of sales and marketing characteristics in G-20 countries. Essential for business travelers, students, and tourists alike if they are to avoid major "cultural collisions" or costly faux pas. Anyone thinking globally at any level should retain a copy of this book as a personal reference."

—*John J. Gerace, Ph.D., P.E.*
Executive Vice President, Energy Edge Technology

"Once again, Morrison has delivered the goods: an informative, current, and reliable guide that is also, mirabile dictu, a pleasure to read. Brava!"

—*Joanne St. John, Former President and Publisher,*
International Academy at Santa Barbara

"When traveling to different countries, people need be conscious of cultural differences, many of which are extremely subtle. When conducting business, you should be prepared for nuances that aren't obvious. *Kiss, Bow, or Shake Hands: Sales and Marketing* is an excellent manual for people working or traveling abroad. There's too much at risk to make faux pas that could be avoided and might very well kill a deal. Terri Morrison's book can demystify the ways others conduct business and more."

—*Karen Fawcett*
President, Paris New Media, LLC (bonjourparis.com)

"*Kiss, Bow, or Shake Hands* is the perfect supplement to my business communications courses: it introduces students to the concept that how we do it 'over here' isn't necessarily how they do it 'over there,' and being unaware of that basic fact can doom your cross-cultural business transactions. Students tell me it's the most important lesson they learn all semester."

—*Kris Swank*
Business Instructor, Northern Arizona University

"For years I've relied upon the *Kiss, Bow, or Shake Hands* book series, especially when entering new global markets. The latest *Sales and Marketing* edition includes very helpful and practical tips and information that every global marketer and sales professional can put to good use."

—*Joseph J. Douress*
Senior Vice President, Global Marketing,
Elsevier Global Medical Research

KISS, BOW, OR SHAKE HANDS:

SALES AND MARKETING

The Essential Cultural Guide—from Presentations and Promotions to Communicating and Closing

TERRI MORRISON AND WAYNE A. CONAWAY

New York   Chicago   San Francisco   Lisbon   London   Madrid   Mexico City
Milan   New Delhi   San Juan   Seoul   Singapore   Sydney   Toronto

1 2 3 4 5 6 7 8 9 10 11 12 13 14 15   QFR/QFR   1 9 8 7 6 5 4 3 2 1

ISBN   978-0-07-171404-4
MHID   0-07-171404-9

e-ISBN   978-0-07-171841-7
e-MHID   0-07-171841-9

Library of Congress Cataloging-in-Publication Data

Morrison, Terri.
    Kiss, bow, or shake hands: sales and marketing : the essential cultural
guide—from presentations and promotions to communicating and closing /
by Terri Morrison, Wayne A. Conaway.
        p.   cm.
    ISBN-13: 978-0-07-171404-4 (alk. paper)
    ISBN-10: 0-07-171404-9 (alk. paper)
    1. Business etiquette.   2. Business communication.   3. Intercultural
communication.   4. Marketing—Cross-cultural studies.   I. Conaway,
Wayne A.   II. Title.

HF5389.M674   2012
658.8—dc23   2011033642

Interior design by THINK Book Works

Homo sum, humani nihil a me alienum puto.
I am human, so nothing that is human is foreign to me.
—Terence

CONTENTS

FOREWORD

Greg Booth, CEO, Zippo

I love my job and suspect a good number of sales and marketing executives would love it too.

I am the president and CEO of Zippo, owner of one of the most highly recognized brand names in the world. When people hear the name Zippo, they invariably think of the iconic American-made lighters that have accompanied soldiers from World War II and Korea to Vietnam and Afghanistan. Campers around the world, concert-goers everywhere, and more than 450 million consumers have relied on Zippos for almost 80 years. Our brand strength is such that customers worldwide instantly recognize the distinctive "click" of our Zippo lighters.

But like any job, mine comes with its challenges as well as its rewards. Many publications write about us, and not just because we are a US company successfully competing in the global market. Our growth strategy—which includes product diversification—makes headlines. Our famous lighters, hand warmers, watches, sunglasses, and writing instruments will be joined by grills and outdoor gear in the near future.

One *Wall Street Journal* article in particular was relevant for multinational executives because it referred to the Zippo "Rippo" factor. Counterfeits and knockoffs have plagued our firm for years. Unscrupulous manufacturers constantly attempt to cash in on our global success by producing cheap imitations and selling them in markets where we are most popular. And since we offer one of the world's few lifetime

guarantees—if your Zippo lighter breaks, we'll fix it free—
these Rippos present a problem when they are sent in for
repair. *You* try and diplomatically deliver the bad news that
a consumer has purchased a fake, and you cannot fix it. It is
disappointing to all concerned. But when you sell more than
12 million Zippos annually, of course the Rippos will try to
infringe upon your market.

These types of situations are common for all salespeople.
They confront similar issues every day. How do you expand
your product line, enter new markets, and simultaneously
protect your brand? You have to be smart and adaptable. And
you have to research your market.

Bookstores are loaded with business guides that promise
success through a variety of sales and marketing techniques.
But selling internationally is more complicated than mastering
a few closing techniques or rising at 5:00 A.M. to consider currency fluctuations. Exporting involves complex variables for
the salesperson—including working with diverse cultures and
languages, unusual advertising regulations, politics, and even
religious and dietary taboos.

These are just a few reasons why *Kiss, Bow, or Shake
Hands: Sales and Marketing* can be so valuable. It combines
the cultural orientations of international clients with sales
techniques in each country. Everyone knows that if you want
to relate to your customer, you must do your research. *Kiss,
Bow, or Shake Hands: Sales and Marketing* can help you understand cross-cultural sales, beginning with the right and wrong
icebreakers from Argentina to the United Arab Emirates. Pick
this book up if you want to know how to pitch the product,
offer the right price, and bring the right gift. Find out whether
your prospect likes golf, rugby, or riding Harleys—and then
buy a Zippo customized with his or her favorite team's logo
emblazoned across it! (OK, it's a sales book, right?)

On a personal note, I was skiing with my family in Utah
last week, and out of the blue, one of my three sons mentioned
the original *Kiss, Bow, or Shake Hands* and how useful it has
been at his company. This particular son is a sales executive at
a very large firm, and you should have seen his jaw drop when

I told him his dad was writing the foreword to the new *Kiss, Bow, or Shake Hands: Sales and Marketing* book! I am telling you, it was priceless. Many say there are no coincidences in this world, and up on that mountain, I believed it.

It is my pleasure to introduce you to the cultural sales issues that differ between Canada and China, Italy and India, and even the United Kingdom and the United States of America. Be ready. Read *Kiss, Bow, or Shake Hands: Sales and Marketing.*

PREFACE

As Greg Booth stated in the foreword, bookstores are loaded with business guides. Often they focus on classical marketing and sales techniques (product, price, promotion, etc.). These very important basics are an excellent start, but they rarely touch the vast cultural differences you will encounter in China, Brazil, India, or Russia. How do you know whether you should negotiate aggressively or if your clients will never say no? Will they expect a gift, or will it be considered graft?

Kiss, Bow, or Shake Hands: Sales and Marketing focuses specifically on the intercultural aspects of marketing and selling your products around the world. What are the best ways to break the ice in the United Arab Emirates? What are the three top sales tips to know when you approach Russian, Japanese, or Italian prospects? Your goal is not just to close one sale, but to gain a loyal client who trusts and relies on you for more than simple business advice. Your goal is to become a credible resource and a trusted friend.

Although the world is more connected than ever, cultural differences are still a reality. Actually, the Internet may be speeding up the rate of intercultural-communications difficulties. A taboo subject will not just stop an individual sale anymore; it may preclude an entire country from viewing your site. Google is keenly aware that governments will prohibit access to them for being culturally or politically offensive. For example, more than a billion consumers have been blocked from seeing Google and its applications (YouTube, Blogger, and Orkut) in these countries:

- China (for permitting access to content that the Chinese government deems politically incorrect)
- United Arab Emirates and Saudi Arabia (for sites with content banned under Islam)
- Turkey (for content that insulted Kemal Atatürk, the founder of Turkey)

Inadvertently selecting the wrong website layout, the wrong sales approach, or the wrong advertising hook can result in lost market share. The information in *Kiss, Bow, or Shake Hands: Sales and Marketing* will help you prevent those missteps. Sometimes what sinks you is the identity element—perhaps something as innocuous and universally beloved as a dog. Animals are incredibly popular in advertisements, from the Geico gecko and Taco Bell's Chihuahua to Toyota's boxer named Buddy (in South Africa). But animals (particularly dogs) are not always just mascots. You may still find dog on the menu in China or South Korea (although it was temporarily banned during the Olympics to avoid bad publicity). In other countries, images of dogs may not be appropriate marketing or design choices for different reasons. A US real estate executive was surprised when he cheerfully offered his business cards at a conference in the Arabian Gulf and saw that they evoked grimaces rather than grins. Why? Because his card featured a sizable portrait of him and his devoted dog (a vizsla). Dogs are considered unclean in much of the Middle East and would not be included on business collateral.

Understanding your client is a basic tenet of sales training, and it should include understanding his or her cultural, linguistic, political, and religious viewpoints. As in our first *Kiss, Bow, or Shake Hands* book, each chapter is organized into a consistent framework. After a few introductory demographics, we move to these sections:

Icebreakers: Brilliant questions or topics to start a meeting—and boorish moves that may bring your meeting to a swift end

What Time Should I Arrive? Perceptions of time and appropriate ways to handle delays

Workweek: Typical appointment times, paid vacation days, and holidays

How Close Should I Stand? Comfortable distances between people in business and social settings

Do I Kiss, Bow, or Shake Hands? Forms of greeting

Business Cards: How to handle a two-dimensional extension of you

Three Tips for Selling: Three important aspects of selling, including controversial issues to watch out for and bits of knowledge that can impress your prospects

Language: Important aspects of the official language(s) in each country and useful foreign phrases

Wow Factor! A special bit of data to close the chapter—and, we hope, your sale

And just as in the original *Kiss, Bow, or Shake Hands*, there are Cultural Notes throughout each chapter, covering everything and anything that will help your sales and marketing process in 20 countries. In addition, you will find notes specifically on sales and advertising.

At the end of the book, we've added a couple of appendices: one on dining etiquette (in a quiz format) and one on international trade. We hope you find them valuable as well as entertaining.

Times change, but cultural sensitivity and professional behavior are more important than ever. World markets are highly competitive, and every bit of research that may help you is worth gathering. It is our desire to continue to provide that extra bit of cultural knowledge, that edge which we hope will add to your success in the global marketplace.

There is a saying in Arabic:

Al kitabu yuqra'a min inwanihi.
The meaning of a book can be judged from its title.

Welcome to *Kiss, Bow, or Shake Hands: Sales and Marketing.*

ACKNOWLEDGMENTS

We are profoundly grateful to all the individuals, companies, governmental entities, and universities that have helped with the research for this book. In particular, we'd like to thank Joanna Savvides, Beth Pomper, Kim Willing, Staci Frantz, Tina Weyant, Giuseppe Pezzotti, Gustavo Espina, PJ Delaye, Nick Santoleri, Michael Cordier, Tony Macaluso, Jorge Cantero, and all the wonderful contributors who are named—and unnamed—in each chapter. Your help and insight are deeply appreciated.

I would also like to thank Gary Krebs, vice president of McGraw-Hill Professional, for this book. *Kiss, Bow, or Shake Hands: Sales and Marketing* was his idea. He is a true professional in a tough industry. Many thanks, Gary. What's next?

Special thanks to the libraries and librarians who have hosted both Wayne and me throughout nine manuscripts. In an increasingly digitized world, it's nice to be able to sit somewhere, surrounded by books.

And to all the readers who found the first *Kiss, Bow, or Shake Hands* of value. Thank you! We hope you find this new *Kiss, Bow* a worthwhile reference too.

*¡Muchas gracias! Merci beaucoup! Gamsahamnida!
Xie Xie! Mille grazie! Imela, yâuwá, Na gode, N'le!
Spasiba! Muito obrigado! Shukran!
Danke schöen! Teşekkür ederim! Arigato-gozaimasu!*

ARGENTINA

Conventional long form: Argentine Republic

Local long form: República Argentina

Local short form: Argentina

Population: 41,769,726 (2011 estimate)

Median age: 30.5 years

Age structure: (2011 estimates)
    0–14 years: 25.4%
    15–64 years: 63.6%
    65 years and over: 11.0%

GDP per capita (PPP): $14,700 (2010 estimated in US dollars)

Suffrage: 18 years old; universal and compulsory

Legal drinking age: 18 years old

Advertising Note

As in most countries, the most popular advertisements in Argentina often use humor, children, or animals—or any combination of the three. However, advertisements that highlight both the intellect and the artistry of Argentineans are very well received, even if they are for a beverage. The soft drink H2O developed a commercial that combined a family meal with comments about tango, rock music, risotto, and neurosurgery—all in one advertisement (http://www.bestadsontv.com/ad/33544/H2Oh-Braids). The ad was effective because it showcased a young man making a good impression on his girlfriend's family by addressing the individual interests of each person in a gently humorous way. Hence, smooth operators drink H2O.

ICEBREAKERS

BRILLIANT!

1. Argentina is the second largest country in South America, but according to the World Bank's 2009 statistics, it has only 40.3 million people, and the vast majority live in urban areas. Professional networks in the cities are strong, active, and so tightly woven that Argentina can feel like a small country. Everyone seems to know everyone else.

   Gustavo Espina, vice president of a Fortune 500 global travel services firm—and a native Argentinean—offered this perspective on breaking the ice in Buenos Aires:

   > In Buenos Aires, as soon as you introduce yourself, the conversation often leads to how you and your associate may be connected to each other—to mutual friends or shared interests. For example, if your prospect has a prominent family name, it would be helpful if you were familiar with it and could ask a question like "Thank you for seeing me, Señor Borges (or San Martin, or Saavedra

Lamas). Would you be any relation to the famous author, statesman, or Nobel laureate?"

Discussing the major universities in Argentina also is a reasonable way to find a connection. Three notable institutions include the highly regarded University of Buenos Aires (UBA)—Argentina's largest public, completely free, university; the Universidad Católica Argentina (UCA), a private, smaller institution; and Universidad de San Andrés, an exclusive, private university. Each institution has its own particular assets, and a conversation about different alumni you may know and the sports they may have played (rugby, soccer, polo, golf, etc.) can give you a solid opening for your first meeting.

2. Argentina's naming conventions are unique in South America. If you are given a business card that says, "Señor Juan Ruiz Martinez," you might say:

"Encantado a conocerle, Señor Ruiz Martinez."
"It is a pleasure to meet you, Señor Ruiz Martinez."

Or you might say:

"Encantado a conocerle, Señor Martinez."
"It is a pleasure to meet you, Señor Martinez."

Either response demonstrates that you understand one major difference between Argentina and all the rest of Spanish-speaking Latin America. Instead of assuming that the father's surname is listed first, you know that the father's side of the family may have two surnames, which is why you might say "Señor Ruiz Martinez." Alternately, the father's name may come last. But in every other Spanish-speaking country, from Bolivia to Venezuela, one's mother's name is last. In that case, Señor Ruiz Martinez would be addressed as Señor Ruiz.

BOORISH

1. Never take offense at being offered a cigarette or cigar, or be disturbed by someone smoking nearby. Argentina and its neighbor Chile have the highest rates of smoking in South America. Despite antismoking efforts, more than a third of Argentine adults still smoke. Additionally, about 25 percent of Argentine teenagers smoke.

   Cigarette companies no longer advertise on Argentine radio or television. They rely on billboards, kiosks, and magazine ads. A survey of 120 convenience stores in Buenos Aires found that all the stores sold cigarettes, and most had the cigarettes in proximity to candy (although cigarette sales to minors are prohibited). Eighty percent of the stores had cigarette point-of-sale advertisements, regardless of the socioeconomic status of the neighborhood.

2. Don't try to adhere to an agenda bullet by bullet or attempt to force a close quickly. Argentineans generally approach topics in a diffuse manner, and avoid risky investments. They tend to examine issues and people from different angles. Personal inquiries demonstrate an interest in the relationship, so never rebuff a question, and never refuse invitations for social events. Let your agenda be driven by your Argentinean contact.

   In their book *Riding the Waves of Culture: Understanding Diversity in Global Business*, authors Fons Trompenaars and Charles Hampden-Turner reported how a Swedish company closed a contract with an Argentine firm—and trounced its US competitor. The Swedes spent their first five days of a weeklong trip simply getting to know the prospect. Only then were the Argentineans willing to talk about business. The US executives allocated only two days for their entire trip and tried to force the Argentineans to negotiate on their schedule. They failed. The Argentineans signed with the Swedes, even though the US company may have had the superior product.

   Another possible reason why the Swedes won was that their negotiating style can be opaque. They believe that "information is power," so they never reveal too much data at once. Not disclosing every detail of their thoughts or their agenda may have proven advantageous in this case.

WHAT TIME SHOULD I ARRIVE?

As a foreigner, you are expected to be prompt. However, punctuality has not been a traditional virtue in Argentina, so do not be surprised if your counterpart is late.

Different rules apply to social events. At parties or dinner, even foreigners are expected to be 30 minutes late. If you are unsure whether you should be prompt, ask, *"En punto?"* ("On the dot?") Of course, you must be prompt for events with a scheduled start time, like sporting events or the theater.

WORKWEEK

The workweek runs Monday through Friday.

Argentine executives are very competitive and often have a long workday. Some routinely work until 10:00 P.M. You might be given an appointment scheduled for an hour that seems unusually late.

In 2011, Argentina had 17 official holidays (which may or may not be paid). In addition, there are minimum requirements for annual paid vacations, based on length of service:

After 1 year	14 days minimum paid vacation
After 5 years	21 days
After 10 years	28 days
After 20 years	35 days

HOW CLOSE SHOULD I STAND?

Stand 1 to 1½ feet from the person with whom you're speaking. Argentineans are not as tactile as some other Latin Americans, but do not be surprised if your associate touches your arm during a conversation.

Argentineans may converse at a closer distance once the discussion becomes more animated. Their doing so demonstrates interest and greater comfort with physical proximity. Be certain not to back away, since it may be interpreted as a rebuff.

DO I KISS, BOW, OR SHAKE HANDS?

SHAKE HANDS

At an initial business meeting, Argentine men offer a brief handshake and a nod to other men. However, if the men are friends, they will also engage in a back-thumping embrace called an *abrazo*. This may be accompanied by a handshake, or it may be bracketed by handshakes at the beginning and end.

Men will also shake hands with women. If they are friends or are being introduced by a friend, they will kiss one cheek. Some Argentine men kiss other men (parents, good friends) on the cheek.

Women generally gently shake hands with other women at an initial business meeting. If they are friends, women exchange kisses on the cheek, even in a business context.

Of equal importance as the handshake is direct eye contact during the greeting. Eye contact conveys trustworthiness; averting one's eyes indicates deception. This eye contact is maintained during one-on-one conversations (which, since they are conducted at such close quarters, may strike some foreigners as uncomfortably intense).

BUSINESS CARDS

- There is no formal Argentine tradition involving the exchange of business cards. However, treat all business cards you receive with respect.
- Your cards should be formatted in advance with Spanish on one side and your native language on the other.

THREE TIPS FOR SELLING IN ARGENTINA

1. Tact
2. Malbec and Beef
3. A Leader of Latin America

1. TACT

Argentineans avoid conflict. Knowing what to say in Argentina is important, but so is knowing what not to say. One thing that makes this difficult is that, in the process of getting to know you, Argentineans will ask your opinion on many topics, including what you think of your country, your country's government, and your country's policies.

Obviously, you want to avoid offending your Argentine counterparts by supporting something to which they may object. For example, if you are from the United States, you should avoid the subject of US support for Israel, since Argentina recognized Palestinian statehood in 2010. There are several other geopolitical details you should be aware of as well. Argentina fought a war in 1982 with the United Kingdom over the Malvinas Islands (never call them the Falkland Islands!), and relations with the United Kingdom remain troubled to this day. Argentine claims over parts of Antarctica also overlap those of several other nations; know whether your country is one of the rival claimants, so you can diplomatically avoid the topic, should it arise. Also, if you do business with Chileans, don't advertise it on your products. Argentina and Chile have had rivalries in the past, and it may not be advantageous for your product to broadcast Chile as its country of origin. (For instance, one company placed the Chilean flag on wine shipped to Argentina, and the wine did not sell well.) While most disagreements between Argentina and Chile are in the past, it is not helpful to compare sports teams, wines, economies, or politics. (Although it may be hard to avoid noting that Chile and Argentina have simultaneously had female presidents, an unusual circumstance in South America.)

Many Argentineans believe they should know the right answer to any question. Perhaps because so much of the population is highly educated, intelligent and convincing responses are valued. The actual query doesn't matter—it can be something as mundane as knowing correct directions—the importance lies in a cogent, thoughtful reply. Of course, if your prospect is wrong, never expose his or her mistake in public.

2. MALBEC AND BEEF

There is no doubt that you will benefit from knowing about two of Argentina's world-renowned products: the country's signature wine, called Malbec, and grass-fed beef.

Malbec is Argentina's remarkable deep red wine. The first Malbec vines were imported in the 1800s from the Cahors region of France, where the grapes were blended with darker Tannat grapes to produce the "Black Wine of Cahors."

Malbec vines flourished in Argentina's dry heat and cool, high altitudes. They became exceptionally productive, particularly in Argentina's northern Mendoza region. Vineyards are planted there, on average, around 3,300 feet above sea level. Argentinean winemakers sometimes compete to have the highest vineyards, and will print their exact altitudes on their labels. One winery in the Andes is planted at more than 9,000 feet above sea level, which makes it the highest commercial vineyard in the world!

The higher you go, the more aromatic and fresher the wine is said to become. Connoisseurs can identify the vineyard where Malbec originates by the character of the wine, which is tied to its altitude. Malbec's dry fruit and spice aromas are considered a perfect complement to Argentina's other specialty—beef.

Demonstrating an appreciation for prime Argentine beef is very useful during a business meal. An *asado* (selection of grilled meats) is an Argentinean staple and can include beef, lamb, and vegetables. The cattle are grass-fed on the pampas and develop a unique flavor based upon their diet, their muscle tone, and the percentage of fat marbleized throughout the

Cultural Note

As in many countries, sports are a popular topic of conversation in Argentina, and famous sports figures are often sought after for commercial endorsements. Football (soccer) is Argentina's biggest sport. The Argentine national team has won two FIFA World Cups, two Olympic gold medals, and many other international titles.

The second most popular sport (tied with auto racing) is basketball. The men's national team has won several important events, including the gold at the 2004 Olympics. Many Argentineans play in the NBA.

Other important sports include rugby, tennis, polo, and golf.

However, the official national sport of Argentina is none of the above; it's a rather obscure sport called *pato*. *Pato* uses a ball with six handles on it; players on horseback try to grab the ball and throw it through a hoop. While *pato* is not overly popular, it is Argentina's only indigenous sport, which is why it was declared the national game in 1953. *Pato* now has players in Europe and the United States, where it is better known as horseball.

meat. Everyone, from executives to tourists, enjoys *asados* in top restaurants throughout Argentina.

Excellent restaurants abound in Buenos Aires, particularly in the Puerto Madero district, the Recoleta, and the Palermo area. If you do business in Buenos Aires, you go out to eat, so expect a selection of *medallion de lomo* (tenderloin), *ojo de bife* (rib-eye), and an array of sausages and sweetbreads—all grilled to perfection.

If possible, take a walk (*dar un paseo*) on a Sunday around 12:30 or 1:00 P.M. The fragrance of hundreds of *asados* on home grills wafts throughout the city and makes Buenos Aires live up to its name.

3. A LEADER OF LATIN AMERICA

Buenos Aires has long been known as the Paris of South America. This designation is quite fitting, as Argentineans consider their country to be a leading nation in Latin America. Argentina has produced a number of famous and accomplished citizens. It can be helpful to be familiar with each of these prominent Argentine names:

- Jorge Luis Borges (1899–1986): Recognized as Argentina's foremost author of the 20th century.
- Diego Maradona (1960–): Football player and coach; considered by most Argentineans to be the greatest footballer of all time.
- Astor Piazolla (1921–1992): Musician and composer; took tango music in a new and controversial direction, which became known as *nuevo tango*.
- Manuel Puig (1932–1990): Author who spent much of his life in exile but is well known due to stage and film versions of his novel *Kiss of the Spider Woman*.
- José de San Martin (1778–1850): Founding father; known as the Protector of the South; led the independence movement that freed the region from Spanish control.
- Mercedes Sosa (1935–2009): Folk singer; well known throughout Latin America and Europe. Her socially conscious songs earned her the title the Voice of the Voiceless Ones.

To date, five Argentineans have received a Nobel Prize:

- Carlos Saavedra Lamas (1878–1959): Lawyer; 1936 Nobel Peace Prize
- Bernardo Alberto Houssay (1887–1971): Scientist; 1947 Nobel Prize in Medicine
- Luia Federico Leloir (1906–1987): Chemist; 1970 Nobel Prize in Chemistry
- Adolpho Pérez Esquivel (1931–): Architect and sculptor; 1980 Nobel Peace Prize
- César Milstein (1927–): Biochemist; 1984 Nobel Prize in Medicine

Cultural Note

The Argentine cowboy, called the gaucho, is the idealized hero of rural Argentina. In Argentine mythology, the gaucho is independent yet loyal, fearless in battle but generous in peace. A favor or an act of generosity can be called a *gauchada*.

Another important cultural component of Argentine tradition is *mate*, a brew derived from a local plant poured in a small, bowl-like receptacle from which people drink in shorts sips—all from the same wood or metallic straw. Although it is not common in a business atmosphere, it is a normal sign of friendship and sharing in social situations.

LANGUAGE

Argentina's official language is Spanish, but it is distinctive on the continent because it has been heavily influenced by Italian. Nearly two million Argentineans are bilingual in English, and there are many German and French speakers as well.

Here are a few phrases that may help you in Argentina. A variety of free Spanish-language programs are also offered through the BBC at http://www.bbc.co.uk/languages.

ENGLISH	SPANISH
How are you?	*¿Cómo está?*
What is your name?	*¿Cómo se llama?*
My name is . . .	*Me llamo . . .*
Good morning.	*Buenos días.*
Good afternoon.	*Buenas tardes.*
Good evening.	*Buenas noches.*
Hello.	*Hola.*
Good-bye.	*Adiós.*

ENGLISH	SPANISH
Please.	*Por favor.*
Thank you.	*Gracias.*
See you later.	*Hasta luego.*
Excuse me.	*Perdóname. / Disculpe.*
Do you speak English?	*¿Habla ingles?*
What is it called in Spanish?	*¿Cómo se llama esto en español?*
Where is . . . ?	*¿Dónde está . . . ?*
How much is it?	*¿Cuánto cuesta?*
I'm sorry, I don't understand.	*Lo siento, no entiendo.*
I would like . . .	*Quisiera . . .*
. . . a glass of wine.	*. . . una copa de vino.*
. . . a beer.	*. . . una cerveza.*
. . . a coffee.	*. . . un café.*
. . . a tea.	*. . . un té.*
. . . fruit juice.	*. . . un jugo.*
. . . water.	*. . . agua.*

WOW FACTOR!

Ever since the Argentine economic crisis of 1999 to 2002, most citizens have avoided using their banks as much as possible. Instead, those who have the means send their savings out of the country and convert it into euros or US dollars.

As you develop your proposals and contracts in Argentina, be prepared to offer creative financing options. Your product or service will look far more attractive if you provide alternatives to Argentina's banking or mortgage financing institutions. Because of prior economic calamities, most Argentineans are fiscally savvy and will welcome your pecuniary alternatives.

AUSTRALIA

Conventional long form: Commonwealth of Australia

Conventional short form: Australia

Population: 21,766,711 (2011 estimate)

Median age: 37.7 years

Age structure: (2011 estimates)
    0–14 years: 18.3%
    15–64 years: 67.7%
    65 years and over: 14%

GDP per capita (PPP): $41,300 (2010 estimated in US dollars)

Suffrage: 18 years old; universal and compulsory

Legal drinking age: 18 years old

Sales Management Note

Sociologists consider Australia to have a highly individualistic culture. That knowledge can be helpful in sales management. Surveys have found that Australian sales executives prefer autonomy, along with fewer controls and greater flexibility in their sales approach. They also appreciate individually based rewards, such as sales contests. The best incentive may be a combination of cash and a trip for two—as long as the winners do not have to travel with their supervisors.

ICEBREAKERS

BRILLIANT!

1. Australians jokingly refer to sports as their national religion. Naturally, sports make a good topic of conversation. You can divide Australian sports into activities and spectator sports. Many Aussies have a favorite activity: they play tennis or golf, cycle, surf, swim, hike, or go boating on a regular basis. (You should, too, when you go to Australia. Expect to be asked, "What's your sport?") Spectator sports, ranked by popularity, range from Australian-rules football—the most popular—to horse racing, rugby, cricket, and football (soccer). Remember also that Sydney hosted the Summer Olympics in 2000.

2. It's a big country, so be aware of the distances between population centers. Australia's 22 million people are concentrated in coastal cities; the interior is sparsely inhabited. Australia is large enough to span three time zones. Questions about travel times or a distribution network will show that you have some appreciation of the country's size.

   Here's an illustration of how big the country is: the massive flooding in northeast Australia that started during Christmas 2010 flooded an area the size of France and Germany combined!

BOORISH

1. Don't blather on or show off your knowledge. Aussies respond negatively to wordiness and pretension—and are vocal in their willingness to attack it. Even a former prime minister, Paul Keating, berated a fellow well-spoken politician, saying that the man "swallowed a [expletive deleted] dictionary when he was about 15." Don't be too intrusive, either; Australians are open-minded but value their privacy.

2. Be aware of some of Australia's current problems—and whether your native country caused any of them. For example, Australia has disputes with illegal immigrants who come by boat. The current crop of immigrants is largely from Afghanistan—and probably wouldn't be trying to escape their home country if the United States hadn't led an invasion of Afghanistan. Australia has also had quarrels with France (over French nuclear testing in the South Pacific) and China (over Chinese purchases of large Australian industries). The majority of Australians are descendants of immigrants from the United Kingdom and tend to have a love-hate relationship with their erstwhile homeland.

WHAT TIME SHOULD I ARRIVE?

Promptness in business situations is very important in Australia. You are expected to arrive on time or early for appointments; being late conveys disinterest and disrespect. Nevertheless, the anti-authoritarian attitude of some Australians sometimes manifests itself in tardiness. This is particularly difficult if you are employing Australians. Some employers claim that, in order to get an employee to be prompt, you must show an employee why being late causes problems.

Different rules apply to social events. It's important to be on time to small gatherings or dinners, whereas at larger parties or barbecues, the timing is a bit more relaxed (although you should not be more than 15 minutes late).

Advertising Note

In both Australia and the United Kingdom, several generations have grown up spreading a certain yeast product on their toast. Australians call theirs Vegemite, and the British call theirs Marmite; both are by-products of beer brewing.

In 1922, the Fred Walker Cheese Company of Melbourne tried to find a way to use the nutrition-rich yeast left over from beer brewing. The company created a yeast concentrate with vegetable flavoring that people found palatable. To publicize the new product, in 1923 the company offered a prize of 50 Australian pounds for the best name. The name Vegemite won, and the product eventually became iconic in Australia. However, achieving that status took years of marketing. The name Vegemite was changed several times. The product was promoted for its health benefits, included in rations for Australian soldiers in the Second World War, and given away free with the purchase of processed cheese.

Vegemite has often been added to cheese sandwiches, so the company marketed a combination cream cheese and Vegemite spread in 2009 under the name iSnack 2.0 (presumably to capitalize on the popularity of the iPhone and similar products). Negative reaction to the name was so strong that within four days of the release, a company spokesman admitted the name was a mistake. Consumers were then invited to vote on a new name online, and the company eventually announced that the winner was Vegemite Cheesybite.

Despite Vegemite's iconic status in Australia, it is no longer an Australian-owned food; it is owned by US multinational Kraft. Vegemite's main local competitor, Promite, was bought in 1967 by the privately owned US candy company Mars International.

WORKWEEK

The workweek runs Monday through Friday in Australia. Although the official workweek is 36.6 hours, Australian executives often work more than 40 hours a week.

Business breakfasts are commonplace, as are early morning appointments.

In 2011 Australia had 15 official holidays (some fell on weekends). In addition to those holidays, workers with 10 years' tenure could receive 20 paid vacation days.

HOW CLOSE SHOULD I STAND?

Between 2½ and 3 feet apart. Don't crowd an Aussie. By and large, you don't need to come any closer than handshake distance.

DO I KISS, BOW, OR SHAKE HANDS?

SHAKE HANDS

Australian men will offer a firm, brief handshake to other men. Men often wait to see if a woman extends her hand before offering to shake. Women may shake hands or not, at their discretion. In a business context, women usually offer to shake hands both with men and with other women.

Of equal importance is direct eye contact during the handshake. Eye contact conveys trustworthiness; averting one's eyes indicates deception.

BUSINESS CARDS

- There is no Australian tradition involving the exchange of business cards. However, treat all business cards you receive with respect.
- Your cards should be formatted in advance with English on one side and your native language on the other.
- Do not be insulted if someone does not offer you a business card. Not all Australians feel the need to have a card.

Cultural Note

In their book *Managing Across Cultures* authors Charlene M. Solomon and Michael S. Schell identify Australians as extremely tolerant of change—more so than people in the United Kingdom, United States, or New Zealand.

Change has been relatively good to Australians, and they see little reason to fear it. Perhaps this is because their national ethos is that of a people who live in a poor, harsh environment and whose life has gotten progressively better over the years (save for a few economic downturns and natural disasters).

THREE TIPS FOR SELLING IN AUSTRALIA

1. Convenience
2. Egalitarianism
3. Multicultural Australia

1. CONVENIENCE

Australians have a reputation for having a laid-back, "no worries, mate!" culture. However, this does not extend to Australian consumer behavior. Australians demand efficient and prompt customer service, preferably 24 hours a day. They hate waiting in line for anything. Twenty-four-hour convenience stores that also offer gasoline (or petrol) and ATMs are common.

Online shopping is becoming increasingly popular—particularly a relatively new option, online mega-malls. Westfield .com is an example of a mega-mall website that bundles hundreds of disparate stores together with one streamlined transaction and one consolidated shipping charge. This offers an effective solution for efficient Australian shoppers.

It is quite possible that the "no worries, mate" attitude has more to do with anti-authoritarianism than a relaxed attitude toward time. Certainly, Australians who interact with polychronic cultures report high levels of frustration. (People from polychronic cultures have a flexible attitude toward time management and are comfortable with overlapping tasks and multiple interruptions.) Most Australian executives are monochronic and have a more orderly, precise attitude toward time management. They would rather address things in a linear, step-by-step manner, and they appreciate obtaining the items they need with a relatively small investment of their time.

2. EGALITARIANISM

As everyone knows, the dominant culture in Australia originated in 1788 as a British penal colony. (Australia's Aboriginal population had already been present for some six thousand years at that point.) For decades, the British looked down upon Australians, even after the majority of Aussies were no longer descended from former prisoners. This attitude helped foster Australians' belief that they were a classless society. Isolated in a harsh environment, Aussies viewed the United Kingdom with both anger and nostalgia: England was a place where life was better, and from where they had been cast out.

During the Second World War, thousands of Allied soldiers were imprisoned by the Japanese in extremely harsh conditions. The Australian mythology about the camps is this: the British prisoners preserved their class structure to the end. The Americans divided into haves and have-nots; some of them became successful capitalists, even if all they had to sell was rice. But the Australians banded together, officers and enlisted men alike, and helped each other. Whether or not this is true, this belief in Australian "fair go" egalitarianism—what some call "mateship"—remains important to this day.

Advertisers can use this sense of egalitarianism to market products and services. But it is also important to make sure you do not run afoul of this philosophy, especially if your product is upscale. For instance, in Australia, a single male passenger is expected to sit in front with a male cab driver. To sit in back implies that you consider the cab driver your servant—and may incite your driver to give you a lecture on Aussie etiquette. (A single woman is not required to sit up front with a male cabbie.)

3. MULTICULTURAL AUSTRALIA

In the old homogeneous Australia, everyone who participated in the economy was descended from England, Scotland, or Ireland. (The Aboriginal population was not a major influence on the economy.) Today Australia is a multicultural nation of some 22 million people. After the Second World War, immigrants came from all over Europe, especially Italy, Greece, and Yugoslavia. Once the "White Australia Only" policy was ended in 1973, immigration from Asia and the Middle East soared. Today, about 15 percent of Australians do not speak English at home; the most common foreign tongues are Italian, Greek, Arabic, and Cantonese. Australia's original inhabitants, the Aborigines, currently number under a half-million people, some of whom still speak a variety of aboriginal languages.

How does this multiculturalism affect sales and marketing? A cross-cultural study asked mothers why they chose presents for their children. White Australian mothers admitted that presents made their children happy and led them to love the gift givers. In contrast, first-generation Chinese and Vietnamese immigrants reported the educational value of their gifts, which they hoped would make their children more successful. It is hard to find more divergent reasons for gift giving, yet advertising targeted at both groups must satisfy the goals of both.

LANGUAGE

Spelling in Australian English tends toward British spelling, but some words are spelled in the American manner. For example, the Australian Labor Party spells its name following the American pattern, not the British *Labour*. Australians usually write *program* and *jail* instead of the British *programme* and *gaol*. However, there is no Australian spelling authority, and both spellings can be found.

Sales Note

Australians elected their first female prime minister, Julia Gillard, in June 2010. Nevertheless, most researchers categorize Australia as having a "masculine" society (ranking it close to that of Great Britain and the United States). In regard to consumer behavior, cultural anthropologist Geert Hofstede identifies the following characteristics of masculine societies:

- Family purchasing is divided by gender: men buy the cars, and women buy the food.
- Couples believe that each partner needs an automobile.
- The status of purchases is important.
- Readers tend toward nonfiction over fiction.

Sometimes Australian English diverges from both UK and US usage. In speaking of what is called a sidewalk in the United States and a pavement in the United Kingdom, Australians usually refer to a *footpath*.

Be sure to have all marketing materials proofread by a native Australian. Using too many US spellings can cause negative feelings toward your product or service at times when Australians are unhappy with the United States.

WOW FACTOR!

In addition to sports played internationally, several sports have been developed in Australia. Australian-rules football is the best known of these, but there are others:

- **Australian handball:** This is a game that looks like squash or racquetball—but without the racket.
- **Campdrafting:** In this stockman's sport, a man on horseback cuts out a cow from a herd and guides it along a predetermined path.

- **Trugo (also spelled TruGo):** Invented by railroad workers in the 1920s, this sport is played on an outdoor pitch. It involves flung mallets and a target made of a rubber ring. Trugo clubs once were highly popular around Melbourne, but today they are closing down for lack of members.
- **Vigoro:** Although invented by an Englishman, this sport is most popular in Australia. It resembles both cricket and baseball, and is primarily played by women.

Advertisers who are looking for images that are uniquely Australian—and who wish to appeal to a sports-loving public—might consider using (or resuscitating) these sports.

Conventional long form: Federative Republic of Brazil

Local long form: República Federativa do Brasil

Local short form: Brasil

Population: 203,429,773 (2011 estimate)

Median age: 29.3 years

Age structure: (2011 estimates)
0–14 years: 26.2%
15–64 years: 67%
65 years and over: 6.7%

GDP per capita (PPP): $10,900 (2010 estimated in US dollars)

Suffrage: Voluntary between 16 and 18 years old and over 70. Compulsory over 18 and under 70. Military conscripts do not vote.

Legal drinking age: 18 years old

Advertising Note

If you would like to inspire rapture in Brazil, weave the "beautiful game" (soccer) into your pitch. Incorporate the spirit of *joga bonito* (play beautifully) in your ads. Nike developed this concept by showing the Brazilian national team playing together before a game. The entire commercial was set to Sergio Mendez's classic samba "Mas que Nada" accompanied by the Black Eyed Peas. You can watch it on YouTube (http://www.youtube.com/watch?v=fRHtq2DTdhk).

ICEBREAKERS

BRILLIANT!

1. Brazil is projected to become the world's fifth-largest economy by the latter half of the decade, surpassing Great Britain and France. Its demographics are young, its natural resources are immense, and its democratic government is stable. *Brasileiros* (Brazilians) are proud of their country and justifiably thrilled about hosting the pending 2014 World Cup and the 2016 Olympics. If you are somewhat familiar with "the beautiful game" *futebol* (soccer), you are welcome to ask questions about it. However, be aware that most *Brasileiros* are *futebol* fanatics, and compared with them, you will have basically no knowledge of the game. Act accordingly.

2. While there may be far less small talk at the beginning of a meeting in São Paulo than in Rio de Janeiro, you should still open with a few comments about the traffic (a common reason for being late), the successful economy, or local cultural events. In Rio, you may ask more extensive questions of your prospect; good general topics include his or her professional career, education, family, etc. The intent is for you to find common ground, some topic around which you can build an alliance. Such topics may include

places you have both visited, sports you have both played, and so on.

BOORISH

1. Avoid comparing sports teams (particularly between Brazil and Argentina). Despite an abysmal performance the night before, an innocuous comment about a team's lack of skill may prove dangerous if your prospect is even marginally related to one of the players! There are more than 29,000 clubs in Brazil registered with FIFA (the Fédération Internationale de Football Association) and millions of registered players across the country. Competitions are organized by the Brazilian Football Confederation, which also administers the national football team.

2. Never refuse an invitation to eat. Relationships are built around meals in Brazil, and restaurants are extremely popular for business meetings. If your sales call is going well and your contact asks you to lunch, the worst possible response is "I'm sorry, I have another appointment. Can I take a rain check?"

   Optimally, you should try to schedule your initial appointment for approximately 10:30 A.M. If it goes well, be ready not only to accept a lunch invitation, but also to have your prospect's favorite table reserved at a preferred restaurant. (Consider asking an administrative assistant for recommendations.) While lunch is usually briefer in São Paulo than in Rio, it is still important.

WHAT TIME SHOULD I ARRIVE?

You will be expected to arrive on time, but your Brazilian counterpart may be anywhere from 15 minutes to an hour late. Never make it obvious that you are distressed over a client's late arrival, and never overbook your day. If you have to cut short—or completely miss—an appointment due to scheduling delays, you may as well eliminate that prospect from your list.

Different regions of Brazil have different perceptions of time. The north is more relaxed than the south (where there are many Brazilians of German heritage). *Cariocas* (people from Rio) may be less punctual than *Paulistas* (people from São Paulo).

Being physically present ensures you have a much greater opportunity to build a relationship and acquire other leads. Whether you're attending a meeting or a meal, be patient and gracious, but also participate in conversations—do not just observe. Relationships rule sales.

WORKWEEK

Monday through Friday is the normal workweek. Business hours vary.

People from São Paulo may have the most rigorous work ethic of all *Brasileiros*. Workdays may start earlier, lunches can be shorter, and work may sometimes be discussed after hours at restaurants, clubs, etc. Decision makers usually begin work later in the morning and stay longer into the evening.

On Fridays, happy hours tend to lure people out of the office earlier than on Mondays through Thursdays. A good bar will not close until the last client leaves.

Avoid doing business around Carnival, Christmas, Easter, or other holidays. In 2011, Brazil had 16 official holidays (which are not necessarily paid), and firms generally offer a minimum of 30 additional paid vacation days.

HOW CLOSE SHOULD I STAND?

Less than 1 foot apart.

Brazil is a wonderful example of a culture that communicates in close proximity. Brazilians may touch you intermittently on the arm, hand, or shoulder during much of your conversation. Never back away from them. They are unconsciously setting up the correct proxemic zone with you, and if you move, they will probably close up the distance at the first opportunity. Let your Brazilian associates define the proper space, or you may find yourself followed around the room.

Many believe that proxemic behavior is driven by sensory responses, which are established in childhood. If you grow up physically close to other people (with multiple people in each room of the house), your sensitivity to reflective thermal heat, scent, and visual stimuli will be set for that distance at a subconscious level. It is exceedingly difficult to change your comfort zone once it is set. Therefore, never expect Brazilians to change for you; you should adapt to their sense of appropriate physical space.

DO I KISS, BOW, OR SHAKE HANDS?

EFFUSIVE GREETINGS

An initial greeting is an exceptional opportunity to connect with your Brazilian prospect. Be enthusiastic at the introduction; give everyone an extended handshake, and repeat this behavior upon departure. Once you know your contacts better, greetings become more effusive, with embraces and air kisses on alternating cheeks. (Brazilians generally lean to the left when kissing each other's cheeks.)

Try to discover everyone's title, name order, and position within the firm before your meeting, so you will not mangle names or misconstrue job responsibilities during the introductions.

BUSINESS CARDS

- Have your business cards formatted in advance with Portuguese on one side and your language (or English) on the other.
- Cards are usually exchanged near the beginning of the meeting, just after everyone has been introduced, and are generally presented with one hand.

Marketing Note

Brazil is the largest country in Latin America, but Brazilians do not consider themselves Hispanic. They are more appropriately called Latinos, South Americans, or Lusophones (which means a person who speaks Portuguese). Although many Brazilians understand multiple languages, a common insult is to assume it is acceptable to try to communicate with Brazilians in Spanish, English, German, or Italian (which are all spoken to some degree in Brazil).

Be very sensitive with your marketing materials, advertisements, and other documentation. Translation blunders between Spanish and Portuguese are common. Have your data vetted in country.

To practice a few phrases in Portuguese before your trip, visit the BBC's language website at http://www.bbc.co.uk/languages/portuguese/talk/index.shtml.

■ If titles such as Doctor or Professor are on the card, use them when addressing business acquaintances. People may sometimes introduce themselves using their titles and first names (e.g., Dr. João).

THREE TIPS FOR SELLING IN BRAZIL

1. The *Jeito* or *Jeitinho Brasileiro*
2. Nepotism and Networks
3. The Indirect Approach

1. THE *JEITO* OR *JEITINHO BRASILEIRO*

Jeito is sometimes translated as a "way" or a "knack," and since *jeitinho* is the diminutive form of *jeito*, it would mean a "little way." The *jeitinho brazileiro* (or the "little Brazilian way") is a cultural nuance, which can refer to many things—from sidestepping a rule to paying for a "favor." It is basically a way to circumvent rules and regulations that can be onerous.

Advertising Note

Although research has shown that Brazilians have a relatively low tolerance for uncertainty and ambiguity, they are open to discussing new concepts and receptive to trying new products. They are also generally more comfortable with short-term goals than long, involved projects. When you develop your contracts, try to break long-term advertising campaigns up into smaller events. Show how a campaign will be developed in stages, over weeks or months, rather than over years.

In Brazil you will encounter several extremely time-consuming policies that are constant reminders of why the *jeito* exists. For example, Brazil's labor code makes it arduous to hire or fire staff. It is so expensive to employ people that many firms decide to just informally add on personnel (under the table). Formal nonwage costs are generally about 50 percent over and above basic salaries, and paying the taxes for genuine employees is so byzantine that more staff must be hired just to comply with complex tax codes. This makes it extremely difficult for legitimate companies in lower-margin industries (like retail or travel) to compete with firms that simply provide cheaper "untaxed employees." One can see how the *jeitinho* evolved.

2. NEPOTISM AND NETWORKS

Nepotism is considered an important obligation in Brazil. While individuals are responsible for their own decisions, family loyalty is a duty. Therefore, when a family member has an influential position in private industry or government, that senior person may feel a true responsibility to help relatives obtain employment.

The family is an exceedingly important institution in Brazil and is key to one's position in society. A Brazilian's *parentela* (kin) is comprised of the relatives that one recognizes from his or her mother's and father's families, as well as the entire family of one's spouse. A *parentela* may include hundreds of individuals. Beyond immediate relatives, there is an even greater network of friends, all of whom define each person's position in the social structure.

Understanding the necessity of nepotism and networks helps explain another priority: interacting in a polite manner regardless of whether a work situation is dire. You never want to ruin an entire network of prospects because of a confrontation with one member of the network.

3. THE INDIRECT APPROACH

Being viewed as *simpatico* is highly desirable in Brazil. Since relationships are so vital, unpleasant facts or feelings may be suppressed in order to protect the feelings of the people they value. They tend to approach problems indirectly, conceal bad news, and be reluctant to commit to a definitive "No."

Therefore, if you are trying to discern whether a Brazilian is not interested in an offer, listen for subtle cues, as in the following statements:

■ Just leave this with me.
■ This may be difficult.
■ It is complicated.
■ I am not sure when we can meet.

Evading a question with an off-topic line, like "I love that restaurant, they have the most delicious . . . ," is also used as a negative response.

Since Brazilians can find aggressive business attitudes offensive, do not be too blunt. Hammering home facts may not help your sale. Facts are admissible as evidence, but Brazilians usually value the personal relationship more than a price point. Once they believe that you are a respectable, valuable, and reliable person, they will invest a substantial amount of time cultivating a relationship with you. Subsequently, the relationship they have with you is as important as your firm. At that point, you *are* the company. And as both the represen-

Advertising Note

In 2007, São Paulo implemented a complete ban on outdoor advertisements in public space. This included not only billboards, but fliers, posters, advertisements on buses, or anything on public streets or transportation. While the move inhibited marketing efforts by some major companies, it received high approval ratings from the general population—and generated some very creative advertising campaigns.

tative of your firm and their personal friend, you may be able to change company policy for them.

If there is bad news to deliver, consider using a third party to act as your intermediary. That will keep you, personally, out of the conflict.

A vice president of sales and program management for a Fortune 500 firm who has been involved in the acquisitions and management of multiple profit and loss centers gave us his view on the simpatico attitude of Brazilians. He is both highly supportive of his Brazilian team and somewhat circumspect:

Brazil is an important market, and Brazilians are rightfully nationalistic. They are proud of being Brazilians and sometimes want to present everything as wonderful, even if it may not be entirely true. Just as in any environment, you need to physically spend the time on-site and deep dive to unearth substantial details—actual statistics—because it can be difficult for them to deliver bad news. Allocate months on-site for any involved tasks, and never assume anything at face value.

LANGUAGE

Portuguese is Brazil's official language. Here are a few phrases that may help you.

ENGLISH	PORTUGUESE
Hello.	*Alô.*
Good morning.	*Bom-dia.*
Good-bye.	*Adeus.*
Excuse me.	*Com licença.*
Good afternoon.	*Boa-tarde.*
Good evening.	*Boa-noite.*
Please.	*Por favor.*
How are you?	*Como vai?*
Thank you.	*Obrigado(a).*
Fine, thanks.	*Muito bem, obrigado(a).*
Yes, please.	*Sim, por favor.*
No, thank you.	*Não, obrigado(a).*
Pleased to meet you.	*Encantado(a).*
I don't speak Portuguese.	*Não falo português.*
What is your name?	*Como é seu nome?*
Do you speak English?	*Você fala inglês?*
My name is . . .	*Me chamo . . .*
What is it called in Portuguese?	*Como se chama isto em?*
Where is . . . ?	*Onde fica . . . ?*
How much is it?	*Quanto custa?*
Could you repeat that?	*Pode repetir o que disse.*
Could you say it more slowly?	*Fale mais devagar, por fa.*
Sorry, I don't understand.	*Sinto muito, não entendi.*
Help!	*Socorro!*
I would like . . .	*Eu queria . . .*
. . . a glass of wine.	*. . . um copo de vinho.*
. . . a beer.	*. . . uma cerveja.*
. . . a coffee.	*. . . um café americano.*
. . . a tea.	*. . . um chá preto.*
. . . fruit juice.	*. . . um suco de fruta.*
. . . mineral water.	*. . . água mineral.*

ENGLISH	PORTUGUESE
I'm . . .	*Eu sou* . . .
. . . from the United States.	. . . *dos Estados Unidos.*
. . . from Canada.	. . . *do Canadá.*
. . . from England.	. . . *da Inglaterra.*
. . . from Australia.	. . . *da Austrália.*

WOW FACTOR!

Being familiar with important Brazilian artists, writers, or musicians will demonstrate a deeper respect for the culture than most salespeople evince. For example, it may be helpful to be conversant about Paulo Coelho, an exceedingly famous Brazilian novelist. His book *The Alchemist* has been translated into nearly 70 languages and has sold more than 60 million copies. Some Brazilian musicians of note include João Gilberto and Antonio Carlos Jobim. João Gilberto's "Bim Bom" was one of the first popular bossa nova releases, which was followed by classics like "*Chega de Saudade*" ("No More Blues") and "*Garota de Ipanema*" ("Girl from Ipanema").

CANADA

Conventional short form: Canada

Population: 34,030,589 (2011 estimate)

Median age: 41 years

Age structure: (2011 estimates)
0–14 years: 15.7%
15–64 years: 68.5%
65 years and over: 15.9%

GDP per capita (PPP): $39,600 (2010 estimated in US dollars)

Suffrage: 18 years old

Legal drinking age: 19 years old in most provinces; 18 years old in Quebec, Manitoba, and Alberta

Cultural Note

Canadians generally test out as being relatively secure. This may be due to the stability and structure of their supportive government services. They are personally highly individualistic but will follow company policies and often opt for immediate results over long-term, multigenerational objectives.

ICEBREAKERS

BRILLIANT!

1. Ice hockey is a vital part of Canadian identity. The Montreal Canadiens have captured 24 Stanley Cups, and Canada has the world record for the sport's most Olympic gold medals (14). If you are from the south, you might bring up Canada's famous win over the United States in overtime during the 2010 Vancouver Olympics. Or you could ask about hockey celebrities, some of whom appear on TV shows like "Battle of the Blades," a program that pairs NHL players with figure-skating champions.

2. Inquire about the city you are visiting, the sites, the political parties, and how they may affect your industry. In Quebec Province (which includes the cities of Montreal and Quebec), a positive comment about French heritage, language, or food would be appropriate. In Vancouver, your prospect may be of Asian descent, and in Newfoundland, he or she may be Irish. Your comments or inquiries should be adjusted accordingly.

BOORISH

1. Never make comparisons between the United States and Canada, and never confuse Canada's seven provinces and three territories. Learn the geography. Although most commerce is still done within 300 miles of the Canadian-US border, the territories are opening up due to global

warming, and you may be supporting mining operations or selling exotic tours to Nunavut in the near future. Michael Kergin, Canadian ambassador to the United States, had this to say about Canadian pride when he addressed the Economic Club of Detroit in April 2001:

> On one side of the border, we Canadians tend to be proud of our differences—sometimes to the point of excess, while on the other side, there is a desire to be proud of your individuality—also occasionally to the point of excess. In short, you are proud of what you are: Americans; we are proud of what we are not: Americans!

2. Be informed about industry news and regulations. A sales representative in the gaming industry was unaware of recent legislation and made an illegal offer for an online gambling venture to a prominent casino manager.

WHAT TIME SHOULD I ARRIVE?

Be a few minutes early. Never waste anyone's time, particularly in Vancouver and Toronto. Meetings generally run for an hour or less, starting and ending promptly. However, you may find that French-Canadian prospects have a different perception of time; do not show any dismay if your prospect is tardy and your meeting runs late.

WORKWEEK

Canadians generally work Monday through Friday from 9:00 A.M. to 5:00 P.M.; banking and shopping hours vary. The Lord's Day Act originally prohibited shopping on Sundays, but some provinces have changed the law, allowing local municipalities to decide whether to allow Sunday shopping. Canada has a 36.5-hour workweek, but many executives exceed those hours.

Canadian firms are expected to offer employees 10 to 15 paid vacation days. In addition, there are approximately 11 official holidays, which may or may not be paid.

HOW CLOSE SHOULD I STAND?

Generally Canadians are comfortable with approximately 2 to 2½ feet of distance between each other. Based upon their ethnicity, you may find some clients backing away somewhat (in Vancouver) or closing up the distance a bit (in Quebec).

DO I KISS, BOW, OR SHAKE HANDS?

GREETINGS VARY

You will probably receive a firm, relatively brief handshake with Canadian executives. However, if you are familiar with French-Canadians of the opposite sex in Montreal or Quebec City, you may receive *les bises* (the kisses). This is more likely upon your departure, after a very successful business meeting.

In Vancouver, there is a slim chance that your prospect may be most comfortable with a bow. However, it is more likely that you will find a westernized Asian greeting there—a warm, if gentle, handshake.

BUSINESS CARDS

- In the province of Quebec, your business cards should be formatted in advance with French on one side and your language (or English) on the other.
- In Vancouver, ascertain the ethnicity of your prospects, and present a card with their native language on one side. Do not assume all Asian clients are ethnic Chinese.
- In central and eastern Canada, cards are usually exchanged near the beginning of the meeting, just after

everyone has been introduced, and are generally presented with one hand. However, in Vancouver, be sure to present your card with two hands if your contact is Asian.

THREE TIPS FOR SELLING IN CANADA

1. **Civility**
2. **Government Support**
3. **Advertising Regulations**

1. CIVILITY

Become familiar with Canada's highly respected, scrupulously honest auditor general, Sheila Fraser. And then expect the opposite. As of 2011, it is rare in Canada to find someone like Ms. Fraser—an individual who is publicly frank and admonishes governmental officials for fiscal irregularities. Unlike this very popular auditor general, individuals who are both candid and forceful in Canada are relatively scarce.

It is far more prevalent to encounter executives who are exceptionally diplomatic and would be taken aback at blunt behavior. According to Beth Pomper, an international marketing and trade expert, you are not likely to hear the statement "That price is too high!"

Canadians will never tell you what to do. They wouldn't want to appear as know-it-alls and will go quite far to avoid conflict. If there is a problem and they are trying their utmost to get you to change your mind, they will probably offer their opinion with a gracious phrase like "You might wish to consider . . ."

While Canada is multicultural, all Canadians take pride in their civility. Making a suggestion is far more acceptable than stating an absolute.

2. GOVERNMENT SUPPORT

The Canadian government is a strong advocate for business. Its support encompasses analysis of business plans, sugges-

Advertising Note

The Quebecois (people from the province of Quebec, including Montreal and Quebec City) treasure their French heritage. All communications, whether billboards, print ads, digital media, or a PowerPoint presentation, must be in the official language of the province—French. Make sure your ads reflect French sensibilities as well. No demands of "Call now!" or "Buy today!" here. However, risqué or seductive advertisements are commonplace. *Bien sûr!* (Of course!)

tions for best global market targets, selection of distributors that are best suited for Canadian products, and final contract agreements. Basically, the government offers Canadian businesses guidance and consulting throughout the entire export process, and the majority of the services are free.

While other governments might not offer the strong assistance to their business operations that Canada does, Canadians are very open to meeting with sales representatives. They will expect to meet with your senior management, so be sure to bring your top executives when you call.

3. ADVERTISING REGULATIONS

The European Union has legislation that regulates misleading or comparative advertising, and protects consumers against its unfair consequences. While this makes it extremely important for corporations to be careful about their ads in Europe, Canada can be even more rigorous for advertisers. In Canada, a set of voluntary codes and guidelines covers many areas, including gender portrayal. Alcohol and tobacco are stringently regulated as well.

The most exceptional advertising prohibition exists in Quebec, where it is illegal to advertise directly to children under the age of 12. The code was developed by the Canadian Association of Broadcasters, in cooperation with an organization called Advertising Standards Canada. If your products

Cultural Note

Any salesperson traveling to Canada should be ready to appreciate Canadian achievements. Canadians are exceedingly proud of their successful citizens. At the least, become familiar with Canadian icons like pianist Glenn Gould and author Margaret Atwood. Online you can find lists of famous Canadians from architects and athletes to magicians and martyrs. Be sensitive to the famous citizens in the provinces you visit, and as mentioned before, never compare Canada with the United States.

are toys, games, food, or other items targeting the under-12 set, your advertisements may be directed to parents, but do not develop marketing or sales programs in print, TV, or any broadcast media for children.

LANGUAGE

Canada has two official languages, English and French. Chinese, the third most commonly spoken language, is concentrated in the Vancouver region. The Inuktitut language is also acknowledged officially in the territory of Nunavut.

It may help to practice a few phrases in French before your trip. There are many websites that offer free French language training, including through the BBC at http://www.bbc.co.uk/languages.

ENGLISH	FRENCH
Hello.	*Salut.*
Good morning.	*Bonjour.*
Good-bye.	*Au revoir.*
Excuse me.	*Excusez-moi.*
Good afternoon.	*Bonjour.*

ENGLISH	FRENCH
Good evening.	*Bonsoir.*
Please.	*S'il vous plaît.*
How are you?	*Comment allez-vous?*
Thank you.	*Merci.*
Fine, thanks.	*Bien, merci.*
Yes, please.	*Oui, s'il vous plaît.*
No, thank you.	*Non, merci.*
Pleased to meet you.	*Enchanté(e).*
I don't speak French.	*Je ne parle pas français.*
What is your name?	*Comment vous appelez-vous?*
Do you speak English?	*Parlez vous anglais?*
My name is . . .	*Je m'appelle . . .*
What is it called in French?	*Comment dit-on en français?*
Where is . . . ?	*Où est . . .*
How much is it?	*Combien ça coûte?*
Could you repeat that?	*Pourriez-vous répéter cela?*
Could you say it more slowly?	*Pourriez-vous le dire plus lentement?*
Sorry, I don't understand.	*Désolé(e), je ne comprends pas.*
Help!	*Au secours!*
I would like . . .	*Je voudrais . . .*
. . . a glass of wine.	*. . . un verre de vin.*
. . . a beer.	*. . . une bière.*
. . . a coffee.	*. . . un café.*
. . . a tea.	*. . . un thé.*
. . . fruit juice.	*. . . un jus de fruit.*
. . . mineral water.	*. . . une eau minérale.*
I'm from . . .	*Je viens . . .*
. . . the United States.	*. . . des États-Unis.*
. . . Canada.	*. . . du Canada.*
. . . England.	*. . . d'Angleterre.*
. . . Australia.	*. . . d'Australie.*

WOW FACTOR!

Know who the "Famous Five" were. Emily Murphy, Irene Parlby, Nellie McClung, Louise McKinney, and Henrietta Muir Edwards were the impetus for the Persons Case of 1929, a decision by the British Judicial Committee of the Privy Council. It found that women are persons and eligible to hold appointed or elected offices. This overturned a prior decision by Canada's own Supreme Court, which unanimously stated that women are not persons and not eligible for appointment to the Senate.

The five suffragettes have monuments dedicated to them in Ottawa and Calgary, and their picture is on a Canadian 50-dollar bill.

CHINA

Conventional long form: People's Republic of China

Conventional short form: China

Local long form: Zhonghua Renmin Gongheguo

Local short form: Zhongguo

Abbreviation: PRC

Population: 1,336,718,015 (2011 estimate)

Median age: 35.5 years

Age structure: (2011 estimates)
    0–14 years: 17.6%
    15–64 years: 73.6%
    65 years and over: 8.9%

GDP per capita (PPP): $7,400 (2010 estimated in US dollars)

Suffrage: 18 years old

Legal drinking age: No official rulings exist across China as of this writing; however, certain cities (e.g., Shenzhen) have reportedly adopted a regulation requiring consumers to be at least 18 years old to purchase alcohol. An ordinance to forbid advertising alcohol reportedly exists in some areas as well.

Advertising Note

China is the most populous nation in the world. Every fifth person on the planet lives in the People's Republic of China.

The world's most populous country is now the world's second-largest advertising market. Yet as of 2011, advertising in China had remained relatively conservative. Chinese advertisements do not often garner international acclaim. (Small markets like the Netherlands win more awards.) The prizes that are awarded for Chinese ads are still concentrated in print and television. However, hundreds of young artists in China are being showcased through a new creative agency called NeochaEdge. NeochaEdge was founded by two Americans who speak fluent Mandarin. The firm represents Chinese member-artists and musicians who design "edgy" campaigns in China for global brands like Absolut vodka. While local Chinese brands are not as experimental yet, the youth-oriented NeochaEdge ads are a fit for multinationals that want to target the 500 million Chinese who are under 30 years old.

The Chinese are enthusiastic users of digital technology, and there is huge potential for the development of innovative promotions in that medium. Copy must be carefully vetted, though, since it must reflect nationalistic viewpoints and avoid incendiary topics.

Every firm that employs celebrities in advertisements shoulders a certain amount of risk, as when Nike signed an endorse-

ICEBREAKERS

BRILLIANT!

1. Do your homework. Not only should you know everything you can about the businesses you plan to work with, know everything you can about your Chinese counterparts. They will know all about you. When Chinese executives go out of the country, they make every effort to thoroughly research the people they will do business with.

ment deal with Liu Xiang, China's famous hurdler, who was injured just before the 2008 Olympics. Also, advertisements that feature celebrities who are politically active can generate a particularly costly uproar in China. For example, in 2008 a Fiat commercial that aired in Italy featured Richard Gere driving a Lancia from Hollywood to Tibet. Even though the commercial never aired in China, the YouTube version and subsequent negative articles quickly created outrage in the PRC, because Richard Gere is a supporter of freedom for Tibet, and of His Holiness the 14th Dalai Lama who lives in exile in Dharamsala, India. Days after the release of the ad, Fiat issued an apology to the government of the People's Republic of China and to the Chinese people.

And in 2011, Groupon went further when the online coupon service exploited Tibetans in a television ad that ran during the Super Bowl. The ad started by stating, "The people of Tibet are in trouble. Their very culture is in jeopardy." The ad then juxtaposed the plight of Tibet with the punch line "But they still whip up an amazing fish curry!" in the setting of a Chicago restaurant. Protests against the ad came from thousands of Chinese, Tibetan activists, and even the owner of the restaurant in Chicago, who stated it was insensitive and unfunny. Ironically, Tibetan Buddhists do not traditionally eat fish—or curry.

In the book *China Safari* by Serge Michel and Michel Beuret, a government functionary in Africa related this story about Chinese executives visiting the Congo:

> I don't know how they do it. They study every manager, every minister. They always build the right relationships. Once, during a dinner given for a Chinese delegation touring Africa, I sat next to a big cheese in the Chinese Ministry of Trade. We got to talking, and it

Cultural Note

A senior female executive from a US Fortune 500 company was sent to China to salvage a project with an important partner. However, no appointments could be scheduled: the president of the Chinese company was so angry at what he perceived as insults coming from her company that he would not confirm a meeting. Fortunately, once she arrived in Beijing, he agreed to a dinner. During the dinner, the Chinese president spoke passionately about the multiple insults her company had committed. She listened politely and intently, even though he was speaking in Mandarin. Meanwhile, her male colleague played with his Black-Berry to show his annoyance that the conversation was not being translated quickly enough.

After listening, apologizing, and assuring the Chinese president that no offense was intended, she asked to come to his office the next day to work with the team and move the project forward, even if not everything had been resolved. When the CEO did not immediately accept, she mentioned that her firm would not have sent her there if it was not serious, and it was unlikely that she would be coming back. This was a moment to rebuild the trust that was lacking on both sides. The Chinese president then turned toward her (away from the male executive who had been looking at his BlackBerry) and said, "We would be very pleased to welcome *you* to our offices tomorrow." The damage was controlled, and ten months later, a delegation from the Chinese partnership arrived in New York City.

turned out that we both loved jazz and Greco-Roman architecture. It really was the most extraordinary coincidence. It turned out that we even had professional interests in common. Then as the delegation moved onward, he called me from South Africa and Angola, and then from China, just to keep in touch, just to check in and see how things were. I mentioned this to some of my colleagues, and lo and behold! they had similar stories. Each one had his own Chinese guy keeping tabs on him!

To cement your relationship with your Chinese counterpart, one of your questions should demonstrate that you share a common interest: "Do I understand correctly that you are a fan of calligraphy/Yao Ming/country music/whatever? So am I!"

2. Thank your hosts. Thank them for their time, admire the facility, compliment them on the tea they will serve you (never pour your own cup), and make sure that you remain calm throughout the proceedings.

BOORISH

1. Bringing out a written contract too soon is the mark of someone who doesn't understand how the Chinese do business. The Chinese have been involved in trade for thousands of years without Western contract law. Success in China requires the patience to establish relationships first. Only then can a contract be agreed upon. Prematurely asking, "Do we have a deal?" demonstrates that you're a naïf.

2. Never omit official titles, and never call your Chinese contact by his or her first name unless you are invited to do so. Chinese names are traditionally listed in the opposite order from names in the West. Family names (or surnames) are written first, followed by the first name. Using the name Li Wu as an example, Li is the person's family name, and Wu is his first name.

To show respect, Chinese are addressed only by their family name and title. Li Wu would be addressed as Director Li or Chairman Li, not as Wu. If a person has no professional title, he or she may be addressed as Mr. or Ms.

Chinese women usually retain their maiden names after marriage. However, to clarify her status to a foreigner, a woman may elect to use her husband's family name.

Assuming that you have obtained a list of all the individuals you will be meeting before your trip, you should ascertain the correct title and family name of each of your contacts. Sometimes the Chinese will adopt a Western-sounding name in order to make you feel comfortable.

Cultural Note

> Not only is the United States China's biggest trading partner, but China is the largest holder of the massive US debt (currently more than $1 trillion in US Treasury bonds). A portmanteau word that describes the intertwined economies of China and the United States of America is Chimerica. The term was popularized by Niall Ferguson in *The Ascent of Money*.

WHAT TIME SHOULD I ARRIVE?

Punctuality is very important in China, even more so for visitors. You are expected to be on time for business and social events. Time is valuable, and to be late is insulting.

WORKWEEK

China is changing so rapidly and is so vast that its work hours seem to be around the clock. Business hours can be extended if necessary late into the evening and over weekends. In general, the workweek is established at 44 hours, Monday through Friday. There is a sliding scale of paid vacation days—from 5 to 15 days depending upon years of service. Additionally, there are approximately 21 holidays.

HOW CLOSE SHOULD I STAND?

Approximately 2½ to 3 feet apart. Give yourself enough space to bow without infringing on your prospect's space.

Cultural Note

A common complaint of foreigners in China is corruption. China's legal system is still developing. In theory, an individual Chinese—or foreign visitor—has many protections under the law. In practice, the powerful and well connected can often act with impunity.

China is a country of rules, thousands of them. There are so many laws that people cannot help but fall afoul of them. Chinese executives know which rules they can get away with flouting, but you do not. For example, China does, in fact, have intellectual-property regulations. But they are enforced selectively. If Chinese regulators consider you to be disruptive, you, as a foreigner, will make an easy target for anyone who wishes to enforce the law, even if it is a law that every Chinese ignores. This can range from a Chinese prosecutor charging your business with violations to a lone Chinese police officer refusing you entry to a subway entrance while allowing thousands of Chinese to pass by. Avoiding confrontation in a public forum is generally advisable.

One indicator that a Chinese official may be corrupt is a reference to him or her as a "naked official." This term refers to officials who have sent their families abroad. Doing so shields their families from shame and removes any pressure that might be brought to bear on them for multiple reasons.

DO I KISS, BOW, OR SHAKE HANDS?

BOW

Typically, Chinese businesspeople bow slightly when greeting another person. In casual situations or when greeting a subordinate, the bow is often abbreviated into a simple nod.

When greeting foreigners, the Chinese often follow up their bow with a handshake.

Cultural Note

As the world's major low-cost manufacturer, the Chinese are large participants in international trade fairs. Chinese trade fairs, which tend to specialize in particular industries, are an excellent resource for finding suppliers and buyers. The Chinese are so eager to export that they hold sourcing fairs both inside and outside of China. Chinese sourcing fairs are held regularly in the United Arab Emirates, India, Singapore, and South Africa, timed to meet the purchasing cycle of buyers.

Attending sourcing or trade fairs outside of China gives you another advantage: your Chinese counterparts will be under the same time pressure that you are. If you both want to complete a deal by the end of the fair, you are both operating under the same deadline. However, many Chinese use these fairs just to introduce themselves to foreign clients, not to complete deals.

Be aware that giving away free promotional items may cause a crowd problem in your booth. Offer attendees tickets to specific screenings, and then distribute the promotional items to participants as they leave your event. Be sure to check that your giveaways are appropriate in China. Avoid green hats (culturally, they imply that your significant other is cheating on you), knives (which can indicate you are severing the relationship), and clocks (older Chinese equate these with another potential termination—death).

BUSINESS CARDS

- Like most aspects of greetings in China, the exchange of business cards should be treated with respect. The Chinese may use two hands. However, there is no strict tradition for exchanging cards.
- Your cards should be should be formatted in advance with Chinese on one side and your language on the other. Gold is the most prestigious ink color.

Cultural Note

Generally, the Chinese do not get right down to business. There may be inquiries into your journey, your health, and your family, but you will likely discuss some other topics before segueing over to the matter at hand. Acknowledgment of China's many discoveries and innovations is always appreciated as a conversational subject.

Topics to avoid include the Chinese record on human rights and anything relating to China's so-called Century of Shame (roughly, from the mid-1800s to the Communist takeover of China in 1949). This is the period that began with Western powers, especially the United Kingdom, annexing portions of China to serve as trading ports, climaxing with the Japanese invasion of China, and ending with Japan's defeat at the end of World War II.

Sports are a safe topic of conversation, although the majority of Chinese are not avid sports fans, despite the Beijing Olympics of 2009. At present, the most popular spectator sports are soccer (football) and basketball.

- If your cards are in your wallet, do not keep your wallet in your back trouser pocket. Men should place the cards in a card holder, or in their wallet, and then put that in an inside pocket of their jacket, to ensure they never sit on them. Women can place business cards in their purse or briefcase, preferably in a card holder.

THREE TIPS FOR SELLING IN CHINA

1. **Tough Negotiations**
2. **Relationships**
3. **The "Long Game"**

1. TOUGH NEGOTIATIONS

There are many types of businesspeople in China. Some believe in win-win deals. Most do not. Others have more interest in establishing relationships than actually completing deals. The one thing they have in common is that the negotiations will be rigorous.

The Chinese expression *bu da bu xiang shi* (loosely translated as "from an exchange of blows, friendship grows") is helpful to keep in mind when preparing for your negotiations. Chinese executives test each other, looking for weaknesses, so of course they will use that approach with you. It is not meant to generate a permanently antagonistic relationship. It is just so you know where you both stand.

If your Chinese prospect appears to get angry during the negotiations, keep your emotions under control. Most Chinese businesspeople can compartmentalize their feelings. You should, too.

Assuming that the deal is complete once a contract is signed is rash. Typically, the Chinese will attempt to extract additional concessions even after a "close." To the Chinese, there is no shame in this; a written contract is an invention of the West. Usually, the foreigner is the one under the time pressure, not the Chinese, so demanding changes right before the foreigner leaves is an accepted tactic. Of course, always be prepared to walk away if the negotiations do not seem to be progressing. Their obdurate stance may change when you approach the door.

Also, understand that the Chinese tradition of hospitality can be a business tactic. Impressive banquets serve two purposes. First, they take time, and the Chinese always assume that foreigners (particularly Westerners) are in a hurry. Second, they place guests under a sense of obligation. Don't yield a negotiating point because they throw you a banquet. But be sure to reciprocate with a banquet of your own.

2. RELATIONSHIPS

In many countries (especially in North America and Northern Europe), personal relationships come after the completion

Cultural Note

The classic military treatise *The Art of War* by Sun Tzu is read by every Chinese student. Certainly, it does encourage fighting hard to get what you want. Many Chinese claim they plan their entire business strategy using its principles.

In truth, there is useful advice for Western businesspeople in *The Art of War*. Knowing that the book regards spies as more valuable than soldiers is helpful, whether you are running an army or a business. Perhaps the most important tactic in the book is involved with the art of deception. You can generally overcome this approach with thorough preparation on your part; get as much information as possible before you arrive.

The use of *The Art of War*'s strategies in business was corroborated during a seminar given by Terri Morrison at the National Defense University in Washington, D.C. When the discussion about doing business in China and *The Art of War* came up, a senior officer offered this comment:

> Terri, business travelers [like you] can be very naïve. We see these precepts in constant use. The Chinese gather intelligence continuously, whether outside or inside China. Many mirrors in hotel rooms in China are two-way. [There are pinhole cameras everywhere.] Every serious meeting is recorded, and every time laptops, zip drives, or printed materials are left unattended, they are copied. You are monitored and analyzed long before your plane touches down, and long after you depart.

of a contract. After doing business repeatedly, you may then, over time, become friends. But in China, while traditions are changing, the relationship and the *guanxi* (see Cultural Note on the next page) it involves generally must still come first. Then a contract can follow.

This relationship is primarily between the Chinese prospect and you—and, by extension, your company. Multinational corporations have sometimes made the mistake of switching their representatives in China at the end of the sales cycle. They assume that final contract issues can be resolved

Cultural Note

Guanxi (pronounced gwan-shee) has had many translations, including networks, relationships, partnerships, and obligations. The characters have been said to symbolize a gate (in the Great Wall) and a family tree. Some Chinese say having it is vital and some (particularly in government) say it's irrelevant. One exceptionally popular way of cultivating elite Chinese networks occurs in business schools like CEIBS, the China Europe International Business School, and the Cheung Kong Graduate School of Business in Beijing. Their exclusive CEO program accepts only 40 students at a time and has generated some of the most valuable alumni networks in China today.

Guanxi can range from trustworthy associates who will always deliver and can be depended upon for minor favors to companies that do business primarily within a mutually obligated network. Businesspeople with *guanxi* consider each other as friends, help each other out of difficult situations, and treat each other with extreme courtesy. In the old Communist China, where slow-moving bureaucrats ran things and it was safer to say no than yes, the only way to get anything done was to have *guanxi* in the government or to go outside the system and rely upon one's friends.

While having *guanxi* in the government is still helpful, private industry connections who follow up on promises and know all the unwritten rules in China can be even more valuable. One aspect of a courteous relationship is keeping in contact with your key associates—through weekly or monthly meetings, or via text or phone (but not e-mail, which the Chinese call "snail mail"). That way relationships and opportunities are continually developed, and trust is sustained.

by legal departments. This can be a costly mistake. Even long after your contract is closed, your personal relationship is expected to continue. When there is a problem, your Chinese prospect may contact you in your home country, rather than talk with your company's current representative in Beijing. This makes it vital for your company to retain you for as long as possible, if you are the one with the Chinese relationships.

3. THE "LONG GAME"

No matter what country you are from, China probably has a longer history than yours does. Their recorded past goes back more than four thousand years. Perhaps this perspective explains why the Chinese tend to be comfortable playing the "long game." If something does not happen right now, it can happen later—years later, if need be. Consider that the Chinese calendar runs in cycles of sixty years, rather than one year or one decade.

Obviously, this attitude is not shared by most Westerners. In the United States especially, time is money. If a deal can't happen now, then the business trip was a failure, the time and money wasted. A very short game is played in the West. The Chinese know this and are willing to use it as a stratagem. They can drag negotiations out as long as possible, knowing that foreigners are under extreme time constraints.

If at all possible, never give your Chinese counterparts too much information about your schedule. Keep your flight arrangements and any deadlines to yourself.

LANGUAGE

China's official language is standard Chinese, which is based upon Mandarin. However, many Chinese will speak other dialects, such as Cantonese, Shanghainese, and Keija. Many businesspeople speak English.

The written Chinese language (which can be understood by speakers of all Chinese dialects) has been simplified in the People's Republic of China. The PRC also changed the direction in which Chinese was written, from vertical to horizontal. Also note that written Chinese has no verb tenses (no past, no future, no subjunctive), so be certain to specify your times and dates in the context of your texts, e-mails, letters, or contracts. (Be aware that Taiwan has not accepted these changes and uses the pre-revolutionary form of writing.)

Cultural Note

The People's Republic of China has more soldiers than any other country. However, the bulk of the Chinese Red Army is not particularly high-tech. Reportedly, Beijing was horrified with the speed at which Allied Forces defeated the Iraqi Army in 1991. It became obvious that the well-trained, high-tech forces of the United States and the United Kingdom could defeat opponents many times their number. Since then, China's military has invested heavily in technology. But China also decided to use the strength of Western countries against them: they would master cyberwar. Western intelligence officials believe that the periodic hacking of foreign companies' websites, security networks, and files in China are simply Beijing practicing cyberwar techniques.

Should armed conflict ever break out between China and the United States and/or United Kingdom, it is expected that China will immediately launch cyber attacks on a wide range of companies and utilities. Electric power grids are considered particularly vulnerable. In preparation for this, intelligence experts claim that China has already placed triggers in the computers of foreign companies and utilities, enabling the Chinese to shut them down at will. Presumably, Western intelligence services have done the same to the Chinese infrastructure.

Why is this significant to your company? Even if your company is too small to be directly attacked, you may be shut down because your local power utility is out of service for weeks, or even months. Armed conflict may be thousands of miles away, in Taiwan or the oil-rich Spratly Islands, but cyberwar can affect you anywhere on the planet.

There could be other reasons for a cyber attack on your company. In 2010, someone managed to breach the firewalls at Google's servers in China. User information was stolen. It is believed that the hackers were working for the Chinese government, which wanted information on the identities of dissidents who were illegally blogging in China.

In the West, most of what is heard about the Internet in China is negative: censorship, government crackdowns, and hacking. The positive side is rarely reported. As of 2010, nearly one-third of China's 142 million Internet users have shopped online. That is about one in every ten Chinese citizens.

As most businesspeople know, the number one search engine in China isn't Google; it's the Beijing-based company Baidu. As of 2010, Baidu had about 63 percent of the Chinese market.

Here are a few phrases that may help you in China. Also, a variety of free Mandarin language programs are offered through the BBC (http://www.bbc.co.uk/languages).

ENGLISH	CHINESE
Hello.	*Ni hao.*
Good-bye.	*Zaijian.*
Excuse me.	*Dui-buqi.*
Good morning.	*Nǐ zǎo.*
Good afternoon.	*Xiawu hao.*
Good evening.	*Wan-shang hao.*
Please.	*Qing.*
Good night.	*Wan'an.*
Thank you.	*Xie-xie.*
How are you?	*Ni zenmeyang?*
Yes, please.	*Hao, xie-xie.*
Fine, thanks.	*Hai xing.*
No, thank you.	*Bu le, xie-xie.*
I don't speak Chinese.	*Wo-bu hui shuo Zhongwen.*
Pleased to meet you.	*Hen gaoxing ren.shi ni.*
Do you speak English?	*Ni hui-bu hui shuo Yingyu?*
What is your name?	*Nǐ jiào shénme?*
My name is . . .	*Wode ming-zi .shi . . .*
Where is . . . ?	*. . . zai nar?*
How much is it?	*Duoshao qian?*
Help!	*Lai ren na!*
I would like . . .	*Wo yao . . .*
. . . a glass of wine.	*. . . yi bei pu-tao jiu.*
. . . a beer.	*. . . pijiu.*
. . . coffee.	*. . . kafei.*
. . . a cup of tea.	*. . . yi bei cha.*
. . . mineral water.	*. . . kuangquanshui.*
Cheers!	*He!*
Bottoms up!	*Ganbei!*

WOW FACTOR!

Most multinationals now know about the color white being associated with death and funerals in Asia. There are multiple examples of blunders in this category. One notable event occurred when a major airline tried to offer white carnations to its passengers for their inaugural first-class flight from Hong Kong. Unfortunately, the little white flowers did not bode well, and no one would embark. The mistake was rectified when airline personnel replaced them with red carnations, and all the passengers boarded.

Red can have sad connotations as well. In Buddhist traditions, the name of the deceased is printed not in black but in red. For this reason, personal names should never be written in red in Asia (unless the person is dead). Printing the name of someone living in red can be highly offensive.

For anything except personal names, red is a good color choice in most of Asia. Red and gold are widely considered lucky colors. Perhaps because of its association with gold, yellow was historically reserved for the highest-ranked people in Asia. In ancient times, only the emperor was allowed to wear yellow. This is no longer the case, although business attire is still in generally subdued colors.

Leatrice Eiseman, director of the Eiseman Center for Color Information and Training (www.colorexpert.com), described a contrast in the use of colors in China:

> I had been invited to speak about color trends to multiple groups in China. One evening, I went to dinner with a group of Chinese businessmen, all formally attired in dark suits and light shirts. I mentioned that I was curious about the significance of the color yellow; I had heard it was historically restricted to the emperor. Most of the senior gentlemen agreed that they would never wear yellow because of the old traditions.
>
> The next day I gave a talk on color trends at Donghua University in Shanghai. Students were wearing fashionable

bright yellow down jackets, T-shirts, and scarves. Young people from 17 to 21 were so excited to hear about worldwide color trends the hall was packed, and they had to put TV monitors out in the halls!

Consult feng shui practitioners for complete details about the location and decor of your office in China and auspicious dates for opening businesses.

Also be sensitive to the use of the number 4 in any configuration (e.g., 4, 14, 24), because the sound of the word is similar to the word for death. There are no operating rooms numbered 4 in hospitals, and new construction in Hong Kong completely bypasses the 4th and 14th floors.

Conversely, the number 8 is exceedingly auspicious. This was demonstrated when the Olympics in China started at exactly 8 seconds after 8:08 P.M. on August 8, 2008.

FRANCE

Conventional long form: French Republic

Conventional short form: France

Local long form: République Française

Local short form: France

Population: 65,102,719 (2011 estimate includes France's four overseas regions)

Median age: 39.9 years

Age structure: (2011 estimates)
0–14 years: 18.5%
15–64 years: 64.7%
65 years and over: 16.8%

GDP per capita (PPP): $33,300 (2010 estimated in US dollars)

Suffrage: 18 years old

Legal drinking age: 18 years old. The age limit for alcohol and tobacco sales was raised in 2009 from 16 to 18 years old. Alcohol ads in print, television, and radio are banned, but online ads are permitted, as long as they are not on websites specifically targeted toward young people.

Advertising Note

Jacques Séguela, a vice president at the French advertising agency Havas, was quoted in the *New York Times* as saying, "American commercials go from the head to the wallet, British ones from the head to the heart, French from the heart to the head." This emotional appeal—straight to the heart—is intrinsic to French marketing. Ads are typically both sensual and witty. Human bodies (even in cartoon form) are often posed in a provocative manner, and nude women are icons in French advertisements: they are beauty incarnate and help evoke instinctual, sensory responses.

If you are selling toothpaste, highlight the sexy, alluring aspect of the product, not the cavity-fighting features. Leave that for Germany.

The French also rely more on Molière than Manhattan, and enjoy little visual tricks or slapstick jokes embedded in ads.

While advertisements may be light on scientific facts and details in Paris, they are heavy on passion, poetry, and piquancy. *Vive la France!*

ICEBREAKERS

BRILLIANT!

1. For centuries, the French language has been cherished not just by the French, but also by the millions of scholars who help make it one of the most commonly studied languages on earth. Polly Platt, author of *French or Foe* and *Savoir Flair*, made an excellent suggestion for an icebreaker. If you cannot speak French, apologize for that flaw—in French:

   Excusez-moi, je ne parle pas français.
   Excuse me, I do not speak French.

   Your apology and your attempt at a phrase or two of French shows respect for the culture and demonstrates your awareness of the importance of the language.

How much do the French revere their language? The *Académie française* (the French Academy), which monitors and protects *la langue français* (the French language), was founded in 1634 by Cardinal Richelieu. It is the most prestigious government-sponsored cultural society, and its 40 members are referred to as "the immortals."

2. Review the latest headlines, and know enough to briefly discuss the news. Topics might range from strikes to taxes to retirement age—or strikes about taxes and retirement age. (Despite a tendency for going on strike and having approximately 40 days off a year, the French are very productive.) Other good options for initial conversations include travel and popular sports like rugby, football (soccer), the Tour de France bicycle race, and the French Open tennis tournament.

BOORISH

1. A loud tone of voice, particularly in a one-on-one conversation, can be tactless in many cultures, but is truly gauche in France. Take note of the conversations around you. The French use many different levels of volume for different circumstances. In a café, one cannot overhear a discussion at the nearest table, even if it is only two or three feet away. Therefore, modulate your own voice to mimic your conversation partner's. Once a group discussion becomes animated, the volume will increase, but the defining word there is *group*.

   Talking loudly has more drawbacks than just appearing boorish. In the 1990s, hidden microphones were reportedly discovered in Air France's first-class cabin. Whether the purpose was industrial espionage or security, conversations were and may be monitored by more than your traveling companions on flights, in hotels, and in offices around the world. Discretion is the better part of valor in public; modify the volume of your voice, and curb the amount of information you dispense in public.

2. You can admire a French person's beautiful attire and accessories, but never inquire about the price. The French

consider it *mal élevé* (vulgar). This aversion to publically discussing money can extend to splitting the bill at a restaurant. If you invite your prospect, you pay. If the other person is the host, you will hear *"Je vous invité,"* which means the person invited you and wishes to pay. Women can still have a difficult time picking up the check, and discussing it in public is distasteful. If you have the expense account, handle the bill discreetly, preferably with the maitre d' before you sit down.

WHAT TIME SHOULD I ARRIVE?

Be punctual, particularly in Paris. Even though your French counterpart may be late, you are the *demandeur* (petitioner) and are expected to arrive on time. The French are generally considered polychronic—that is, they may engage in multiple tasks simultaneously—and are comfortable with interruptions and changes in their activities. Therefore, a French manager may not feel it necessary to apologize for being late to an appointment with you, when it is obvious that she or he is juggling many events at once. At the end of the day, the French will feel satisfied that all of their obligations have been met, just not in a step-by-step, linear manner.

Most sales are accomplished between fall and springtime. If you leave a deal pending until late June, it may languish on the desks of vacationing Parisians until September. Close as much business as you can in the cold weather.

WORKWEEK

Office hours are generally standard Monday through Friday, but there is a great variation with small businesses, public museums and offices, and restaurants. Be very careful to confirm all your business appointments several days before your arrival.

If you wish to tour Paris, or eat, be aware that restaurants may be closed on Sundays, and museums may be closed on

Mondays or Tuesdays. The museums of the city of Paris are open every day except Mondays, from 10:00 A.M. to 5:40 P.M. National museums, like the Louvre, are closed on Tuesdays . . . except for Versailles, the Trianon, the Rodin Museum, and the Orsay. The website of the French tourism bureau can clarify this for you at http://www.francetourism.com/practical info/museums.htm.

French corporations are normally generous with their paid vacation days. Most firms offer four to six weeks' vacation, which the French generally take in July and August. Indeed, except for the tourist industry, France virtually shuts down in August. Restaurants and shops may close for the entire month, while their staff goes on holiday. Beyond the paid vacation days, the French celebrated 14 holidays in 2011 (some of which may be paid as well). The entire compensated package can come to 37 days of paid leave a year.

However, there has been substantial movement toward fuller employment in the past few years. In 2008 France's parliament passed a reform that ended the compulsory 35-hour workweek and allowed for firms to negotiate independently with unions for additional work hours.

HOW CLOSE SHOULD I STAND?

Stand about 2 feet apart at the first meeting. After the initial handshake, personal space may contract based upon the formality or informality of the situation, the age of the participants, and the volume of your voice. The louder you are, the more space the French may give you. The closer they approach, the better the rapport.

DO I KISS, BOW, OR SHAKE HANDS?

GREETINGS VARY

French women are more likely than men to perform *les bises* (the kisses). They may kiss men at work on the cheek as

Cultural Note

US executives should remember that France was the first significant military ally of the fledgling United States of America. French philosophers like Montesquieu and Voltaire inspired the founding fathers as they developed the US Constitution and the Bill of Rights. Since the French are often well versed in history, it would behoove any US salesperson to develop some appreciation of the history between the two countries.

well—after a few meetings. French men do not generally kiss other male professional acquaintances unless they know them very well.

The number of *les bises* can vary—even within France. In Paris, it is usually two kisses—one on each cheek. In northern France, it can go up to four kisses, and in the southeast (including Marseilles), you may receive *trois bises* (three kisses).

For a first encounter, extend your hand, but do not use a vise-like grip. Always look your contact straight in the eyes when you speak to him or her. State your full name (the French may state their last name first), and smile pleasantly (don't display an enormous grin—you may look overeager or simple). You will shake hands again with everyone as you leave.

Both sexes kiss their close friends and family members. If you receive a hug, it may be a gradual embrace. It is a touching moment—not an awkward, backslapping encounter.

BUSINESS CARDS

- Business cards are often exchanged near the end of the initial visit.
- French business cards often conform to the rectangular size of a credit card, without the rounded edges. This stan-

dard size has been adopted in many countries, except for Japan, Hungary, and the United States. (Business cards in the United States are smaller.)

■ Make sure your card is attractively designed and on good stock. Even though most French executives understand English, it is still of benefit to have your card translated into French on the back.

■ The card is generally presented with one hand.

THREE TIPS FOR SELLING IN FRANCE

1. **University, Business, and Governmental Connections**
2. **Repartee**
3. **Epicureans and Oenophiles**

1. UNIVERSITY, BUSINESS, AND GOVERNMENTAL CONNECTIONS

In France, personal connections are paramount—and they equal power. Networks can be elite and are often based upon clubs that start in France's top universities. Know about the premier institutes of higher education in France, particularly the *École nationale d'administration* (ÉNA) and *École Polytechnique*.

ÉNA was founded by Charles de Gaulle in 1945, with the concept of offering brilliant graduate students access to training for senior governmental positions. University costs are covered by the state, as long as the student accepts a senior French official post for five years after graduation. Many graduates opt for elite positions in private industry before or after their five years are up. If you meet with a French CEO or senior French official in Paris, the odds are good that he or she went to either ÉNA or the *École Polytechnique*.

There are many other notable universities—like *École Normale Supérieure*, the *Université Pierre et Marie Curie* (UPMC), and the *Université Paris Sorbonne* (also called Paris IV). The latter two were part of the University of Paris before it was divided up into thirteen successor universities following the

Cultural Note

While French university graduates are happy to network with other alumni, they have not historically shown off their alma maters by wearing university garb. College sweatshirts, keychains, baseball caps, and bumper stickers have been the domain of North American and UK universities. Educational institutions in France have not commonly promoted themselves in that manner, until now.

President Nicolas Sarkozy's administration has implemented changes. French universities have greater funding and hiring responsibilities, and are venturing into the new realm of globally promoting their brands. They are aggressively competing for top students and faculty members, and they need name recognition. As of this writing, ÉNA has a new online boutique, which offers a sweatshirt, rugby shirt, T-shirt, mug, pen and pencil set, and PC bag. No fuzzy mascot?

student strikes in 1968. The French invest great weight on serious educations, and being able to network through a university connection is exceedingly helpful.

Of course, there are many other means of building connections. The Freemasons are strong in France, and clubs in many fields of interest abound.

In a sales call, high-level connections are indicative of another key asset in France: your communication skills. The more articulate and capable you are, the larger your executive network will be. Being adept at communication is vital, since eloquence can inspire and unify a group during negotiations. France is a high-context culture, and most executives will have chatted multiple times with their networks before they ever enter a meeting. Never get caught not knowing a basic answer in France. You are supposed to be well informed.

2. REPARTEE

The French appreciate a well-educated person who excels at repartee. However, there is a fine line between demonstrat-

Cultural Note

A person who passionately believes in a premise (whether or not the person is right) will engage the French. The way you present your case is critical for success. Exude interest and belief in your concept. Tell anecdotes about it, make it an emotional story, and use all five of your senses when you describe it.

A young executive for a food company in France believed so firmly in a new product, and presented his case to the board in such an eloquent and passionate manner, he was permitted to try the launch. This was despite a technically difficult development cycle and a downturned economy. He was so emotionally engaging, the rules were broken for him.

Earning the respect of your French prospects may be difficult, but if you believe that your product is intensely different, radiate intensity. Your presentation should evoke the phrase *Je me sens* (I sense it; I feel it) from your audience. In France, some products are bought on intuition alone.

ing your erudition and being dull. Never lecture the French. Never be boring. They will encourage you to debate a topic, but not to be pedantic. Allow for any objections to your proposal to be expressed, and expect some to be rhetorical. It is not necessary to respond to each and every comment, just welcome them all. Do not feel compelled to explain every step. Let the French deduce an outcome. (A frequent French complaint about US citizens is that they lecture instead of converse.)

Arguments tend to be made from an analytical, critical perspective, but emotions are also permitted. While philosophical discussions don't often arise in North American meetings, they may in France. One of the required tests for all French high school students is a four-hour written philosophy exam known as *le bac du philo*. The French respect a person who not only is familiar with philosophy and the arts but also can defend a viewpoint with wit, precision, and subtlety. One-

Cultural Note

Les vrais amis (true friends) are true cognates, or words that are extremely similar in both spelling and meaning between French and English. *Intelligence, instinct, situation, absent,* and *accident* are examples of *les vrais amis*. *Faux amis* (false friends) are false cognates, or words that look similar but are not equivalent in meaning. They can generate a good deal of embarrassment if used incorrectly. See if you can match the French *faux amis* with their English translations:

French	English
A. *Bribes*	1. Corner
B. *Chair*	2. Reading (matter)
C. *Coin*	3. Disappointment
D. *Déception*	4. Fragments
E. *Lecture*	5. Flesh

Answers: A. 4; B. 5; C. 1; D. 3; E. 2

word answers won't do. Repartee and the art of debate have been considered an aspect of true civility since Louis XIV.

3. EPICUREANS AND OENOPHILES

It is crucial to go to lunch (or breakfast) with your clients. It is not as common to go out for drinks or dinner after work in Paris as it is in Buenos Aires or Boston. The French enjoy their family life and rarely let work infringe upon it during the evening hours or the weekends—or during their well-known holidays. Lunch is the major opportunity to get to know them and to enjoy what so many of them enjoy: exquisitely prepared food.

Many French are epicureans and oenophiles, and they will notice whether you observe proper dining etiquette. Expect long, excellent meals, often with select wines. (Statistically, however, the French are not drinking as much wine as they did ten years ago.) Appendix A contains a review of dining etiquette.

In Paris, good restaurants will be booked three weeks or more ahead of time, so be certain to make your arrangements far in advance. Representatives from different industries eat in different restaurants; ensure that your reservation is at one of your prospect's favorite establishments, and at his or her favorite table.

LANGUAGE

Here are a few phrases that may help you in France. A variety of free French-language programs are also offered through the BBC (http://www.bbc.co.uk/languages).

ENGLISH	FRENCH
Hello.	*Salut.*
Good morning.	*Bonjour.*
Good afternoon.	*Bonjour.*
Good evening.	*Bonsoir*
Good-bye.	*Au revoir.*
Excuse me.	*Excusez-moi.*
Please.	*S'il vous plaît.*
How are you?	*Comment allez-vous?*
Thank you.	*Merci.*
Fine, thanks.	*Bien, merci.*
Yes, please.	*Oui, s'il vous plaît.*
No, thank you.	*Non, merci.*
Excuse me, I don't speak French.	*Excusez-moi, je ne parle pas français.*
What is your name?	*Comment vous appelez-vous?*
Do you speak English?	*Parlez vous anglais?*
My name is . . .	*Je m'appelle . . .*

ENGLISH	FRENCH
What is it called in French?	*Comment dit-on en français?*
Where is . . . ?	*Où est . . . ?*
How much is it?	*Combien ça coûte?*
Could you repeat that?	*Pourriez-vous répéter cela?*
Sorry, I don't understand.	*Désolé(e), je ne comprends pas.*
I would like . . .	*Je voudrais . . .*
. . . a beer.	*. . . une bière.*
. . . a coffee.	*. . . un café.*
. . . a tea.	*. . . un thé.*
. . . fruit juice.	*. . . un jus de fruit.*
. . . mineral water.	*. . . une eau minérale.*

WOW FACTOR!

The French government prohibited private advertising on public television (which included every station) until 1968. And recently, President Sarkozy banned ads on public stations again—at least during the evening. Another general prohibition is a "Call now!" phone number displayed in a hard-sell ad. You need special justification to load a phone number on the screen. The French generally resist any hint of being forced or manipulated, and being sold to is equivalent to being told what to do.

And of course, you may never directly denigrate a competitor's product. Unfavorable comparison advertising is not generally permissible in many parts of the European Union.

GERMANY

Conventional long form: Federal Republic of Germany

Conventional short form: Germany

Local long form: Bundesrepublik Deutschland

Local short form: Deutschland

Population: 81,471,834 (2011 estimate)

Median age: 44.9 years

Age structure: (2011 estimates)
0–14 years: 13.3%
15–64 years: 66.1%
65 years and over: 20.6%

GDP per capita (PPP): $35,900 (2010 estimated in US dollars)

Suffrage: 18 years old

Legal drinking age: 16 years old to purchase beer or wine; 18 years old to purchase spirits. Laws are primarily directed toward sellers, rather than the minors.

Advertising Note

German citizens save twice as much money every year as people from the United States. When Germans do shop, they usually go for items they have already researched, seeking out the lowest price. When they find what they want, they often buy it and go home. In general, Germans do not consider shopping to be a form of entertainment; aimlessly wandering through store after store is wasteful to them. If you want to motivate Germans to buy something, provide as much scientific detail as you can about the item in the ad or on your website. The more serious information (not hype!) that your marketing materials and advertisements offer, the better your chances of loosening up some of those savings accounts.

ICEBREAKERS

BRILLIANT!

1. Your prospects may begin the meeting with small talk or by immediately getting down to business. Follow their lead, and be prepared.

   If there is an opportunity to chat, be familiar with the local sites and culture, musical heritage, local foods, beers, wines, etc. Pick out something interesting that is indigenous to that area, and learn about it in detail. For example, if you are in Munich, you should try the *Weisswurst*. This famous white sausage is made fresh every day, cooked (not boiled) for ten minutes in hot water, and then cut off at the ends to be eaten straight out of the casing (or cut down the center if you're feeling prudish). Dipped in sweet mustard, it is customarily eaten before noon, perhaps accompanied by a huge soft pretzel and, often, a beer. *Weisswurst* is a Bavarian dish and not available everywhere throughout Germany.

2. There are several reliable options for topics of discussion with Germans. Sports are a good subject, since Germans

are huge football (soccer) fans. Many also personally enjoy skiing, cycling, hiking, tennis, and ice sports.

Germans tend to be well informed about international affairs as well, and some of them might have strong opinions about your native country. Do not be surprised or offended if they offer some criticisms. Their opinions will be about a nation or its government, not you personally. Be prepared with some general responses about your homeland's policies that will keep the conversation going.

BOORISH

1. Leave your sense of humor at home. Germans do not consider business an appropriate place for levity. Serious business takes place in offices. Germans do have a sense of humor (as evidenced at the BBC's website about the German language, http://www.bbc.co.uk/languages/german/comedy/jokes.shtml), particularly for slapstick. However, they are very good at compartmentalizing it. Anything that distracts them from focusing on business is unwelcome.

   While it is common in the United States and the United Kingdom to begin a presentation with a joke or humorous anecdote ("A funny thing happened to me . . ."), this is not the appropriate way to start a speech in Germany.

2. All Germans know about their history in the two world wars. They study it in school. Thousands of Germans have researched all aspects of the wars. But they don't talk about it, especially not with foreigners. Bringing it up—especially any aspect of the Third Reich—is considered impolite and unwelcome.

WHAT TIME SHOULD I ARRIVE?

As Goethe said, "There is nothing more terrible than ignorance in action" (*"Es ist nichts schrecklicher als eine tätige Unwissenheit"*). Therefore, be early. There are few countries in the world where promptness is more important than Germany. It is considered an insult to be even a few minutes late

Cultural Note

Literature is important in Germany—as evidenced by the annual Frankfurt Book Fair, the largest of its kind in the world. If the subject comes up, you might like to show some appreciation for these two giants of German literature:

- Johann Wolfgang von Goethe (1749–1832) is considered the first of the great German writers. His masterwork is *Faust*, the story of a man who makes a pact with the devil.
- Friedrich von Schiller (1759–1805) was a contemporary of Goethe. He wrote plays and essays as well as the poetry for which he is best remembered.

Germany has produced a great number of Nobel Prize winners, in all categories. Recognizing the work of some of these winners of the Nobel Prize for Literature might help your overall appreciation of Germans and Germany:

- Gerhart Hauptmann (1862–1946) was a novelist and playwright. His small-town birthplace in Silesia is now Polish territory. Awarded the Nobel in 1912, he is best remembered for the drama *The Weavers*, about an uprising of Silesian weavers in 1844.
- Thomas Mann (1875–1955) was a writer from a family of writers. He is best known for *Buddenbrooks* and *The Magic Mountain*, as well as the novella *Death in Venice*. The latter has been made into both a film and an opera. Mann was awarded the Nobel in 1929.
- Hermann Hesse (1877–1962), the winner of the 1946 Nobel, was one of the few German authors to achieve international popularity in modern times. His novel *Steppenwolf* was made into a film in 1974.

to a business meeting, particularly if you are in the subordinate position. You can expect your German counterpart to be prompt as well.

If you are meeting with a *Geschäftsführer* (a CEO or executive director), give yourself enough time for the administrative assistant to greet you, announce you, and escort you into the executive's office. The door will probably be closed

- Nelly Sachs (1891–1970) and her mother fled Nazi Germany on the last plane to Sweden in 1940. Her plays and poetry often expressed the tragedy of the Jews in Nazi Germany. She was awarded the Nobel in 1966, but her life was marred by mental health issues, although she kept writing even when institutionalized.
- Heinrich Böll (1917–1985), drafted into the Wehrmacht, was wounded four times before being captured by the Americans. His writing often focused on the Second World War and its aftermath; his work has been described as *Trümmerliteratur* (the literature of the rubble). He won the Nobel in 1972.
- Günter Grass (1927–), winner of the 1999 Nobel, often writes of his birthplace of Danzig, which is now in Poland. He is most famous for his Danzig Trilogy, the first book of which is *The Tin Drum* (made into a film in 1979).
- Herta Müller (1953–), awarded the 2009 Nobel, is the second German woman laureate in literature. She was born in Romania, and her work often portrays the oppression of the ethnic German minority in Communist Romania. Her 2009 novel *Everything I Possess I Carry with Me* depicts the deportation of Romanian Germans to the Gulags in the Soviet Union under Stalin.

Knowing the names of Laureates in chemistry or medicine is not expected, unless you are in those fields. But many Germans who won the Nobel Prize in Physics are known to every student, such as Max Planck (1918), Albert Einstein (1921), Werner Heisenberg (1932), and Max Born (1954). And the very first Nobel Prize awarded, for physics in 1901, went to a German: Wilhelm Conrad Röntgen (1854–1917), the man who discovered x-rays.

when you arrive. Never just open a door and walk in; privacy is extremely important. At the end of the meeting, if your German prospect does not see you out to the door, be sure to close it behind you as you leave.

Social events begin on time as well. Interestingly, the German insistence on punctuality applies primarily to face-to-face meetings; it does not extend to delivery dates. Prod-

Cultural Note

If there is one thing everyone can agree upon about the German character, it is that Germans like things to run smoothly. Everything from your initial sales presentation to your product advertising should be clear, detailed, and orderly. Negotiations proceed in an organized manner as well. Germans like to be linear: one point follows another point. And once a point has been resolved, you should never revisit it.

Remember the German saying *Alles in Ordnung* (All in order).

ucts may be delivered late without either explanation or apology.

WORKWEEK

Business hours are generally 8:00 or 9:00 A.M. to 4:00 or 5:00 P.M., Monday through Friday. Late-afternoon appointments are not unusual, but try not to schedule appointments on Friday afternoons; some offices close early. Many people take long vacations during July, August, and December, so check first to see if your counterpart will be available. Also be aware that little work gets done during regional festivals, such as Oktoberfest or the three-day Carnival before Lent.

Germans have been known to have shorter workweeks than many other countries, but this is offset by Germany's gross domestic product (GDP), which is consistently in the top five worldwide. The expansion of the German workweek has been under discussion as well, due to the recovering economy, but whether it is during an abbreviated 37.5-hour or an extended 42-hour week, make sure that your meeting with German prospects will be an efficient, orderly use of their time.

Advertising Note

After World War II, most major German corporations hired foreign-owned (English-speaking) advertising firms. There were several reasons for this:

- The omnipresence of propaganda in Nazi Germany left Germans suspicious of advertising in general. (Of course, Communist propaganda was common in the former East Germany.)
- Many Jewish advertising professionals fled Germany or were killed by the Nazis. An entire generation of marketing and advertising agents—and the merchants who hired them—were lost.
- Finally, Germans pride themselves on their intellectual heritage. The profession of advertising was seen as insubstantial, frivolous, and unworthy of a first-class, disciplined mind. Until recently, few Germans wanted to go into advertising.

HOW CLOSE SHOULD I STAND?

Germans prefer a slightly larger personal space than the British or North Americans. One way to gauge a comfort zone is to stand about 6 inches beyond handshake distance.

This expanded distance applies not just to Germans personally, but also to their cars, furniture, and groceries. (Wal-Mart discovered this when German customers took umbrage at checkout clerks who tried to bag their food.) Never move a chair in a German executive's office, and never lean on, or even touch, the exterior of a German's car. Many Germans check their cars daily for scratches or nicks.

And refrain from massaging anyone's neck—particularly the Chancellor's—as former president George W. Bush briefly did at a G-8 summit in 2006.

DO I KISS, BOW, OR SHAKE HANDS?

SHAKE HANDS

Most Germans shake hands at the beginning and the end of a business meeting. The German handshake is brief, moderately firm, formal, and accompanied by direct eye contact—but not a big smile. Stand up straight, and keep your hands out of your pockets. Some Germans also add a very slight nod of the head to a handshake.

Remember that Germany has a very hierarchical business culture. The highest-ranking executive has the right to offer to shake hands first, then the second-highest, and so on.

There are other greetings in Germany worth noting. Staci Frantz, international sales manager at W. R. Case & Sons Cutlery, describes an especially interesting social one:

> German pubs and restaurants often seat people at large tables, where they share their meal with friends—or sometimes total strangers. If a German joins a party that is already seated, you may notice him give a couple of raps to the tabletop. This was traditionally a means of saying hello or good-bye, in lieu of interrupting the group to personally shake each individual's hand. While it is not as common as it once was, it is an acceptable and efficient way of greeting, or leaving, friends who are already at the table.

BUSINESS CARDS

- Like every aspect of business, the exchange of business cards in Germany is orderly. One does not simply toss cards out on the table like a poker deck. However, aside from proceeding in the order of precedence, no traditional ceremony is involved. Exchange cards with the highest-ranking (or oldest) person first.
- Your cards should already be translated into German on one side. In fact, all written materials, from business cards to technical data sheets, should be translated into Ger-

man. This is true even though most German executives speak multiple foreign languages—especially English and French—fluently.

- If your company has been in business for a long time (100 years or more), consider including the date of its founding on your card.
- If you have a Ph.D., you may include that on your business card.
- Bring plenty of cards; if you run out, it looks as though you were ill-prepared.

THREE TIPS FOR SELLING IN GERMANY

1. **Be Exhaustively Prepared**
2. **Take Advantage of Conferences**
3. **Let Germans Proceed at Their Own Pace**

1. BE EXHAUSTIVELY PREPARED

To sell in Germany, you need to be able to provide data on every aspect of your product or service. Germans will ask every question you can imagine and some you can't. They consider this interrogation a necessary and integral part of doing business. Extensive preparation is considered one of the reasons for the quality of German products.

If you put yourself in the position of having to send an inquiry back to your company headquarters after every question, you will not be taken seriously as a business partner. And to be labeled "not serious" is a serious allegation in Germany.

Remember that all written material must be translated expertly into German before delivery. Do not depend upon computer translations, even when you are pressed for time.

If you are in advertising, you must also research German advertising regulations, which are extensive. For example, if you suggest advertising during children's television programs, you will lose all credibility, as German law prohibits interrupting children's programming for advertising. As in other coun-

Cultural Note

Germans dislike surprises, even good ones. Surprises are an affront to order; worse, they show that their preparation was not sufficient to foresee the surprise, which can be embarrassing.

During the course of a business negotiation, if something unexpected happens that would result in you being able to offer a better deal, consider not telling the Germans. Even if it is positive news, the new data will result in delays while they conduct new research to vet your conclusions.

tries of the European Union, it is also prohibited to compare your product with a competitor's product in advertisements.

2. TAKE ADVANTAGE OF CONFERENCES

German celebrations—from Carnival (*Fasching*) before Easter to Oktoberfest in the fall—draw thousands of visitors. But Germany's trade fairs and conferences draw even more. The country hosts an average of 80 major fairs and exhibitions per year, for everything from automotives to textiles to nanotechnology. The famous Frankfurt Book Fair dates back to the 15th century and usually draws more than a quarter million visitors.

If you want to do business in Germany, you should take advantage of conferences, exhibitions, and trade fairs in your field. Be ready to book far in advance, since local hotels fill up for major conventions a year ahead.

There are multiple environments that can help you prepare for your exhibit in Germany. Meetings and exhibition management firms can provide you with information and support for transportation and customs issues, as well as safety and green regulations for the construction, installation, and dismantling of your booth. There are many fire safety regulations that will affect your construction; for example, inflammable foam rubber padding is prohibited in Germany. Associations including Successful Meetings, The Professional Convention

Advertising Note

The various forms of direct marketing are alive and well in Germany. These include Internet and/or e-mail, telephone marketing, and direct mail. However, both Germany and the European Union have strict rules about privacy protection. Consult a knowledgeable lawyer before you even compile a list of names to contact. You must also honor do-not-call/do-not-contact lists.

How extensive are the privacy laws? In 2010, the German legislature considered additional privacy legislation that would prohibit an employer from viewing a prospective employee's Facebook page (or any other social networking site).

Google's Street View feature has come under fire from hundreds of thousands of Germans who do not want their homes or streets displayed on Google Maps. Germans consider it a form of surveillance, which thieves could use to identify targets, security firms could incorporate into sales presentations, or potential employers and banks could use to scrutinize job candidates' and loan applicants' homes.

Management Association, and Meeting Professionals International are excellent resources for accessing industry leaders in convention, exhibition, and destination management worldwide.

Since food and drink are generally offered in booths, consider what you might want to supply. The larger the booth, the more elaborate the refreshments. While some venues require permission to serve liquor, alcohol is usually available in large exhibits. Be aware that the drinking age is based on the type of alcohol. For beer and wine, it is 16 years old, and for hard liquor, 18.

3. LET GERMANS PROCEED AT THEIR OWN PACE

The German reputation for producing quality products is well known. To accomplish this, German companies need to do painstaking research on every question. Obviously, this takes time.

Cultural Note

Foreign companies have made more than a few blunders when trying to market their products in Germany. Often the problems come from difficulties in translation. For example, Puffs facial tissues did not do well when introduced in Germany. The reason was that the word *puff* in German can mean brothel. (Another word with an odd translation is *gift*, which means poison in German.)

German companies are not immune from blunders. As they expand and purchase foreign firms, the potential for missteps increases. Volkswagen executives were less than pleased when their subsidiary Skoda started producing cars, which competed directly with VW's own. Skoda, a Czech company that was acquired by VW in 1991, was expected to sell low-priced, entry-level cars. But the 2010 Skoda Superb large family car not only competes directly with the VW Passat, it surpasses it. Built using VW technology, the Skoda Superb is slightly larger and more luxurious while costing a few thousand euros less. The Skoda Superb even won a comparison test in the German automotive magazine *Auto Bild*. It seems likely that the successor to the Skoda Superb will be smaller and less luxurious and will not compete directly with any VW models.

The only way you can speed up the research that precedes the decision making is to have all the answers in hand. This will require extensive effort on your part. It is also a good reason to bring one or more of your technical staff with you.

To keep track of the German team's progress, ask questions. Germans tend to respect people who pose intelligent questions. These inquiries show that you are remaining involved and on top of the situation.

Don't frame issues in the good news/bad news format that is common in English-speaking countries. Avoid trying to lessen criticism by first saying something positive. These combinations of positives and negatives tend to confuse Germans and will just make the process longer by requiring you to backtrack and explain yourself again.

LANGUAGE

Germany's official language is German (Deutsch). There are various dialects, including the accepted national dialect High German (Hochdeutsch), Low German (Plattdeutsch), and Bavarian.

Here are a few phrases that may help you in Germany. A variety of free German language programs are also offered through the BBC (http://www.bbc.co.uk/languages).

ENGLISH	GERMAN
Hello.	Hallo.
Good morning.	Guten Morgen.
Good-bye.	Auf Wiedersehen.
Excuse me.	Entschuldigung.
Good afternoon.	Guten Tag.
Good evening.	Guten Abend.
Please.	Bitte.
How are you?	Wie geht es Ihnen?
Thank you.	Danke.
Fine, thanks.	Danke, gut.
Yes, please.	Ja, bitte.
No, thank you.	Nein, danke.
Pleased to meet you.	Schön, Sie kennenzulernen.
I don't speak German.	Ich spreche kein Deutsch.
What is your name?	Wie ist Ihr Name?
Do you speak English?	Sprechen Sie Englisch?
My name is . . .	Meine Name ist . . .
What is it called in German?	Wie heißt das auf Deutsch?
Where is . . . ?	Wo ist . . . ?
How much is it?	Was kostet es?
Could you repeat that?	Könnten Sie das wiederholen?
Could you say it more slowly?	Bitte sagen Sie es langsa?
Sorry, I don't understand.	Ich verstehe es leider nicht.

ENGLISH	GERMAN
Help!	*Hilfe!*
I would like . . .	*Ich möchte . . .*
. . . a glass of wine.	*. . . ein Glas Wein.*
. . . a beer.	*. . . ein Bier.*
. . . a coffee.	*. . . einen Kaffee.*
. . . a tea.	*. . . einen Tee.*
. . . fruit juice.	*. . . einen Saft.*
. . . mineral water.	*. . . ein Mineralwasser.*

WOW FACTOR!

Germans are at the forefront of recycling and environmental sciences. Marketing your product as "green" will appeal to German consumers. However, you will have to back up your green credentials with data.

Even toys in Germany are marketed as green. Some are not only made of recycled or environmentally friendly materials, but also teach children about the environment. Green products, of course, usually cost more to produce, but they are often more durable as well (an important marketing point in Germany). A 2010 survey by the Nuremburg Toy Fair revealed that about a third of German consumers would be willing to pay 10 to 20 percent more for toys made from sustainable products.

One example of an award-winning green ad opened with a large, rough-looking Frenchman dressed in a black turtleneck, pants, and a bowler hat. He describes, and the viewer sees in flashbacks, his former behavioral problems: how he threw sand in a little girl's face, slapped windows shut, messed up women's hair, and whisked up dresses. Ultimately, it is revealed that this character is the wind. It is a clever ad for EPURON, a renewable German energy company: http://www.youtube.com/watch?v=2mTLO2F_ERY.

INDIA

Conventional long form: Republic of India

Local long form: Republic of India/Bharatiya Ganarajya

Local short form: India/Bharat

Population: 1,189,172,906 (2011 estimate)

Median age: 26.2 years

Age structure: (2011 estimates)
0–14 years: 29.7%
15–64 years: 64.9%
65 years and over: 5.5%

GDP per capita (PPP): $3,400 (2010 estimated in US dollars)

Suffrage: 18 years old

Legal drinking age: Varies from state to state, but minimum ages for buying and drinking alcohol are between 18 and 25 years old. Alcohol is prohibited in Gujarat and Mizoram, and throughout the country there are many days (e.g., religious holidays) that are intended to be dry.

Cultural Note

In 2007, the United Nations Department of Economic and Social Affairs released demographic data showing that India comprised 17 percent of the world's population. If you add in the other BRIC countries (Brazil, Russia, and China), their populations collectively came to 42 percent:

- Brazil: 3 percent
- Russia: 2 percent
- India: 17 percent
- China: 20 percent

In contrast, five of the leading economically developed nations made up only 10 percent of the world's population:

- United States: 5 percent
- United Kingdom: 1 percent
- Germany: 1 percent
- France: 1 percent
- Japan: 2 percent

Considering these demographics, this is a brilliant time to enter the Indian market. Every trade seems to be expanding. For example, India's film industry is now the largest in the world. Both Bollywood and India's advertising industry are based in Mumbai.

Additionally, past barriers to doing business are now being turned into opportunities. For example, the formerly appalling telecommunications sector has leapfrogged land lines for cell phones, and the potential for advertising on smart phones is prodigious.

ICEBREAKERS

BRILLIANT!

1. Whether you work in a high-tech firm or Bollywood, you will need a strong network in your industry segment. Be ready to invest in frequent face-to-face meetings, and build long-term relationships in order to succeed. Before your meeting, prepare a variety of comments and inqui-

ries about current trade events, the city you're visiting, the economy (the stock market) and the culture (from music and museums to places of worship).

In addition to its 4,000-year history, India is a stable democracy in a part of the world where democracies are rare. Your hosts will probably be righteously proud of India—as they should be. They may even want to show you a few local sites of interest. Allocate a bit of extra time for sightseeing.

2. Be prepared to reveal some personal information. Your Indian associate may begin the meeting with inquiries into your journey, your health, and your family. You should be ready with gracious answers and reciprocate with questions about your prospect's favorite hobbies, travels, sports (cricket is big), and so forth.

BOORISH

1. Never complain about India's infrastructure, even though the traffic is horrendous in the cities. As in other rapidly developing countries (like China), India has too few good thoroughfares. But Indian governmental and business leaders know this; they are building roadways as fast as possible. The project known as the Golden Quadrilateral (GQ) is a superhighway linking the four cities of Mumbai, Chennai, Kolkata, and Delhi. The GQ project represents the largest infrastructure project in India since the British built the Indian railway network in the 1850s.

That said, hire a good driver, allow for additional time to make your appointments, and do not be surprised at gridlock—sometimes due to free-roaming sacred cows, which can be traffic hazards.

2. There are multiple conversational topics you must avoid. Be particularly careful about discussing any of the following:

- Disturbances and terrorism in India
- The Indian caste system
- Indian disputes with its neighbors, especially Pakistan, with which India has fought three wars

- India's belief systems, particularly Hindu-Muslim relations
- India's poverty, politics, or red tape

If you do feel compelled to bring up any debatable topics, be aware that Indians will fervently defend India's social, economic, and political structure. Real or imagined slights against India can quickly ruin a deal—or your company's reputation.

WHAT TIME SHOULD I ARRIVE?

As a foreigner, you are expected to be on time. Although punctuality is not a traditional virtue in India, many Indian businesspeople are prompt.

Remember that Indians are always conscious of social hierarchies. While higher-ranking people may keep lower-ranked ones waiting, the reverse is not true. As a foreign supplicant, you may be in the subordinate position.

WORKWEEK

While there is no absolute standard for workweeks, business hours are generally 9:30 A.M. to 5:30 P.M. Monday through Friday. Lunch is usually from 1:00 to 2:00 P.M. Banks and governmental offices are often open on Saturdays, but with limited hours. Senior Indian executives may prefer late-morning or early afternoon appointments, between 11:00 A.M. and 4:00 P.M. Many Indians work long hours and are accustomed to receiving work calls during weekends or in the evenings.

Corporations generally offer approximately two weeks of paid vacation, and many observe the multiple holidays in India (27 in 2011). However, they may not compensate employees for all of them.

Advertising Note

As of this writing, more than 65 percent of ad revenues in India are spent on television advertising. Other major venues are magazines and newspapers, the Internet, and radio. TV ads are usually directed at the Indian middle class. Although English is widely spoken, more and more TV advertising is being done in the Hindi language. Advertisers believe that they can better appeal to their customers' impulses and emotions in Hindi.

Some major Indian television networks intend to make their programs available on cell phones. At that point, advertising on cell phones will spike, and design elements will need to be modified for the smaller screens.

HOW CLOSE SHOULD I STAND?

Two to 2½ feet apart is standard. Initial meetings are formal, but Indians may move closer after they have initially greeted you.

DO I KISS, BOW, OR SHAKE HANDS?

SHAKE HANDS OR PERFORM A *NAMASTE*

Many Indian businessmen who are familiar with international customs will shake hands. However, the handshake is not an indigenous tradition. The most common greeting among Indians is the *namaste*. To perform the *namaste*, put the palms of your hands together in front of your chest, fingertips pointing upward. You may hold your fingertips just under your chin, and bow your head slightly. The *namaste* is frequently executed both on arrival and departure, and is the traditional greeting of Hindus and Sikhs. It is not always performed by Indians of other religions.

Cultural Note

India has more than 200 special economic zones (SEZs) set aside specifically for foreign companies to make products for export using Indian workers. Tax incentives and new infrastructures make SEZs alluring to many firms.

Physical contact between the sexes is not as common as in many countries. Businessmen generally shake hands with other men, but they may not shake hands with women. Or they may wait to see if the woman extends her hand first. Unrelated Indian women do not usually have physical contact with other Indian women.

Overt, close physical contact (big hugs and kisses) is frowned upon by Indians of many belief systems, including Hindus, Muslims, Sikhs, and Buddhists. Refrain from hugging or kissing your Indian counterparts in public.

BUSINESS CARDS

- Remember to present your card with your right hand, receive your associate's card with your right hand, and treat all business cards with respect.
- Since English is the unifying language of India, your cards should be translated into English on one side and Hindi on the other.
- Many Indians are vegetarians, and pig products are prohibited to observant Muslims. Consider purchasing a non-leather wallet or card case.
- If your cards are in your wallet, do not keep your wallet in your back trouser pocket. A card holder that goes into a jacket pocket may be a good investment.

Cultural Note

Be certain to use formal titles in first business meetings, even for yourself. You will lose credibility if your Indian contact introduces him or herself as "Dr. Gupta" and you respond with "Hi, I'm Buddy."

Indian Hindu names have historically been tied to one's social background, or caste. Brahmin names are generally recognized and can be advantageous when applying for admittance to prestigious universities or applying for desirable positions. Some Indians now change their last names in order to distance themselves from lower caste affiliations. Names have become far more inventive as well. Some people adopt monikers that reflect a current or past profession (e.g., Rajesh Pilot, a former Indian government minister) or find inspiration for their children's names in celebrities, literature, or even the periodic table of the elements (like Iodine).

THREE TIPS FOR SELLING IN INDIA

1. **Hierarchy**
2. **Understanding Yes, No, and Patience**
3. **Taboos, Revered Animals, and *Vaastu***

1. HIERARCHY

You will want to meet with the most senior personnel possible while you are in India. Final decisions generally rest with one person, often with the title of director, owner, or president. If you do not meet with this individual during your visit, you may not be near the final close. Therefore, it is vital to gain this decision maker's confidence and support.

During your first visit, midlevel managers may ask you personal questions in order to confirm the status they may have already accorded you. This is important both personally and professionally. There are multiple factors that define your social standing in India. Do not be surprised if your contacts inquire about your family, your education, your title, how many people you manage, your home, hobbies, any sports you may have played, and any private clubs to which you belong. If you have any impressive accomplishments, it is acceptable to mention them.

Since hierarchies and formal chains of command are still prevalent in India, senior executives and officials command far more respect than in other, more egalitarian environments. J.D., a former vice president of publishing operations for a US-based, global information services company, was somewhat surprised at how far the differences extended during a recent trip to multiple cities in India:

> We were in the final stages of evaluating potential vendors for business process outsourcing work in India, and when we arrived in Kolkata at 2:00 A.M. on a Sunday morning, a team from one of the vendors was there waiting for us. They escorted us to our hotel and came back again to pick us up in a small touring bus later that morning. The quality of the interpersonal relationship is paramount in India. They wanted us to trust them, and so they set up a half day of tours through local points of interest to develop that relationship.
>
> One aspect of the hierarchical system that is very evident—and different—is the fact that our hosts completely sidestepped the very long lines at the tourist attractions and went right to the front of the queues. It actually made us somewhat uncomfortable, but there wasn't any graft or questionable behavior going on; it was just the culture and was accepted behavior. There is an obvious difference in the way people of different status are treated. Conversely, their senior executives only expect to meet with our senior management.

2. UNDERSTANDING YES, NO, AND PATIENCE

The word *no* has harsh implications in India. It is considered dismissive and insulting. Do not use it, and do not expect to hear it from your prospects, contractors, or associates.

Cultural Note

To no one's surprise, Indians are unhappy when foreigners attempt to profit from concepts Indians consider their intellectual property. The Traditional Knowledge Digital Library was established to help fight attempts to patent traditional Indian medicine. In one case, a US patent on using turmeric to heal wounds was withdrawn after India objected. The Traditional Knowledge Digital Library has expanded its reach and is filming yoga poses, so no one can claim yoga as his or her intellectual property.

Consequently, getting truthful answers can be difficult in India. Traditional politeness keeps Indians from stating outright objections. You may be working on a business deal and assuming your Indian clients are in complete agreement, only to find out at the close that they have been repeating a polite yes rather than upset the process by coming out with a blunt "No!"

Indirect refusals may sound like this: "I'll try," or "Possibly," or "That may be difficult." These responses or a complete evasion of the topic can be safely interpreted as meaning no.

One way to get at the truth is to solicit a response from someone older or higher-ranking than yourself. It is considered acceptable for such a person to say no to someone younger or inferior.

Once you have established a solid personal relationship with your Indian counterparts, they will be more comfortable saying no. (Of course, some Indians trained in foreign business methods have no problem saying no.)

It is paramount to understand that all communication takes time, and Indian businesspeople cannot be rushed. Exercise patience in every situation, because every negotiation is a personal, intuitive process. Indians do not give as much credence to scientific data and statistics as Westerners may, so any decision must be built on positive feelings and a solid rapport. The pace may seem leisurely to you, but never try to force a close.

3. TABOOS, REVERED ANIMALS, AND *VAASTU*

There are many taboos in India—both in person and in the media. India is the world's most populous democracy and is home to the world's largest population of Hindus, as well as the world's second-largest population of Muslims. Sikhs, Buddhists, Jainists, Catholics, Jews, and basically every other religion are represented in India. It is a serious challenge for advertisers to avoid upsetting any particular group. Here are some guidelines:

■ Be careful when you depict a man and a woman alone in an ad. Physical proximity and gestures may imply more intimacy than you want associated with your product. Strict Muslims as well as some Hindus may be sensitive to this.

■ Never show the sole of someone's foot in an ad. It is insulting. Never show anyone eating with the left hand. It is considered unclean.

■ The cow is revered. Bovine traffic jams are common, but do not denigrate them; those same cows may be used in a blessing for your new office! Cows should be depicted appropriately in any advertisements. If you must eat beef, try not to do it in front of your Indian prospects. While it may not destroy a potential sale, watching you consume a steak may not leave a good taste in the mouth of your vegetarian prospect. Never underestimate the gravity of insensitivity toward cows. A former member of parliament and ex–foreign minister, Shashi Tharoor, flippantly tweeted that he was happily traveling in "cattle class" (economy class) on an airplane in 2009. His Twitter post was rebuked by his Congress Party for being "unacceptable" and in poor taste. Some party members felt it was not only inconsiderate of social hierarchies in their locale, but also a tactless reference to a holy animal.

■ As the national animal of India, *Panthera tigris* (the Bengal tiger) is a popular symbol found in Indian advertising. Found throughout most of India, as well as in a few neighboring countries, it is now an endangered species. India has established more than 25 reserves to arrest the tiger's decline.

■ Inquire as to whether there is a traditional time of year to purchase the product you advertise. For example, many Indians consider the month of October (before the festival of Diwali) to be an auspicious time to buy an automobile.

■ While Hindi is written left to right, another popular language in India is Urdu, which is written from right to left. Urdu is spoken by more than 48 million Indians in the northern state of Jammu and Kashmir. If you happen to run any ads there, or anywhere near the Pakistani border (where Urdu is the national language), remember to adjust your marketing graphics to correspond with the right-to-left script.

■ *Vaastu* is an ancient Indian manner of analyzing buildings, land, and the layout of rooms, furniture, and gardens in order to encourage harmony and balance. The concept is similar to feng shui in Asia. If your environment is conducive to peace, positive energies will flow. *Vaastu* considers the Five Elements, Cosmic Energies, and human actions. It offers many guidelines for construction of an ideally balanced dwelling and takes into consideration appropriate directions for each room, window, and door. For example, one premise is that the sunrise from the east should hit the front door. Here are some additional tips on orientation and construction:

□ Plots (and houses) should be square.
□ Use high-quality woods and construction materials.
□ Don't plant tall trees close to the house. Tree roots and branches can endanger the building and block sunlight. Herb gardens are a better choice, and good for your health.

Cultural Note

When visiting India, expect sensory overload, especially on your first trip. The throngs, the noise, the weather, the unfamiliar scents, the indecipherable native alphabets—all of them tend to overwhelm. You can deal with it, but don't expect to be able to perform at 100 percent efficiency. Never schedule an important meeting too soon after arrival. You must be rested, sharp, and prepared for the intense bargaining that goes on continually in India. No one expects to pay full price for anything. Be ready to negotiate.

□ Sleep with your head to the east or the south.
□ Eliminate clutter.

If you are involved in real estate, it may behoove you to contract with an experienced *Vaastu* practitioner before breaking ground or opening your business. It always helps to get an auspicious start to any project.

LANGUAGE

The online edition of *Ethnologue* (http://www.ethnologue.com) lists more than 400 extant languages in India. Of those, Hindi and English are acknowledged as India's official—or national—languages. However, individual states in India have the right to establish additional "scheduled" languages, and they include Assamese, Bengali, Bodo, Dogri, Gujarati, Hindi, Kannada, Kashmiri, Konkani, Maithili, Malayalam, Marathi, Meitei, Nepali, Oriya, Eastern Panjabi, Sanskrit, Santali, Sindhi, Tamil, Telugu, and Urdu.

WOW FACTOR!

Direct mail in India is constrained by a slow postal service. Private delivery services are relatively new, so catalog and online sales are also limited. But India still has millions of door-to-door salespeople. If your product or service is suitable for door-to-door sales, you can achieve tremendous market penetration. Be certain that your merchants have a sufficient supply of the product with them, since the sale will either occur quickly at the door or not at all. Your sales team should also be ready to bargain; homeowners often expect to negotiate the price down by 40 or 50 percent!

INDONESIA

Conventional long form: Republic of Indonesia

Local long form: Republik Indonesia

Population: 245,613,043 (2011 estimate)

Median age: 28.2 years

Age structure: (2011 estimates)
0–14 years: 27.3%
15–64 years: 66.5%
65 years and over: 6.1%

GDP per capita (PPP): $4,300 (2010 estimated in US dollars)

Suffrage: 17 years old; universal; as well as all married persons regardless of age

Legal drinking age: 18 to 21 years old, depending upon the region. However, Indonesia is a predominantly Muslim country, and Islam prohibits the production, sale, and consumption of alcoholic beverages. Be aware of your surroundings. Halal restaurants will not serve alcohol.

Advertising Note

Unless you are of the opinion that "there's no such thing as bad publicity," the last thing you want is street protests and boycotts caused by your advertising campaign.

You will need native Indonesians to vet your ads and your products with an eye to circumventing any potential offense among the country's most conservative citizens. In general, these will be religious Muslims.

The Turner Broadcasting Network did this when it launched its 24-hours-a-day Cartoon Network in Indonesia. When the company discovered that Muslims abjure pork and pork products, it agreed to remove Porky Pig from the roster of cartoon characters to be broadcast into Indonesia.

Indonesia has the largest population of Muslims in the world, so be sensitive to the layout, colors, graphic elements, and taboos involved in marketing and selling to Muslims here.

ICEBREAKERS

BRILLIANT!

1. Estimates vary, but there are at least 13,000 islands in Indonesia's archipelago, and more than 700 languages! As you become familiar with the vast geography of this polyglot nation, you will appreciate the challenges of marketing and selling to Indonesia's myriad ethnic groups. In business, you will probably interact primarily with Indonesians of Chinese, Malay, Indian, and European heritage. If your contacts, agents, or distributors are Chinese, you may get down to business quickly. If not, let your contact lead the conversation. If it moves toward business, a general question about the prevailing economic and political climate, and how it may influence your products can be helpful.

   For example, if interest rates are rising, you will want to discuss possible low-interest options or discount pricing you can offer through your distributors or franchise networks. Or if there is an undercurrent of resentment against your particular country for any reason, you may want to forgo large advertisements in local media outlets for a month or two.

2. Good general topics of conversation include tourism, travel, food, and sports. Indonesians love racket sports, particularly badminton (the country's athletes have repeatedly won Olympic gold medals in badminton). Other popular sports include soccer (football), Australian-rules football, golf, and polo.

BOORISH

1. Do not get down to business too quickly. As we alluded to already, unless your prospects or contacts are all ethnic Chinese, you may not discuss work at all during the first visit. If you appear too eager, or if you push for yes-or-no answers, your visit may be cut short. Indonesian conversations traditionally begin with inquiries into your journey, your health, and your family. Questions of a personal nature (about your job, your education, your age, etc.) may help your Indonesian associate ascertain your status in society. Blunt yes-or-no questions are considered confrontational and are totally inappropriate at the start of a relationship.

2. Many Indonesians have negative feelings about much of the West. In general, avoid discussing anything related to colonialism. Indonesians continue to resent their former Dutch colonizers, and non-Chinese Indonesians particularly begrudge the way the Dutch favored Indonesia's ethnic Chinese over ethnic Indonesians. Indonesian Muslims may also object to US, UK, and NATO intervention in Middle Eastern Muslim countries, such as Iraq and Afghanistan.

WHAT TIME SHOULD I ARRIVE?

As a foreigner, you are expected to be on time. Although punctuality is not a traditional virtue in Indonesia, many Indonesian businesspeople are prompt. Others may abide by

Advertising Note

In 2007, the Indonesian government issued a regulation requiring all broadcast advertising to be created entirely by Indonesians. However, as of this writing (2011), the law has yet to be enforced.

the indigenous casual attitude towards time, *jam karet* (rubber time), and arrive very late.

Different rules apply to social events. Indonesians know exactly where they stand in the cultural hierarchy. If you invite Indonesians to a social event, they may ask who else is coming. Then they may make a point of arriving before higher-status guests but after lower-status guests.

WORKWEEK

The majority of Indonesians are Muslims, but Indonesian businesses do not follow the traditional Islamic workweek pattern of taking off either Thursday and Friday, or Friday and Saturday. Since Friday is the Islamic holy day, many people go to a mosque on Fridays at noon, but the standard workweek is Monday through Friday. Also, remember that many business owners are ethnic Chinese, few of whom are Muslim, so they may conduct business after lunch hours on Fridays and often are open a half day on Saturdays.

Business breakfasts are commonplace, as are early morning appointments. Many Indonesians prefer business meetings early in the morning. On the island of Bali, where the tourist industry has a plethora of hotels, breakfast meetings may start as early as 6:30 A.M.

Twelve days of paid vacation are standard. Approximately 20 days of holidays may be observed as well, but not all 20 Indonesian holidays are necessarily part of the compensation package.

HOW CLOSE SHOULD I STAND?

Approximately 2 feet apart. If your Indonesian business associate is ethnic Chinese, allow room for a bow.

DO I KISS, BOW, OR SHAKE HANDS?

SHAKE HANDS

Indonesian men usually shake hands with other men. Their handshakes tend to be relatively gentle and last for an extended period of time. After the handshake, a Muslim Indonesian may place the right hand over his or her heart. Some observant Muslim men will not shake hands with a woman (or touch her at all). Most Chinese businesspeople will shake hands with men and women, and may bow as well.

Instead of shaking hands, observant Hindus may prefer the *namaste* greeting, which does not involve touching. (Information on performing a *namaste* is in the chapter on India.)

BUSINESS CARDS

- Treat all business cards with respect, and remember to present your card either with two hands or just with your right hand. The left hand is considered unclean in many parts of Asia.
- Your cards should be in your native language on one side, with the other side translated into Bahasa Indonesian.
- Pork and pig products are prohibited under Islam. Do not keep your cards in a pigskin card case or wallet.
- Pictures or logos of dogs, pigs, or inappropriately attired people are not acceptable. If you display your picture on your cards, do not include any pets in the photos.
- If your cards are in your wallet, do not keep your wallet in your back trouser pocket. Just as in many parts of Asia, your business card is an extension of you and should not be written on, bent, or sat upon.

Cultural Note

Some 45 percent of Indonesian men are smokers. There is a cultural taboo against women smoking, so few women do so publicly. According to the World Health Organization (WHO), Indonesia is one of the 10 nations that account for two-thirds of the world's tobacco consumption.

Some 85 percent of the tobacco market is controlled by Indonesian companies (most owned by ethnic Chinese). These companies have a solid grasp of what appeals to the Indonesian market. Would-be advertisers in Indonesia would do well to study Indonesian cigarette advertising.

At this writing, there are few laws in Indonesia restricting the advertising of smoking. Tobacco advertisements often target youth, equating manliness and adulthood with tobacco usage—i.e., "You aren't a man until you learn to smoke." Cigarettes are also sold individually in Indonesia, allowing youths to smoke even without enough disposable income to buy a pack.

Much of the tobacco advertising is done via billboards. Billboard advertising is ubiquitous in Indonesia, especially along streets which are heavily used and have daily traffic jams.

THREE TIPS FOR SELLING IN INDONESIA

1. **Respect Indonesian History**
2. **Understand Indonesian Languages**
3. **Follow Their Social Agenda**

1. RESPECT INDONESIAN HISTORY

The Republic of Indonesia became an independent country in 1945, so it is natural to regard it as new. However, Indonesia encompasses hundreds of cultures, some with written histories more than a thousand years old. Indeed, Indonesia was occupied by precursors of modern humans. The remains of a *Homo erectus* skeleton found in Indonesia—popularly known as "Java Man"—date back to 2 million years ago.

Advertising Note

Indigenous music is sometimes used in Indonesian commercials. A popular form of Indonesian music is called *dangdut*, which fuses Malay, Arab, and Hindu musical traditions, along with Western forms such as pop and hip-hop. *Dangdut* bands include a singer backed by both traditional and contemporary instruments, even synthesizers. *Dangdut* evolved among working-class Indonesian Muslims in the 1970s and has also become popular in Malaysia and the Muslim (southern) part of the Philippines.

As is common for youth-oriented music, adults are often offended by *dangdut* lyrics and sexuality. *Dangdut* performances in Indonesia have been denounced as pornographic and have inspired street protests among religious Muslims. Advertisers intending to use *dangdut* music or performers should be aware of such controversies.

A number of kingdoms ruled over portions of Indonesia's 6,000 inhabited islands. There is archaeological evidence that a Hindu kingdom existed in Indonesia in the first century A.D. (The island of Bali remains the primary home of Hindus in Indonesia.) The last large non-Muslim kingdom was the Hindu Majapahit in the 13th century. Since then, most of Indonesia's rulers have been Muslim.

These kingdoms used several forms of writing, derived from either Arabic or Hindu scripts. A substantial body of literature developed, especially on the island of Java. Latin script did not come into use until Western colonization. The Portuguese conquered the Sultanate of Malacca in 1512. They were eventually replaced by the Dutch East India Company, which arrived in 1602.

Viewed from a historic perspective, even the 350 years of Dutch colonization are recent history. And the ethnic Chinese who dominate many Indonesian businesses are also recent immigrants.

2. UNDERSTAND INDONESIAN LANGUAGES

The national language of Indonesia is known as Bahasa Indonesian (which means "Language of Indonesia"). It is not technically correct to refer to the tongue as Bahasa, since this simply means "language."

Bahasa Indonesian is a Malay tongue that has been a lingua franca throughout the archipelago for centuries, although it was only formalized in the decades since independence. Because it is taught in every Indonesian school, virtually all Indonesians are now familiar with it.

Most Indonesians speak more than one language, and their other language is usually the indigenous tongue of their island or region, such as Javanese or Sundanese. Each of these regional languages may be spoken by more people than live in your native country: Javanese is the native language of more than 75 million people! There are many written scripts in use in Indonesia, but the Indonesian government has found ways for most Indonesian languages to be written using the Latin alphabet.

Many Indonesian businesspeople speak English. Indonesia is a former Dutch colony, but the use of the Dutch language is dying out. (Its use was never widespread, and some Dutch learned Bahasa Indonesian.) Ethnic Chinese businesspeople sometimes speak a version of Chinese as well. However, they do not necessarily speak Mandarin Chinese; most Indonesian Chinese originally came from Southern China and spoke southern variants collectively known as Min Nan.

Although many Indonesian businesses are owned by ethnic Chinese, it can be difficult for a foreigner to identify Indonesian Chinese by their surnames. Anti-Chinese legislation was adopted by the Suharto (spelled Soeharto in Indonesia) regime; in 1966, all Indonesian Chinese were ordered to adopt "Indonesian-sounding names."

Chinese traditionally put great value on their family names, so this was an oppressive blow. Some Chinese adopted Indonesian names, which encompassed their original names. For example, the Chinese surname Lin—also spelled Lim and

Liem in the Roman alphabet—could become Halim, Salim, Limanto, Limantoro, Limijanto, Alim, Limawan, or Ruslim, among others. Other Chinese translated their names into the Indonesian equivalent. And to make matters more complicated, the law was revoked after Suharto's resignation. Some Chinese kept their pseudo-Indonesian names, while others reverted to their original family names.

Clearly, with all the language permutations in Indonesia, all your marketing materials, advertisements, and presentations should be carefully translated and vetted locally.

3. FOLLOW THEIR SOCIAL AGENDA

Before business conversations begin, let your Indonesian contacts drive the agenda. This is their turf until the work starts, and meetings tend to be leisurely, starting with small talk and many cups of tea. Indonesian businesspeople cannot be rushed. Decisions will be made on their own time, which may proceed at a pace significantly slower than in your native country. However, Indonesia is a dynamic country, with a median age of 27.9 years. As younger Indonesians come into positions of power, the pace of business may accelerate.

Because of Indonesians' resentment of the imperialistic/ Western approach, it is very important to leave any rigid viewpoints aside. Keep in mind that there are factors that may remain hidden from you, such as political concerns. If you adapt to your prospect's agenda, though, you will make an exceptional impression and gain an advantage over your competition.

Here is an example: International sales manager P. J. Delaye was met at the Jakarta International Airport by his prospective distributor, who happily announced, "I canceled your hotel room; you're coming to my house for the weekend!" While this major change in plans was startling, it turned out that the contact was married to a daughter of former President Soeharto (Suharto) and their family's home was palatial. After Mr. Delaye spent an entire weekend following his prospect's agenda (seeing the country, meeting family, etc.),

Cultural Note

Indonesia contains the most volcanoes of any country in the world. More than 70 are historically active, including Krakatau (or Krakatoa). Significant volcanic activity occurs on Java, western Sumatra, and on many more islands. Indonesia's "Decade Volcano" has been in eruption since 2010 and is being studied by the International Association of Volcanology and Chemistry of the Earth's Interior because of its explosive history and close proximity to human populations.

he was offered a durian—a vile-smelling local fruit that many Indonesians consider a delicacy. Mr. Delaye, who is of French descent, thought the stench was deplorable but gamely tried the fruit. His feat so impressed the Indonesian distributor that he exclaimed, "You are the first Caucasian I've met who ate the durian!" Dining on the durian closed the deal.

LANGUAGE

Indonesian (Bahasa Indonesian) is the official language and is used in business, school, and government. However, there are more than 700 languages in existence throughout the thousands of islands of Indonesia, and most citizens revert to their primary languages at home.

Here are a few phrases in Bahasa Indonesian that may help you in Indonesia:

ENGLISH	BAHASA INDONESIAN (INDONESIAN)
Hello.	*Selamat siang.*
Pleased to meet you.	*Senang bertemu dengan Anda.*
Good morning.	*Selamat pagi.*
Good afternoon.	*Selamat siang.*
Good evening.	*Selamat sore.*

ENGLISH	BAHASA INDONESIAN (INDONESIAN)
Good night.	*Selamat malam.*
Good-bye.	*Selamat jalan.* (to the one leaving)
Good-bye.	*Selamat tinggal.* (to the person staying behind)
Yes.	*Ya.*
No.	*Tidak.*
Please.	*Silakan.*
Cheers / Good health!	*Pro! / Tos!*
Bon appetit!	*Selamat makan.*
I don't understand.	*Saya tidak mengerti.*
Excuse me.	*Maafkan saya. / Permisi.* (to pass by someone)
Sorry.	*Maaf.*
Thank you.	*Terima kasih.*
You're welcome.	*Kembali.*

WOW FACTOR!

Perhaps because of Indonesia's distance from the European Union and from North and South America, customer support and after-sales service are extremely important factors to consumers. If you are going to launch a product, you must make sure that your local distributor or partner is given sufficient resources to be a strong provider of product support. While your brand may be highly recognizable, it will not inspire loyalty if you do not develop a reliable local maintenance program with quick-response capabilities.

ITALY

Conventional long form: Italian Republic

Local long form: Repubblica Italiana

Local short form: Italia

Population: 61,016,804 (2011 estimate)

Median age: 43.5 years

Age structure: (2011 estimates)
0–14 years: 13.8%
15–64 years: 65.9%
65 years and over: 20.3%

GDP per capita (PPP): $30,700 (2010 estimates in US dollars)

Suffrage: 18 years old; universal (except in senatorial elections, where the minimum age is 25)

Legal drinking age: Varies by region from 16 years old (in Milan) to 18 years old for the purchase of alcohol. In general, minors can drink with parental supervision.

Cultural Note

Selling to Italy can be complicated, but selling Italy to others may be even more complex. Independent regional viewpoints can make it difficult for the country to gain a consensus. According to a *Wall Street Journal* article by David Berretta, regional differences may be a key reason why Italy lost its primacy as a tourist destination, affecting the country's economy and image worldwide. (In 2010 Italy was behind France, Spain, the United States, and China in terms of numbers of visitors and tourism revenue generated.) In 2004 the government set aside more than $66 million (45 million euros) for a tourism website, logo, and advertising campaign. But neither the money nor the time was sufficient to gain a consensus among the 20 regions involved in the decision about the website design and content. Eventually, the government reorganized the project, and the Italian Tourism Ministry developed an official site at www.italia.it.

ICEBREAKERS

BRILLIANT!

1. Italians are exceedingly aware of fashionable attire and appreciate *la bella figura* (a refined, beautiful image). They have a discerning sense of style and will recognize brand names, from shoes to sunglasses. So in a way, your first icebreaker is your entrance in beautifully fitting clothes. Many executives consider attractive clothing just another investment that will make everyone feel comfortable and respected.

2. Italians love to *comunicare* (talk) and *mangiare* (eat). A successful first visit should involve both. In Naples or Palermo, you may talk for two or three hours before any business comes up at all. Follow the client's lead with polite questions about the region's cultural sites, art, history, music (opera), sports, literature, local foods and restaurants, or family. Italians respect accomplishments and knowledge beyond just the workplace.

Then know enough about the politics to ask probing but reasonable questions. For example, you might say, "Tell me about your prime minister and how his party may influence our business."

BOORISH

1. The kingdom of Italy was established on March 17, 1861. In 2011, plans for a major celebration, Italia 150, included a multitude of festivities. Ironically, strife between northern and southern Italy made headlines at the same time. There is some antipathy between Italy's northern "economically profitable" region and the less prosperous southern half of the country. Wherever you are, be sensitive about expounding upon your work with—or your appreciation for—other regions.
2. Avoid speaking in a monotone. Although a controlled, modulated tone of voice may communicate respect in many Asian cultures, it will not impress many Italians. Your tone of voice should not be devoid of enthusiasm, nor should you sit as still as stone. Rather than showing respect, subdued speech may communicate a lack of interest or, potentially, a dull mind.

WHAT TIME SHOULD I ARRIVE?

Be on time, particularly in the north. Executives in Milan often start meetings promptly and spend less time on pleasantries than in the south. At the same time, though, it's important to know that personal priorities can override professional schedules. Flexibility with agendas (and with contracts) is a key characteristic of Italians, and they will appreciate that quality in you. Your appointment may start within 15 minutes of the planned time in Rome, but being kept waiting for thirty minutes is not remarkable. Accept delays without rancor, and never reveal a sense of urgency to wrap up a meeting or close a contract. Impatience is a weakness.

Cultural Note

Personal obligations tend to take precedence over established rules in Italy, particularly when the rules involve deadlines. Italians respect individuals more than regulations. In particular, they admire anyone who can outmaneuver Italy's byzantine governmental regulations (which can go back to ancient Rome).

If a critical delivery of goods, a new financial system cutover date, or some other important deadline is looming, be sure you take the time to check in with all involved parties—in person, if possible. Show interest in the value of each participating individual. Deadlines without a person behind them can be viewed as arbitrary and may not be considered a top priority.

The concept of time does not directly apply to the sales process in Italy, but it is true that closing large orders can take six months to a year. This is more about the research and consultation that goes on in the *cordata* (the line of the decision making) than the hours of operation.

WORKWEEK

Monday through Friday is the normal workweek, but many businesses may be open Saturday mornings. Banking hours may be 8:30 A.M. to 1:30 P.M. and then 3:00 to 4:00 P.M., Monday through Friday. Family-owned firms are commonplace, and their hours of operation are not always rigid.

Meetings can run hours over schedule, so never overbook your day.

The month of August is the height of the holidays, so appointments generally stop in August and resume in September. Each major city observes a feast day for its patron saint as well, and celebrations around Christmas and Easter can bridge several weeks.

Marketing Note

When Procter and Gamble introduced its popular Swiffer wet mop into Italy, it failed so badly that the product was soon removed from the shelves. After additional research, P&G found that Italian women spend more than 20 hours a week on household chores—not including cooking—and prefer strong cleaning products rather than time-savers. They did not believe that a little mop with a paper cushion on it would cut grease or produce the kind of deep clean they wanted. However, Italian women did like the concept that you could wax an already-scrubbed floor easily with a Swiffer mop. When Swiffer added beeswax to the mop (just for the Italian market), the product became popular. Its sales, combined with sales of other Swiffer products (like the duster), made Italy the biggest European market for the brand.

Other products, such as dishwashers, also have to be adapted for the Italian market. If a machine cannot clean plates as well as a person, and dishes have to be thoroughly rinsed before you put them in the dishwasher anyway, why bother? Some manufacturers adapted their dishwashers with an option for extra-hot water, which has alleviated some of that concern, but in general, Italians like to have more control over their cleaning and cooking processes and will reject some labor-saving devices if they don't think the end result will be as good as they can do by hand.

A standard paid vacation package is a generous 20 days, with approximately 12 additional holidays as well.

HOW CLOSE SHOULD I STAND?

There is a definite physical shift between initial formal introductions, at a distance of approximately 2 feet, and subsequent greetings. Once you become acquainted, expect to be approximately 1½ feet away from your Italian associates, or even closer.

Cultural Note

Italians are highly aware of scent, so if your new product includes a fragrance, you may want to study a report published in the *Acta Otorhinolaryngologica Italica* (the official journal of the Italian Society of Otorhinolaryngology). This report demonstrated that some odors are difficult for Italians (and other Europeans) to identify because they are atypical in that region of the world. For example, a University of Pennsylvania Smell Identification Test (UPSIT) worked well in the United States, but it was culled down for Italian subjects. Six odors out of 40 were unfamiliar in Italy. The mystery odors were root beer, cheddar cheese, wintergreen, turpentine, pickle, and gingerbread. Root beer is easily recognized in Memphis, but not in Milan. Another scent that stumped some Italian test subjects was cloves. They were able to pick the odor out of four options by process of elimination: "It isn't cinnamon, it isn't mustard, it isn't pepper . . . it could be cloves!" Don't expect your root-beer-, wintergreen-, or clove-flavored gums to fly off the shelves in Firenze (Florence).

DO I KISS, BOW, OR SHAKE HANDS?

GREETINGS VARY

Shaking hands is very important both when arriving and departing. After the first meeting with a male Italian associate, don't cut off the handshake abruptly; he may be about to grasp your arm with his other hand as well.

Kisses are not ubiquitous at initial business meetings, but businesswomen often kiss each other on the cheek upon departure.

Constant eye contact is part of being engaging in Italy. Do not let your gaze wander aimlessly. You may appear easily distracted and superficial.

Cultural Note

Whether you are in Sicily, Florence, or Rome, be certain to invite your prospects to lunch. A good meal is the way to build a relationship and is also an opportunity for you to make a good impression with your Italian contacts. Being able to discuss fine wines and Italian cuisine is important, as is your knowledge of dining etiquette.

Formal meals do not simply have more glassware and more cutlery. They involve more protocol. Wait for your associates to start eating before you begin. One of them may offer up a *"Buen provecho"* or *"Bon appétit!"* Since pasta is served at most meals, practice how to maneuver a forkful into your mouth as gracefully as possible (without using a big spoon to twirl it). Eat inconspicuously, without disturbing other diners. And refrain from cutting your salad up into little bites; Italians don't slice at their lettuce, they fold it.

Being a pleasant dining companion will endear you to your Italian associates, who will bring up business when they are ready. Very few of us follow all the rules of etiquette all the time. However, you should know what the rules are. Further dining guidelines can be found in Appendix A.

BUSINESS CARDS

- Have your business cards printed on excellent stock, but do not adorn them with too many embellishments.
- Italian cards are often designed with simple, clean lines; white backgrounds with black print are common. Be sure your name is legible, and avoid fonts with flourishes.
- Senior executives may put very little data on their cards.

THREE TIPS FOR SELLING IN ITALY

1. **Maintain an On-Site Presence**
2. *Il Sangue Non e Acqua* **(Blood Is Not Water)**
3. **It's Not Business, It's Personal**

1. MAINTAIN AN ON-SITE PRESENCE

Your long-term commitment to Italy should include regular contact between your corporate officers and senior Italian managers. However, that does not replace an Italian sales representative and/or distributor on-site. These individuals must be available for the day-to-day personalized service that Italian customers will expect. No matter how frequently you travel back and forth to Italy, it will not be enough to consistently monitor your customers' needs or navigate the onerous governmental regulations that go with virtually every major transaction.

It also helps to provide attractive marketing collateral in Italian for your products. Even if your clients speak your language, they will appreciate the effort you take to have your promotional and technical materials elegantly designed and printed in Italian.

2. *IL SANGUE NON E ACQUA* (BLOOD IS NOT WATER)

La famiglia (family) is not just nuclear in Italy. It's allegorical. It extends from close friends and professional associates to sports teams. It involves loyalty to figures of authority and power, as well as the *cordata* of coworkers that leads up to them.

Because of this loyalty, it is very possible that your top Italian sales representative would rather not be singled out for a large bonus if his or her coworkers—or even worse, his or her Italian boss—did not receive one.

Like Italy's strong, authoritarian leaders, Italian brands can inspire intense loyalty. Armani, Dolce & Gabbana, Prada, Versace, Gucci—all of these generate a level of devotion that is personal. During the World Cup, every Italian feels like part of Italy's national football *famiglia*. Familiarize yourself with

Cultural Note

When US artist Nicholas Santoleri visited Italy, he went to see several relatives in the region of Abruzzi. In the town of Letto-palena, he was impressed that the village's physical layout, architecture, and culture revolved around not only the church, but the church's graveyard. Seeing fresh flowers and gleaming sepulchers, he assumed they were recent interments. When he examined the Carrera marble crypts, he was shocked that several were for his ancestors who had been dead for decades. Obviously, his Italian relatives visited and maintained these gravesites weekly. It demonstrated the enduring support and connections that Italian families share:

Chi si volta, e chi si gira, sempre a casa va finire.

No matter where you go or where you turn, you will always end up at home.

the Forza Azzurri. (The word *Azzurri* is derived from azure, for the team's blue jerseys.)

While the nuclear family is getting smaller, *la famiglia* is still the major source of security, stability, and order in Italy. Even exceedingly efficient northern Italian executives buy and sell based upon the quality of their relationships and the trust they put in suppliers, many of whom are related to one another.

3. IT'S NOT BUSINESS, IT'S PERSONAL

Emotions are inextricably linked to decisions, and all business is personal. There is rarely a demarcation between personal feelings and quantitative data in a proposal. Therefore, when an idea is offered, it is an extension of the individual presenting it. If you negate the idea out of hand, you dismiss the person as well. Everything is internalized, everything matters deeply. Listen carefully to the opinions of your Italian colleagues, and always start with the points of agreement in each discussion.

Advertising Note

Television advertisements dominate all other media in Italy. More than 55 percent of advertising dollars goes toward TV commercials, a far higher figure than in most other European Union countries or North America. This predominance may be based upon somewhat slow Internet connections or declining newspaper and magazine circulations. Due to the woeful service of the Italian post office, magazines have few subscribers; readers purchase them at newsstands. But some believe it reflects the control that a huge media firm, Mediaset, holds over broadcasting. Mediaset was founded by the Berlusconi family.

There is competition for broadcast advertising, notably a pay-TV provider called SKY Italia (owned by News Corporation). But the influence of the Berlusconi family's holding company is considerable.

Conversations are not always linear in Italy, and ideas can be offered simultaneously by multiple participants. When engaged in a conversation, be comfortable with being interrupted, and know that it is not a show of disrespect.

LANGUAGE

Italy has been the name of this region for more than 3,000 years. It became a politically unified kingdom in 1861 and has only been a constitutional republic since 1946. Its ethnic diversity stems from the geographic influence of its surroundings. For example, France and Germany border the northern region of Italy and have had an effect on the languages and traditions there. In the east there can be a Slavic orientation from across the Adriatic Sea. And Arabic influences can still be found in parts of southern Italy.

Italy was a group of city-states for far longer than it has been a unified country. Although the media and the school systems are slowly diminishing the importance of ancient dialects, there are still major differences among Italy's 20 regions. Italians are often still proud of their local languages and cultures. Natives from the island of Sicily are known to identify themselves as Sicilians before they say they are Italians. The dialects of Sicily at one end of Italy and the Piedmont at the other are distinct enough to be classified as separate languages and are mutually unintelligible. In the Piedmont region alone, children may hear one of three dialects at home before they are taught Standard Italian in school: Piedmontese, Occitan (if they live in the Occitan Valleys), or in the heights of the Alps, they may speak Franco-Provencal. Other disparate dialects include Abruzzese, Pugliese, Umbrian, Laziale, Molisano, Aquilano, Venetian, and Lombard. The Napoletano dialect of Napoletano-Calabrese is reportedly not even comprehensible with Standard Italian.

Because each region has its distinct history and ethnicity, be sure to use the right terms, display the right graphics (Genovese meals look different than Roman), and know the right people in each region.

Here are a few phrases that may help you in Italy. A variety of free Italian language programs are also offered through the BBC at http://www.bbc.co.uk/languages.

ENGLISH	ITALIAN
Hello.	*Salve.*
Good morning.	*Buon giorno.*
Good afternoon / evening	*Buona sera.*
Good-bye.	*Arrivederci.*
Excuse me.	*Mi scusi.*
Please.	*Per favore.*
How are you?	*Come sta?*
Thank you.	*Grazie.*
Fine, thanks.	*Bene, grazie.*
Yes, please.	*Sì, prego.*
No, thank you.	*No, grazie.*

ENGLISH	ITALIAN
Pleased to meet you.	*Lieto di conoscerla.*
I don't speak Italian.	*Non parlo italiano.*
What is your name?	*Come si chiama?*
Do you speak English?	*Parla l'inglese?*
My name is . . .	*Mi chiamo . . .*
Where is . . . ?	*Dov'è . . . ?*
What is it called in Italian?	*Come si dice in italiano?*
Is it nearby?	*È vicino?*
How much is it?	*Quant'è?*
Could you repeat that?	*Potrebbe ripetere?*
Could you say it more slowly?	*Potrebbe dirlo più lentam?*
Sorry, I don't understand.	*Mi dispiace, non capisco.*
Help!	*Aiuto!*
I would like . . .	*Vorrei . . .*
. . . a beer.	*. . . una birra.*
. . . a glass of wine.	*. . . un bicchiere di vino.*
. . . a coffee.	*. . . un caffè.*
. . . a tea.	*. . . un tè.*
. . . fruit juice.	*. . . un succo di frutta.*
. . . mineral water.	*. . . dell'acqua minerale.*
I come . . .	*Vengo . . .*
. . . from the United States.	*. . . dagli Stati Uniti.*
. . . from Canada.	*. . . dal Canada.*
. . . from England.	*. . . dall'Inghilterra.*
. . . from Australia.	*. . . dall'Australia.*

WOW FACTOR!

Fine wines are an important aspect of dining in Italy, and being knowledgeable enough to suggest selections for a meal can leave a very positive impression on your important prospects.

Giuseppe Pezzotti, a senior lecturer at the Cornell University School of Hotel Administration, has a refined approach to learning about wines and the associated aspects of business entertaining. Professore Pezzotti offered the following viewpoint about becoming familiar with wines:

It can be wise to pick one variety of grape or one type of wine to learn about at a time. Start with lighter, less complex whites, and then move to the more multifaceted, robust reds. Find out everything you can about that particular grape—the strengths and weaknesses of the variety, the vineyards, the altitudes where they grow, the rainfall and climates of the regions of the world that grow them.

When you taste a wine, you use all your senses. The process of training your palate has a regimen:

- **Sight:** Examine the color, it should be the right shade and clear, not cloudy.
- **Swirl:** Swirl to aerate the wine and enhance the flavor and aroma. Notice if it adheres to the sides of the glass. If the wine is very light or does not doesn't have the complexity, it will not have rivulets or "legs."
- **Smell:** Pick out the subtle aromas—from fruits, vanilla, the oak, etc. If the aroma is "off," it may be oxidized, maderized (overheated), or "corked" (infused with TCA, or trichloroanisole).
- **Sip:** Bring the first sip in with some air to enhance the scent and taste.
- **Savor:** Assess the finish after you sip. Does it linger? Is there an aftertaste?

When you are hosting a dinner, try to find out about your guests' level of interest in wines in advance of the meal. If they are wine connoisseurs, ask the restaurant about its wine cellar before the lunch or dinner. (You can consult with the sommelier or wine steward if there is one.) Understand the options for good wines in each category, and be prepared to make some suggestions once your guests decide upon their meals. Consider what they are ordering and their preferences for dry or sweet wines. If your budget allows, order a sophisticated wine that will be decanted at the table. This may be costly for a well-aged wine (30 to 60 years), but you will be remembered for the mood you evoked and the excellent care you took of your prospects. Wine is like music: it is a wonderful accompaniment to a meal, and the people sharing it with you can all participate in the performance.

> *Si fueris Romae, Romano vivito more; si fueris alibi, vivito sicut ibi.*
> When you are at Rome, live in the Roman style; when you are elsewhere, live as they live elsewhere.
> —St. Ambrose (c. 340–397)

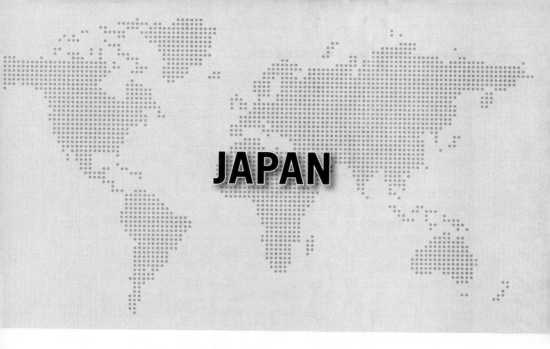

JAPAN

Local long form: Nihon-koku/Nippon-koku

Local short form: Nihon/Nippon

Population: 126,475,664 (2011 estimate)

Median age: 44.8 years

Age structure: (2011 estimates)
    0–14 years: 13.1%
    15–64 years: 64%
    65 years and over: 22.9%

GDP per capita (PPP): $34,200 (2010 estimates in US dollars)

Suffrage: 20 years old; universal

Legal drinking age: 20 years old

Cultural Note

Vending machines are extremely popular in Japan. Some of them have been equipped with visual facial recognition software, allowing the machine to postulate a customer's gender and age. The vending machine then uses that information to make appropriate buying suggestions on its sign.

Another version of facial recognition software is employed for the opposite effect: since it is now illegal to sell tobacco to persons under the age of 20 in Japan, the Kyoto firm Fujitaka programs vending machines to refuse to sell to customers it determines to be underage.

Other potential applications for the software range from marketing on billboards to security at airports, in hotels, and at universities.

ICEBREAKERS

BRILLIANT!

1. In general, you will be introduced to senior executives by a third party. This could be your representative in Japan, your interpreter, or one of the managers who works for the senior executive. If you can, learn the Japanese phrase for "Pleased to meet you": *Doozo yoroshiku* (doh-oh-zoh yo row' she coo).

   Then your interpreter should express your thanks for the executive's time and the opportunity to talk together about your mutual companies. "Thank you" is an important phrase for you to learn as well: *Arigatoo-gozaimasu* (ah ree gah' to go zai'mahs).

   These preliminaries will occur in conjunction with the exchange of cards, which is a key element of the introduction, and can set the tone for the entire visit. The business card (*meishi*) exchange is described later in this chapter.

2. If you are meeting multiple Japanese managers at a conference or other public venue, they may not dive right into a conversation. They will need to understand your level in

the hierarchy of the firm, and your social position. No one is precisely equal with anyone else in Japan. (Even twins are born seconds apart, so there will always be an elder brother or sister, and in Japanese society, this distinction can be significant.)

To ascertain your status, Japanese people may ask you many questions. Some may seem intrusive. It is certainly not their intention to be rude; the questions are part of an important process. They help your Japanese associates understand your role and give you the appropriate honorific in Japanese (which does not translate into English). Any of these questions would be legitimate in Japan:

- How old are you? (The older the better, since age is respected.)
- How many people report to you?
- Are you married? Do you have children?
- How much do you earn?

Never take offense. If you do not wish to respond, simply evade the question. Offer an innocuous comment to move the conversation in another direction and take the attention off of you, such as "This is such a beautiful facility!" The Japanese are not obtuse; they will understand that you do not want to respond. Bluntly refusing to answer a question, in contrast, is unacceptable. That would embarrass everyone concerned, and the consequences could include an early termination of your visit with a viable prospect.

BOORISH

1. Never be a businessperson not bearing gifts. Your prospect has just handed you a beautifully wrapped present, and all you have are company brochures. Instead of looking cheap and ill prepared, be sure to at least have an initial present from your firm to theirs. An iPod loaded with a customized message from your CEO to theirs, or music from accomplished local musicians would be a very nice

introductory gift. Whatever you offer, be sure it is made in your country, preferably in your state or province, thereby investing the gift with a certain significance. (While iPod components are manufactured in a variety of countries—including Japan—they are considered a US product.)

Some multinational salespeople advocate giving the gift almost immediately, right after the exchange of cards. No one is seated yet, and you still have direct access to the executive. It may be an appropriate way to generate goodwill for the rest of the meeting and open the lines of communication. Never expect that the gift will be opened while you are there. Many Japanese might feel that doing so would make them appear greedy.

Other executives believe that the gift should come at the end of the initial meeting, after some rapport has been built. This prevents you from looking overly enthusiastic at the start of the meeting. Some firms are more formal than others, so ask your Japanese representative for his or her advice before the meeting. Just be prepared with a variety of gifts, from smaller but high-quality items like Zippo hand warmers to iPads. Whatever you give, be sure it is exceptionally well made, and not emblazoned with your corporate logo.

2. Professors in Western classrooms often inquire whether their students comprehend a topic before they move on. They expect interaction throughout the lesson, and at the end of the class, teachers often close with "Does everyone understand?" or "Do you have any questions?" Westerners are trained to question their professors, and, subsequently, their bosses. Employees brainstorm, question authority, ask for help, and stop meetings if they don't understand.

However, since early childhood, the Japanese are trained to blend in with their peer group. This overriding conformity to the group means that no student would say to a professor, "Excuse me, I don't understand, could you explain it again?" For the Japanese, this thinking suggests a selfish desire to have the lesson repeated, in a custom-

Cultural Note

In North America, many people believe that meeting a person's gaze conveys honesty and that avoiding direct eye contact is a sign of evasion or weakness. However, in Japan, prolonged eye contact is considered impolite (at best) or aggressive (at worst).

This personal cultural behavior may transfer to static images in advertising. Psychologists who study how we look at faces found that Westerners focus primarily on the eyes and mouth. But neuroimaging eye-tracking studies found that Japanese and Chinese subjects targeted completely different facial features. The East Asian volunteers concentrated their gazes around the bridge of the nose! Further research is being done to validate these findings, but it represents another factor that advertisers in Japan must consider. How do you sell mascara in three seconds (a high span of attention for a print ad) when Japanese women may not focus their foveal vision (sharp, central vision) on the eyes in the ad at all?

Many universities are studying applied neuroimaging to help eliminate much of the risk in marketing research, new-product development, and advertising. The engineering and technology group at the University of Warwick has a variety of videos and podcasts on the subject at http://www2.warwick.ac.uk/newsandevents/podcasts/engineering-technology/41-neuromarketing.

ized fashion, for one person. Not only would the student be implying that the teacher is not a good enough instructor, he or she is admitting a total lack of comprehension and imposing that shortcoming on the entire classroom. The class now has to wait for the embarrassing moment to pass.

If your presentation fails to communicate important data clearly or your sales call goes poorly because you were inadvertently rude, Japanese executives will never stop you to deliver the bad news in front of a group, if at all. To find out the truth, you can use Japanese intermediaries who will extract accurate information after hours from the prospects for you. Or you can go out after work with your prospects yourself and stay clear-headed enough to remember the important chats you had over multiple alcoholic beverages. If you are fortunate, at least one of your Japanese associates will be comfortable enough to tell you the truth in private.

WHAT TIME SHOULD I ARRIVE?

Be early. It is better to arrive 5 to 10 minutes before your appointment is scheduled to begin, so that everyone will be comfortable and begin promptly. Being late is insulting, and the Japanese do not like surprises. A whole group would probably have to change their schedule if you are late.

WORKWEEK

While the standard workweek may officially be 9:00 A.M. to 5:00 P.M., Monday to Friday, many employees work far later into the evening and will attend after-hours events with coworkers and/or business clients. Socializing after hours is essentially mandatory to conduct business in Japan.

In 2011, there were 18 holidays in Japan—all of which may be observed and paid for as well. Avoid scheduling appointments during the three major holiday breaks, because many people travel, hotels are more expensive, and work can be difficult to accomplish. The three significant holidays are New Year (January 1st), Golden Week (which falls between the end of April and the beginning of May), and Obon (around the middle of August in most of Japan). Obon is a Buddhist festival that commemorates Japanese families' ancestors. Many people leave the larger cities and return to their hometowns during Obon.

Most companies offer 10 paid vacation days for their employees and add more days after the employees have substantial tenure with the firm. Due to Japan's aging workforce,

Cultural Note

Confucianism underpins Japanese society, and one of the tenets of Confucianism is a hierarchy based on age. Always defer to elders and show them respect. How important is this hierarchy? Sony is one of the few companies to have a non-Japanese as its CEO: Welsh-born Howard Stringer. In 2009, Stringer broke with tradition and promoted four high-achieving Japanese middle managers over their older bosses. Usurping the hierarchy was so traumatic that the four Japanese managers were reluctant to accept the promotions.

On a practical level, you will show respect for the elderly by greeting them first, allowing them to enter a room first, and never interrupting them.

the government has started subsidizing companies to help keep senior workers employed.

HOW CLOSE SHOULD I STAND?

Start between 2½ and 3 feet away from the other person. Be far enough away that a slight bow from the waist will not intrude on your associate's space. After the bow, you can move closer to shake hands and exchange business cards.

DO I KISS, BOW, OR SHAKE HANDS?

GREETINGS VARY

Greetings are verbally enthusiastic in Japan. A lukewarm, listless "Hello" conveys apathy and will be received somewhat like a limp handshake would be in Germany.

However, traditional greetings do not involve touching anyone, ever. Be certain not to touch, hug, kiss, or in general be physically demonstrative with anyone in a work environment.

Corporate employees may bow several hundred times a day. There are multiple degrees of bowing, and Japanese learn all the intricacies from childhood or at *juku* schools. Watch what others do, and attempt to emulate them.

Men place their hands by their sides and bow, while women clasp their hands in front of them. Bow from the waist. The junior person always bows lower than the senior executive. Your efforts will be appreciated.

You are also generally welcome to shake hands in Japan. Do not use an overly aggressive grip. Japanese handshakes are relatively gentle and may last for five seconds or more. Respond in kind. Never assume that a weak grip is indicative of weak negotiating skills, and never break a grip too quickly.

BUSINESS CARDS

- A business card (*meishi*) is a physical extension of you. Never offer a bent, dirty, or less-than-perfect version of yourself to a prospect.
- Have your *meishi* translated into Japanese on one side. If your firm is extremely large or particularly old, consider adding those statistics to it.
- Bring boxes of cards. You may go through hundreds in a comparatively short time. Never run out; a lack of cards may imply you have no job.
- When you get to Japan, buy an attractive *meishi-horuda*, a business card holder. Keep your cards inside, and place it in your jacket pocket or your purse. Never put it in your pants pocket.
- Have your *meishi-horuda* easily accessible, because the exchange of cards happens during the introduction.
- Always start with the most senior member of the Japanese team.
- If you are offering your card first, present it with two hands, with the Japanese side facing forward. Keep your fingers on the corners of the card, and try not to cover any important data with your thumbs.

Marketing Note

A professional association had carefully selected a primary graphic element to use on marketing materials for an annual conference in Japan. It was to be one exquisite cherry blossom. Cherry trees in bloom are an auspicious symbol in Japan, and the conference coordinators thought the graphic would communicate their appreciation for the culture. Unfortunately, the visual disturbed some of the Japanese. Although cherry trees in bloom *are* beloved in Japan, culling one single flower made it look oddly isolated and did not bode well. Japan is a consensus-based, cooperative culture, and highlighting one lone flower from a branch that would normally hold many blossoms was like singling out one person from an entire group.

It took some effort for the US coordinators to discover why the Japanese members objected to the graphic. But when one Japanese associate finally explained the problem, they were able to salvage the campaign by changing the graphic to a spray of blossoms. Fortunately, the marketing team had submitted the concept in plenty of time for review in Japan.

- Receive cards with two hands, with a slight bow. If the executive you are meeting is extremely senior, an assistant may accept your card for him or her, and will dispense one to you.
- If you are exchanging cards simultaneously, offer the card with your right hand only. Never present a card with your left hand. You receive your contact's card with your left hand and then hold it with both hands. Thank him or her for the card, look at it closely, and make a polite comment or two about it.
- Business cards are put on the table at meetings in an orderly manner. Don't scatter them around or play with them. Bending or writing on a card is an insult to the owner of the card.
- When it is time to go, carefully pick up all the cards and place them in your *meishi-horuda*.

THREE TIPS FOR SELLING IN JAPAN

1. Confucianism and Harmony (*Wa*)
2. Subtleties and Silence
3. Apologizing

1. CONFUCIANISM AND HARMONY (*WA*)

Confucian and Buddhist principles guide many aspects of Japanese behavior. Of the five constant virtues of Confucianism (kindness, righteousness, courtesy, wisdom, and *xin*), *xin* is key for salespeople. *Xin* refers to personal service, faithfulness, and integrity (keeping one's word). Japanese salespeople strive to exhibit a high level of service and faithfulness by visiting their prospects repeatedly—but keeping the sales calls relatively short. By their consistent, reliable presence, they cultivate the buyer's trust. In some high-tech industries, this can happen quickly—in others, in can take years. But once a harmonious relationship is established, try not to change your sales representative.

The preservation of a tranquil, harmonious environment is important in Japan. The word *wa* is difficult to define, but it reflects the smooth, tranquil operation of every aspect of a group. It is like a perfect game, work of art, or musical composition. Everything is in sync.

One way salespeople maintain *wa* is to take a low-key approach. Traditionally, they tend toward the soft sell, virtually apologizing for interrupting the executive's day. They try to establish pleasant moods rather than burden the top executive with a plethora of facts. The executive will hear about the details from his or her group, if the group decides to take your proposal seriously.

2. SUBTLETIES AND SILENCE

Many cultural anthropologists divide countries into low-context societies (like the United Kingdom and the United States) and high-context societies, like Japan. In low-context cultures, information is predominantly communicated in an overt, frank manner. But in Japan, a high-context society, a

Cultural Note

As in most countries, many of Japan's business leaders are from old, established families. The power elite of Japanese business-men are known as the *Zaikai*. But even the *Zaikai* do not work alone. Since Japan is a highly collectivistic society, the concept of a single decision maker is not acceptable. The Japanese see the entire sales process as a complex flow of interaction.

Products and services must be marketed to the group and accepted accordingly. It would disturb group harmony if one member openly acquired an "unapproved" item. Proposals go through multiple levels of consensus building. In effect, you sell to the team, and the team sells to the CEO.

When you are in the final negotiation stage, avoid introduc-ing any major changes to the proposal. Since every aspect of the contract has already been predetermined by the Japanese, a spontaneous idea or major change will not receive a positive reaction.

great deal of information is transmitted nonverbally, with sub-tle, indirect cues. Therefore, key points often go unsaid but are clearly understood by the Japanese.

In Japanese, what you do not say is just as important as what you do say. Omissions, pauses, and evasions are just as communicative as words. Many Japanese executives are comfortable with silence. A respectful pause may last ten to fifteen seconds and does not signal either acceptance or rejec-tion. Westerners generally have an aversion to silence during sales calls and often resume talking before the Japanese pros-pect has the chance to respond.

Subtleties and restraint in communications are ingrained, so that highly dynamic presentations can be exceedingly dis-tracting. An animated speaker may fail in his or her message, because the Japanese will pay attention to the dramatic body language and emotions—and may not actually hear the data being communicated. The book *Doing Business with Japanese Men* related a situation where the exaggerated facial expres-

Marketing Note

National pride does play a part in decision making. Be sure that your product or service is not seen as un-Japanese before you invest in marketing it. The way you approach the market can actually make your product part of Japan's culture.

Understanding that the Japanese have adopted some Western holidays, especially Christmas and Valentine's Day, the company KFC (formerly known as Kentucky Fried Chicken) achieved a marketing coup by developing marketing that suggested the traditional American Christmas dinner consisted of fried chicken. This marketing campaign was so successful that you must now reserve your Christmas takeout meal from KFC well in advance of the holiday. Signs in front of KFC stores notify customers how many reservations are still available for December 24th or 25th. And the image of Colonel Sanders has become so popular that statues of him are often dressed up in kimonos or costumes for photo opportunities outside the stores. KFC has been so thoroughly accepted in Japan that some Japanese bloggers seem unsure of whether or not KFC exists in the United States.

sions and gesticulations of a North American presenter mesmerized the Japanese audience so completely that one attendee in the front row actually started to unconsciously imitate the speaker! Restraining yourself both physically and emotionally in Japan is an important sales and speaking skill. Develop your poker face.

3. APOLOGIZING

While apologizing has many negative ramifications in other countries (an admission of guilt can make one look weak or liable for dismissal or legal action in the United States), apologies are far more common in Japan. Most Japanese apologize a dozen times daily, whether or not the occurrence is their fault. Prime ministers and CEOs have offered their public apologies for problems as varied as the economy to car recalls.

Cultural Note

Reading left to right may be wrong. How do advertisers know how to design and lay out ad copy in Japan? It depends upon the ad vehicle. Traditional Japanese was written vertically, in columns read from the top to the bottom, and then right to left (called *tategaki*). This method is still used in many areas: on street signs, for the text in *manga* (Japanese comic books), in newspapers, and in some books. (Art and calligraphy books are often bound on the right-hand side and read "back to front.") This reading style may affect how you design some of your marketing materials.

The more common format is *yokogaki*, a horizontal layout, read left to right. However, to complicate things, you may see a combination of both formats in the same ad, or even right-to-left horizontal writing on captions of illustrations, in headlines of newspapers, and along the sides of vehicles.

In certain circumstances, apologies are required in order to continue doing business in Japan. If Citibank Japan CEO Douglas Peterson and Citigroup CEO Charles Prince had not bowed in apology in 2004 on Japanese television for being lax on manipulative sales, lending practices, and money laundering, they would never have been able to reenter the Japanese marketplace.

Apologizing also helps to reestablish harmony in the work environment and allows business to proceed. On October 2, 2009, the president of Toyota, Akio Toyoda, apologized profusely at Japan's National Press Club for the four deaths that were thought to be the result of faulty Toyota floor mats, and the resulting recall of 3.8 million cars. He also expressed sorrow for closing Toyota's factory in California and not being prepared for the global economic crisis. At the time, the extent of his list of regrets surprised even the reporters at the Press Club. But it was just the beginning of the apologies necessary to reestablish Toyota as a trustworthy brand.

LANGUAGE

Most sentences in Japanese can be expressed in at least four different levels of politeness. Japanese women almost always use one of the more deferential forms. Here are a few, generally polite phrases that may help you do business in Japan.

ENGLISH	JAPANESE
Hello.	*Konnichiwa.*
Good morning.	*Ohayoo-gozaimasu.*
Good-bye.	*Ohayoo-gozaimasu.*
Excuse me.	*Sumimasen.*
Good afternoon.	*Konnichiwa.*
Good evening.	*Konbanwa.*
Please.	*Onegai-shimasu.*
How are you?	*Ogenki desu ka?*
Thank you.	*Arigatoo-gozaimasu.*
Fine, thanks.	*Hai, okage-sama de.*
You're welcome.	*Doo itashi-mashite.*
How do you do?	*Hajime-mashite?*
No, thank you.	*Iie, kekkoo desu.*
Pleased to meet you.	*Doozo yoroshiku.*
Yes, please.	*Hai, onegai-shimasu.*
I don't speak Japanese.	*Nihongo wa wakarimasen.*
What is your name?	*Onamae wa?*
Do you speak English?	*Eego ga wakarimasu ka?*
My name is . . .	*Watashi no namae wa . . . desu.*
What is it called in Japanese?	*Nihongo de nan desu ka?*
Where is . . . ?	*. . . wa doko desu ka?*
Is it nearby?	*Chikaku desu ka?*
How much is it?	*Ikura desu ka?*
Could you repeat that?	*Moo ichido itte-kudasai?*
Could you say it more slowly?	*Yukkuri itte-kudasai*

ENGLISH	JAPANESE
Sorry, I don't understand.	*Sumimasen, wakarimasen.*
Help!	*Tasukete!*
I'm . . .	*. . . shusshin desu.*
. . . from the United States.	*Amerika . . .*
. . . from Canada.	*Kanada . . .*
. . . from England.	*Igirisu . . .*
. . . from Australia.	*Oosutoraria . . .*
I would like . . .	*. . . o onegai-shimasu.*
. . . a glass of wine.	*Gurasu wain . . .*
. . . a beer.	*Biiru . . .*
. . . coffee.	*Koohii . . .*
. . . tea.	*Koocha . . .*
Thank you. (before eating/ drinking)	*Itadakimasu.*
Cheers!	*Kanpai!*
Thank you. (after eating drinking)	*Gochisoo-sama-deshit.*

WOW FACTOR!

The relationship between a seller and a buyer in Japan has been compared to that of a son and a father. The seller, of course, is in the inferior position of the son. The buyer is willing to accommodate the seller—but only after the proper relationship has been established.

In the US negotiating tradition, the longest and toughest part of the negotiations is the actual sale: the back-and-forth over price, delivery dates, and other conditions. But in Japan, the most critical part of the negotiation is at the beginning: the establishment of the proper relationship. Without that relationship, including the acknowledgment that the seller is in the inferior position, no sale will happen.

MEXICO

Conventional long form: United Mexican States

Local long form: Estados Unidos Mexicanos

Population: 113,724,226 (2011 estimate)

Median age: 27.1 years

Age structure: (2011 estimates)
  0–14 years: 28.2%
  15–64 years: 65.2%
  65 years and over: 6.6%

GDP per capita (PPP): $13,800 (2010 estimates in US dollars)

Suffrage: 18 years old; universal and compulsory (but not enforced)

Legal drinking age: 18 years old

Sales Note

If you want to start and run a business in Latin America, Mexico was the World Bank's number one choice in its 2011 "Doing Business" report. (Singapore was ranked as the best country worldwide.) Mexico's rating moved up six levels in one year due to their implementation of online options for business registrations and tax payments. To analyze and compare 183 countries worldwide in the "Doing Business" report, the World Bank evaluated the following criteria (rendered verbatim from the report at www .doingbusiness.org/reports/global-reports/doing-business-2011).

- Ease of starting a business
- Dealing with construction permits
- Employing workers
- Registering property
- Obtaining credit
- The ease of trade across borders
- Enforcing contracts
- Protecting investors
- Closing a business

Mexico's improvements in business regulations were encouraging for entrepreneurs both within their country and internationally.

ICEBREAKERS

BRILLIANT!

1. In Mexico, your first appointment with a key decision maker is most likely the result of a personal introduction. Therefore, chatting briefly about your mutual contact may be the best way to begin the conversation. Your prospect will probably ask where you have been in Mexico and what sites you have seen. This is a very good reason to arrive well ahead of your appointment and spend some time visiting the major sites in Mexico City—or wherever your sales calls take you.

Cultural Note

The correct amount of eye contact can be a delicate affair. Whether it is between a superior and a subordinate in business, a man and a woman, or a child and a parent, extended periods of eye contact can communicate anything from insolence to intimacy to adoration. Be aware of the ramifications of your nonverbal communication in Mexico.

2. Keep your questions formal, but explore mutual interests you may have. The higher status the topic, the better. You might want to discuss exotic trips your client has taken, prestigious clubs you both belong to, sports you both enjoy, or luxury items you both admire (or own).

BOORISH

1. Never try to move too fast into the business part of the discussion. Many people say 80 percent of their first few business visits in Mexico are primarily efforts at building *confianza* (trust), and 20 percent are business.
2. Never refuse a social invitation. Weekends can be far more important than workdays for building relationships and closing deals. If you are invited to a personal gathering and you reply, "Thank you, but I have a previous commitment," you have just lost the opportunity for entering the social circle of your client.

WHAT TIME SHOULD I ARRIVE?

Your Mexican contacts may be late for appointments—sometimes considerably so. However, you do not have that luxury. It is important to allocate far more time than you think necessary to make your meeting on time. Traffic in Mexico City is atrocious. Gridlock is ubiquitous, cars are only permitted to

Advertising Note

Political correctness is not as sensitive an issue in Mexico as in some countries. Mexicans can be very comfortable laughing at stereotypes, as long as they are clever. For example, an ad campaign for a Mexican football (soccer) lottery featured Landon Donovan, a star USA player "disguised" in a colossal sombrero, fake moustache, and striped poncho, sneaking into Mexico from the United States of America so that he could play the lottery. When he claims he is *Mexicano*, an enormous Mexican border guard peels off the hat and the moustache and states, "No, you're Landon Donovan." Eventually, the border guard banishes him home, back through the hole from which he crawled. The witty aspects of this ad would never play in reverse in *el Norte* (the North/the USA) where border patrols and immigration issues are horribly controversial, but it was appreciated on Mexican TV.

drive on certain days of the week (to combat pollution), and people often schedule only two appointments a day.

Traffic is the most common excuse for a major delay, but if your client is only a half hour late, do not expect it to be mentioned at all. Always take work with you, relax, expect to wait, and be happy when the prospect does arrive. Mexicans are well aware of North American and European Union attitudes toward time and will be watching your reaction to normal delays.

Among themselves, Mexican businesspeople may gibe the first person to arrive at work or to a meeting with a comment like *"Llegaste a barrer?"* ("Did you arrive with the janitor?")

Be aware that your Mexican prospect may be considering how his or her organization might handle your proposal during your visit. Mexican executives often think about personnel decisions during the sales cycle, as in "If we accept this project, who among my employees will be responsible for it?" Relatively rapid delegation is normal for managers in Mexico.

Social events may start anywhere from a half hour to an hour later than announced. Never arrive promptly to a party.

Deliveries can be protracted as well. Build extra weeks into your deadlines to accommodate inevitable delays.

WORKWEEK

Monday through Friday is the normal workweek. Business hours vary.

Paid vacation days generally start at 6 days the first year, 8 days the second year, 10 days the third, 12 the fourth, and 14 days for years five through nine.

Most years there are 7 official holidays. These are complemented by 12 "civic" holidays, which are not paid but are often observed. A multitude of local festivals and celebrations, which include Valentine's Day, Mother's Day, and religious holidays, will also compete with your schedule. Try to close your contracts well before the month of December. It is filled with celebrations—from *La Dia de la Virgen de Guadalupe* (the Day of the Virgin of Guadalupe) on December 12 (in honor of the Virgin Mary's appearance to Juan Diego Cuauhtlatoatzin) to weeklong processions for *Las Posadas* (in honor of Mary and Joseph's trip to Bethlehem and search for shelter). *Nochebuena* (Christmas Eve) and *Navidad* (Christmas Day) lead into New Year's Eve and the *Dia de los Reyes* (or Epiphany) on January 6.

Sometimes long weekends or holidays are referred to as *puentes* (bridges). The longest example of this is *Puente Guadalupe Reyes*, which extends from December 12 to January 6 (see above for the holidays).

HOW CLOSE SHOULD I STAND?

At the first introduction, you may stand anywhere between 1 and 2 feet apart. As soon as you start to develop a rapport,

Cultural Note

Regarding phone messages—particularly on ubiquitous cell phones—do not take offense if executives do not return your calls. They generally expect that you will call them back if it is important.

your Mexican prospect may approach closer and remain in a space near enough to touch you during much of the meeting.

Female executives may find that men are very attentive and solicitous—far more so than in Canada, northern Europe, or the United States of America. This is not meant to be patronizing or insulting. Successful Mexican businesswomen have a reputation for competence and efficiency while maintaining their feminine comportment.

DO I KISS, BOW, OR SHAKE HANDS?

GREETINGS VARY

Men consider shaking hands a standard initial greeting, and most Mexican businesswomen will shake your hand. However, be sure to lighten up on your grip with female colleagues. Women often just touch each other on the arm or shoulder in greeting.

As soon as you are more than an acquaintance, you will get a hug or kiss on the cheek.

If you go to lunch during your first meeting and are lucky enough to be included in a group of people who know each other, you may be immediately accepted as a friend and get the better greeting.

Marketing Note

Mexicans may not even enter big-ticket environments like car dealerships or real estate offices unless they know someone who works there. If you want to attract buyers, put your firm's representatives and products out where your prospects shop, work, or play. Make it easy for prospects to have access to *amable* (friendly) and nonthreatening sales or service representatives. Brand loyalty is huge, and since buyers often collaborate with friends and family throughout a decision-making process, your product's reputation will travel far beyond your initial investment.

BUSINESS CARDS

- Have your business cards formatted in advance with Spanish on one side and your language (or English) on the other.
- Before your visit, ask an administrative assistant for a list of everyone you will meet, and learn their titles and correct surnames before your visit. As in most of Latin America, the father's name is listed before the mother's on a business card; never call your contact by the wrong (mother's) last name. For example, as of this writing, the president of Mexico is Felipe de Jesús Calderón Hinojosa. He would be properly addressed as President Calderón, not President Hinojosa (which is his mother's name).
- Be certain to use titles; they are exceedingly important in executive circles. Sometimes businesspeople will use generic titles like *licenciada* or *licenciado* if they are not certain of a person's proper one. Never move to a first-name basis until your prospect does.

THREE TIPS FOR SELLING IN MEXICO

1. The Relationship
2. Eating
3. Debt Aversion

1. THE RELATIONSHIP

Sometimes salespeople are trained to figure out the "in"—in other words, divine the hook that will interest a prospect in talking about your product. In Mexico, if you do not have a personal relationship with your prospect, you have no "in."

One way to think about how important the relationship is in Mexico would be to consider that Mexico has the largest upper middle class of all the countries in its region, and the majority of them are related to one another. The top network of key decision makers is exclusive and somewhat guarded. If you are meeting with a decision maker in Mexico's elite network of senior executives, you already have an advantage over salespeople who cannot gain access. One strong relationship, based upon *confianza*, can grow multiple contracts within the entire network.

Nepotism is common and should not be viewed skeptically. Mexicans are somewhat risk-averse, and it has been postulated that the nepotism alleviates concerns about risk for Mexican executives. Your family defines you; it is integral to your identity, so family members are the most trustworthy people in your life. Who better to work with? The concept of family can also be extended to include people beyond the nuclear unit. They may not be real relations, but are *compadres*. Your goal is to develop *compadrismo* or *personalismo* with each of your prospects. Eventually, your clients will attach more value to your friendship than to the firm you represent.

Once you close a sale in Mexico, you are considered to be someone who can be depended upon for more than just that product. You may be consulted in many aspects of life. For example, if your client is considering sending a child to college in your country, you should be ready to help with advice and, possibly, accompany the client and son or daughter on some campus visits. Strong professional relationships come with a level of leadership in multiple areas—not just your role at work.

Conversely, there is a phrase that encapsulates the repercussions of insulting anyone, privately or publicly: *Quien a uno castiga, a ciento hostiga* (He that chastens one, harasses one hundred).

2. EATING

First, remember that Mexico City is 7,349 feet above sea level. This high altitude does not combine well with alcohol for visitors. Give yourself a day to acclimate, and then if you drink, pace yourself.

Business breakfasts do occur, but lunches are more common, more convivial, and will give you more of an opportunity to bond. Lunch in Mexico City is enjoyed for several hours and may not start until 1:00 or 2:00 P.M. On Fridays, a late lunch may develop into an event that precludes returning to work.

Dinners also are a key element of doing business. Reservations are never made before 8:00 P.M., and the meal can go on well into the night.

One caveat for women: If you invite a male prospect out for dinner alone, you may inadvertently put yourself in a compromising position. Always include spouses or other associates at dinners.

3. DEBT AVERSION

Family is often the top motivating factor when a Mexican is considering a large purchase. This is not only because Mexicans want the best for their families, but also because the money for larger expenditures often comes from a pool. Extended families often contribute funds to monthly pools, which are used to help each other with specific expenses. Whether it is a car, college tuition, or *una casa* (a home), Mexican families often make payments together rather than

Advertising Note

Specific color combinations have a tremendous impact in many cultures. After the attacks of 9/11, there were a multitude of red, white, and blue themes in the United States of America. Similarly, in Mexico, color combinations can be so powerful that they influence voters and sway elections. Professor Jorge Contreras from the University of Monterrey in Mexico described a situation where this occurred:

> The Mexican flag has three vertical bands of color: green, white, and red. At election time, each political party adopts a particular flag, which is prominently displayed at voting booths. One of the most important parties in Mexico, the Partido Revolucionario Institucional (PRI), used to generate controversy during every election because the colors it used on its campaign flags were green, white, and red. This confused people in rural sections of Mexico. Since some people may not read or are not well educated, the colors of the PRI flag were said to make them think they were voting for the flag of Mexico.

While politicians may have been delighted to influence an election by virtue of their flag in the past, the adverse reactions resulting from the misuse of the flag or its colors may have had some impact on the elections in 2000.

That year, the 71-year winning streak of the PRI's flag ran out, and the PRI lost the presidential election to PAN, the *Partido Acción Nacional* (National Action Party).

go to lending institutions. Like many Hispanics, Mexicans often have an aversion to debt and would rather avoid the grueling machinations involved in acquiring car loans or mortgages (although mortgage-backed real estate transactions are growing). Therefore, medium to large financial obligations may involve many members of a family. Always provide explanations as to how your product will benefit the prospect's family.

LANGUAGE

The official language of Mexico is Spanish. English is often spoken in many Mexican firms, and you will be able to find an English-speaking executive nearby, should you need assistance. Nevertheless, here are some helpful phrases in Spanish:

ENGLISH	SPANISH
Hello.	Hola.
Thank you.	Gracias.
Good-bye.	Adiós.
Good morning.	Buenos días.
Good afternoon / evening.	Buenas tardes.
How are you?	¿Cómo estás?
What is your name?	¿Cómo se llama?
My name is . . .	Me llamo . . .
Excuse me.	Perdóneme. / Discúlpeme.
Please.	Por favor.
See you later.	Hasta luego.
Yes, please.	Sí, por favor.
No, thank you.	No, gracias.
I don't speak Spanish.	No hablo español.
Do you speak English?	¿Habla inglés?
What is it called in Spanish?	¿Cómo se llama esto en español?
Where is . . . ?	¿Dónde está . . . ?
Is it nearby?	¿Está cerca?
How much is it?	¿Cuánto cuesta?
Could you repeat that?	¿Puede repetir lo que dijo?
Could you say it more slowly?	¿Podría decirlo más despacio?
Sorry, I don't understand.	Lo siento, no entendí.
Help!	¡Socorro!

ENGLISH	SPANISH
I would like . . .	Quisiera . . .
. . . a glass of wine.	. . . una copa de vino.
. . . a beer.	. . . una cerveza.
. . . a coffee.	. . . un café.
. . . a tea.	. . . un té.
. . . fruit juice.	. . . un jugo.
. . . mineral water.	. . . agua mineral.
I am . . .	Soy . . .
. . . from England.	. . . de Inglaterra.
. . . from Australia.	. . . de Australia.

WOW FACTOR!

If you want to impress your Mexican contacts, you should know some of Mexico's famous artists, authors, and leaders. Read about Octavio Paz, Sor Juana Inéz de la Cruz, Diego Rivera, Frida Kahlo, and other cultural icons. Your familiarity with political, business, artistic, and historical leaders will demonstrate an exceptional level of interest and respect for the ethos of Mexico. At the least, you will not be a one-dimensional sales rep.

RUSSIA

Conventional long form: Russian Federation

Local long form: Rossiyskaya Federatsiya

Local short form: Rossiya

Population: 138,739,892 (2011 estimate)

Median age: 38.7 years

Age structure: (2011 estimates)
    0–14 years: 15.2%
    15–64 years: 71.8%
    65 years and over: 13%

GDP per capita (PPP): $15,900 (2010 estimates in US dollars)*

Suffrage: 18 years old; universal

Legal drinking age: 18 years old

*As of 2011, Moscow had more billionaires than any other city in the world.

Advertising Note

Before the breakup of the USSR in 1991, the Eastern Bloc produced its own consumer goods—and one brand fit all. Since shortages were common, there was no need to advertise consumer goods inside the USSR. Basically, few premium-quality Soviet products existed, but two that the world would buy were vodka and caviar. Unfortunately, one of the two staples of entertaining in Russia—black caviar—was taken off the market for nine years because of overfishing in the Caspian Sea and the Volga River. Epicureans were pleased when farm-raised sturgeon caviar became available again in 2011.

After 1991, foreign goods flooded Russia, along with Western advertising. The rest of the 1990s was a spirited time for sales and marketing. (Of course, this was also a time of economic dislocation in Russia, because few people had any disposable income.) Before 1991, the Russian people had never been targeted by advertising and were highly susceptible to even the oldest sales techniques. Russian advertising firms were new and amateurish: ads often consisted of little more than lists of prices.

Those days have ended. A little more than two decades after the fall of the Soviet Union, Russian consumers are highly sophisticated and hard to impress. Russia is as challenging a market as any major power. However, Russians still appreciate brand names, big firms, and large-scale promotions. In Russia, size matters.

ICEBREAKERS

BRILLIANT!

1. Russians are exceedingly proud of their country's accomplishments. You should have no trouble finding something in Russia to admire and discuss: art, music, literature (particularly from pre-Soviet days), and major scientific achievements, especially as exemplified in Russia's space

program. Express a desire to visit cultural sites such as Red Square in Moscow or the State Hermitage Museum in Saint Petersburg, even if you never find the time to actually get there. You should also have some familiarity with the names of great Russian artists and some Russian winners of the Nobel Prize in Literature:

- Ivan Bunin (1870–1953), author of *The Village* and *Dark Avenues*, was awarded the prize in 1933. He emigrated to France in 1919, fleeing the Russian Revolution.
- Boris Pasternak (1890–1960) wrote *Dr. Zhivago*. His Nobel was announced in 1958, but he was forced by the Soviet government to decline the prize.
- Mikhail Sholokhov (1905–1984), writer of *The Silent Don*, was awarded the prize in 1965. A writer in the socialist realism style, he was the only laureate approved by the Soviet government.
- Aleksandr Solzhenitsyn (1918–2008) is famous for *One Day in the Life of Ivan Denisovich, The Gulag Archipelago*, and other works. He was awarded the prize in 1970. He was imprisoned, then exiled from the USSR, but in 1990 his citizenship was restored and he returned to Russia in 1994.
- Joseph Brodsky (1940–1996), author of *Less than One* and *On Grief and Reason*, was awarded the prize in 1987. He was imprisoned and then exiled from the USSR in 1972.

There are also Russian laureates in all the other Nobel categories (including peace).

Three more towering Russian authors who characterized the Russian soul, or *dushá*, were Nikolai Gogol (author of *Taras Bulba* and *The Overcoat*), Leo Tolstoy (*War and Peace* and *Anna Karenina*), and Fyodor Dostoyevsky (*Crime and Punishment* and *The Brothers Karamazov*). The Russian soul is a philosophical and religious perspective, which defines Russians. It encompasses their sensitivities, their stubbornness, patience, honesty, emotions, intellect, and capability to survive extreme hardship and suffering. Nikolai Gogol expresses this beautifully in *Taras Bulba:* "No, brothers, to love as the Russian soul loves, is to love not with the mind or anything else, but with all that God has given, all that is within you."

Some Russians might also appreciate a discussion of the Novgorod Codex, just discovered in 2000. It is a palimpsest—a wax codex, which was scraped or cleaned off repeatedly and reused, estimated as having been written between A.D. (or C.E.) 988 and 1030, which makes it the oldest wooden Russian book in existence.

2. Despite the breakup of the USSR, Russia is still the largest country on earth (almost double the size of Canada, the second-largest country). To many, Russia's enormous dimension makes the country appear like a Goliath externally. But internally, this size means that Russia has millions and millions of indefensible kilometers to protect from invasion. This is one source of Russian xenophobia: knowing that you are surrounded by enemies yet unable to adequately defend your own borders.

Outsiders rarely show any understanding of Russian suspicion toward non-Russians. You can try to bridge that divide by attempting to comprehend Russia's vast geographic responsibilities. It shares boundaries with 14 countries, from Norway to North Korea, and is bordered by three oceans and 13 seas.

If you feel accomplished just driving through Moscow, the third most congested city in the world (behind Beijing and Johannesburg), imagine taking a sales trip to Provideniya, more than 4,000 miles away on Russia's far eastern shore. Just don't try to get driving directions from Google Maps; you will be disappointed. Provideniya is close to the international date line and has the closest Russian airport to the United States. (However, most Alaskans cannot actually see it.)

BOORISH

1. Russians have a word for boorish behavior: *nyekulturny*. Many behaviors that are normal in Western countries (especially the United States) are considered by Russians to be *nyekulturny*. For example, whistling is *nyekulturny* in Russia, as is standing with your hands in your pants pockets. Sitting with the legs spread, or with the legs crossed so that the sole of a shoe is visible, or with an arm resting over the back of a chair—these are all *nyekulturny*. Russians have even called people *nyekulturny*.

   When Bobby Fischer was playing chess (and beating World Champion Grandmaster Boris Spassky), the Soviet press created a variety of tags for Fischer, including "a temperamental child" who was definitely *nyekulturny* (uncultured). In general, if you want to avoid earning this tag yourself, keep your posture straight, and observe and mimic the behavior of your prospects and clients.

2. In 2008, Moscow surpassed New York to become home to more billionaires than any other city in the world. Moscow's super-wealthy have another distinction: they are all self-made. And like many nouveaux riches, many enjoy the material benefits of wealth. Designer clothes are common, as are expensive watches, cars, homes, etc.

   No matter what you may think about this excess, you should ensure that your image is commensurate with that of other executives in Russia. Wealthy Russian businesspeople will not respect you (or your company) if your appearance is ordinary or you stay at less than first-class hotels. First impressions are exceedingly important.

WHAT TIME SHOULD I ARRIVE?

As a foreigner, you are expected to be prompt. However, punctuality was not a traditional virtue in the old Soviet Union. Modern Russians seem to be getting more punctual, but being 15 minutes late is still very common. Do not expect

Cultural Note

Historically, the most chaotic times in Russia were those without a strong leader in charge. By and large, the Russian people accept that the largest nation in the world needs an authoritarian, strong man. This leader also needs to be predictable; a capricious boss is not reassuring.

Similarly, Russian businesses tend to be run by strong managers. If you find yourself in charge of Russian employees, be decisive. It is not as important that your orders are correct; what is important is that you give orders.

an apology if Russians are less than 30 minutes late. Also, allow for the possibility that your appointment will start late and finish behind schedule.

WORKWEEK

In April 2011, the news agency RIA Novosti reported that a notable Russian businessman, Mikhail Prokhorov, proposed that the workweek be increased from 40 to 60 hours a week. However, Russian Premier Vladimir Putin opposed the proposition, and Prokhorov later recanted his statement, saying he had been misunderstood and simply wanted employers to be able to manage their labor force freely. For now, the 40-hour week is still the standard.

Business hours are generally from 9:00 A.M. to 5:00 P.M. Monday through Friday, but hours can vary widely by industry and level of employee. Banks have expanded their hours to the weekends, as have many stores, particularly in tourist areas. Some shops may be closed for lunch.

Paid vacation days can vary in different areas of Russia, with employees in the extreme northern regions receiving additional paid leave. It is reported that generally there are

Marketing Note

During the days of the Soviet Union, Russians were put on years-long waiting lists to buy locally made automobiles. Now Russia is awash in imported cars. Thanks to oil wealth, Russia became the largest car market in Europe in 2008. Russia's roads are now jammed with foreign cars, which contributes to Moscow's gridlock. Many US, European, and Japanese car companies have manufacturing plants in Russia.

approximately 25 paid vacation days. While Russia had 18 holidays in 2011, they are not necessarily all compensated, as some fall on weekends.

HOW CLOSE SHOULD I STAND?

Approximately 1½ feet apart. Surprisingly, Russians stand at a distance similar to that of southern Europeans. North Americans and northern Europeans may find this distance a bit close for comfort. Do not back away if you find the proximity disconcerting. If it is the proper distance for your Russian counterpart, it is just fine for you, too.

Remember that Russians tend to be suspicious of most forms of communication, including phones and e-mails. (In fact, it may even be wise to assume that some of your communications are being monitored.) Expect to be doing business on a one-to-one basis often. Learn to be comfortable speaking to Russians at close quarters. Hopefully, it will help you develop the social relationships and the connections you are seeking. As a foreigner, you will need these relationships and the larger networks they will lead to.

Cultural Note

Russians do not have one single word that encompasses all the colors that are called blue in English. They distinguish the color spectrum that we call blue into two colors: *goluboy* (light blue) and *siniy* (dark blue). Beyond these two divisions, Russians, of course, have the ability to identify discriminate variations of *goluboy* and *siniy*. So what's your favorite color? *Goluboy?* Or *siniy?*

DO I KISS, BOW, OR SHAKE HANDS?

SHAKE HANDS

Russian men sometimes hug and kiss other men on both cheeks, but they reserve these greetings for close friends. (Interestingly, greetings are the only time Russians typically exhibit physical contact in public. For example, it is uncommon for Russian couples to kiss in public.)

Russian men shake hands with other men. They may wait for a woman to extend her hand before shaking.

Russian businesswomen usually shake hands with other women.

Typically, upon first meetings, Russians will state their name when shaking hands with someone. You should do the same.

Direct eye contact is key. Do not let your gaze waver. And do not be taken by surprise if Russians stare at you.

BUSINESS CARDS

- There is no Russian tradition involving the exchange of business cards. However, treat all business cards with respect.
- Your cards should be translated into Russian on one side.

Cultural Note

Be certain to register with your embassy before you arrive in Russia. While kidnappings of wealthy businesspeople are not the norm, they do occur, particularly in Moscow. Unfortunately, the Russian police cannot always be relied upon for protection. They are frequently distrusted by the Russian people, and it is believed that commercial kidnappings could not take place without the collusion of police officers.

Businesspeople have been convicted on false evidence—a dire fate in Russia. Russian prisons have barely changed since Stalin's time. Few prisoners are kept in cells; most are kept in roughly built barracks housing around 100 men. At night, the barracks are locked and the prisoners left to their own devices.

Russian President Dmitri A. Medvedev (who trained as a lawyer) has promised an overhaul of the penal system. Prime Minister Vladimir Putin has also publicly mentioned that vices like taking bribes and abusing power are chronic problems in Russia that need to be addressed in the future.

- Take a large supply of business cards with you; you will need them.
- If your cards are in your wallet, do not keep your wallet in your back trouser pocket.

THREE TIPS FOR SELLING IN RUSSIA

1. Classic Mercantilism
2. What's New?
3. Negotiating as a Game of Chess

1. CLASSIC MERCANTILISM

Russians are mercantilists in the classic sense. That is, they believe resources are always limited; for them to gain, someone else must lose. They play a zero-sum game and are very direct about it. It can be helpful for you to highlight the

Cultural Note

If you look at the *Dramatis Personae* page in a long Russian novel, you may despair at ever getting Russian names correct. Most Russians have a bewildering variety of names, nicknames, and diminutives. Fortunately, many of these nicknames are reserved for intimates. Name usage in business is somewhat easier.

Russian names are listed in the same order as names in the West: first name, middle name (or patronymic), and then surname. The Russian patronymic is a name derived from the first name of one's father. Suppose you meet Igor Ivanovich Shuvalov. His first name is Igor, his patronymic is Ivanovich (son of Ivan), and his surname is Shuvalov.

Among themselves, Russians often address each other by their first name and patronymic. If you were extremely close friends with the prime minister of Russia, Vladimir Vladimirovich Putin, you might address him as Vladimir Vladimirovich. (Vladimir has been translated to mean "great, glorious ruler.")

Male and female patronymics have different endings. Male patronymics are usually the father's first name plus -*ovich*; women's are the father's first name plus -*ovna*. So if a man named Victor had two children, a boy named Dmitri and a girl named Elena, the boy's patronymic would be Victorovich (son of Victor), and the girl's would be Victorovna (daughter of Victor).

Surnames vary between genders as well. Most ethnic Russian women add the suffix -*a* to the end of their surname.

You, as a foreigner, are welcome to address anyone by his or her title and surname. You can even use the English Mr. or Mrs. or Ms. if the person does not have a title.

However, eventually you should learn to use patronymics. Russians may ask you the first name of your father so that they can decipher your own patronymic. Eventually, you may acquire a Russian nickname as well.

When you begin to learn Russian, you will note that there are formal and informal forms of the word for "you." Never move to the informal form before you are asked to do so.

Conventional Russian first names are often derived from the name of a Russian Orthodox saint. The name day is the feast day of that saint on the Russian Orthodox calendar. Most Russians celebrate their name day. You might like to congratulate your associate on his or her name day.

potential profit for them, repeatedly, and consistently validate the figures. Do not compromise on a deal too soon. Since the concept of a win-win deal is not intrinsic to Russian nature, they do not often seek compromises. Some believe that compromise is inherently wrong.

Russians can become very emotional during meetings. The volume of the discourse can rise, and walkouts may occur. Patience, equanimity, and modesty are key during these sessions. You must explain with great clarity why your position is firm. Having the evidence to justify the position is important, but your relationship with your Russian contacts will be more crucial than the statistics.

This is why it can be difficult to negotiate with Russians, but to many Russian executives, if people don't take a hard stand, they are not truly negotiating.

2. WHAT'S NEW?

Russians love technology. Pitch your Russian prospects your current offerings, and allow them a glimpse at some future concepts as well. Do not expose too much of your research, but decide with your technical team what you can reveal without potential damage. Never take complete specifications on a laptop or zip drive, unless you want them to have the data.

If you are from the United States, there are some barriers you may have to overcome just to get in the door:

- **Distance:** Russians may prefer to work with Europeans because they are closer geographically for support.
- **Consistency:** Standards, such as metric measurements and pharmaceutical approvals, have been established with European markets for years.

One way of surmounting these obstacles is by providing superior research and technological advances to your Russian prospects. Russians have a multitude of highly educated scientists, engineers, and information technology (IT) special-

Cultural Note

Russians usually do not get down to business immediately. This can be part of the "feeling out the opponent" phase, when you are being judged on your conversation and responses to questions. If you are part of a negotiating team, be aware that the Russians are looking for any opportunity to sow discord among your team. Always present a unified front.

Initial conversations can include popular team sports like soccer (football), basketball, ice hockey, and bandy (imagine ice hockey with a small round ball instead of a puck, played on an ice rink the size of a soccer field).

ists. Let them voice their opinions. Many Russian firms are more excited by inventions and future technology than the reliable options of the past. When shortages were common several decades ago, Russians used to invent solutions themselves for everything. They appreciate the potential to work with sophisticated and complex tools—and the flexibility to enhance them—even if your solution may be the more expensive option.

Small gifts of technological devices or other benefits are also a common way to help the evaluation process proceed.

The IT sector is generally advanced in the metropolitan areas, although Internet penetration may be limited in Russia's vast rural areas. However, Internet marketing is poised to explode. The Russian search engine Yandex claims to be the world's second most popular non-English search engine (second only to the Chinese service Baidu). This puts Yandex in the top ten search engines worldwide.

3. NEGOTIATING AS A GAME OF CHESS

Lenin loved to play chess and officially promoted it in the USSR. It was considered a dynamic, skillful game of war that anyone could play—inexpensively. Training started in elementary grades, and large-scale tournaments were held regularly in factories, offices, and schools. As an intellectual pursuit, it dovetailed with the USSR's pride in its cerebral capabilities.

Chess still has an important place in the Russian psyche. Many political and business leaders have played and look at every negotiation as a game. They believe that in comparison to Russia, other countries (particularly the United States) play simplistic games like Monopoly, which is all about the materials—getting the most hotels on the board.

In contrast to a linear game like Monopoly, chess involves cognitive processes that can be circuitous and involve many connections. Tactics abound, like the double threat, which is a single move that presents the opponent with two dangers. The opponent appears forced to defend against both threats. However, a counter threat is possible. Instead of defending any pieces, the opponent can attack, as long as the attack endangers an even more important piece (usually the queen or king).

Hundreds of moves are considered in each game. Strategies involve taking the center, allocating materials, gaining space to maneuver, and exploiting time. Materials, space, and time are the three resources of chess and can be interchanged to gain advantage. Time may be the most powerful variable your Russian counterpart can control. How long can you afford to stay in Moscow and sit in negotiations? Russians are adept at sitting, staring, and smoking—and can stretch out a game for their profit. In the early 1900s, world champion Emanuel Lasker was known to repulse opponents with fetid cigars. Mikhail Botvinnik, a later world champion, would prepare by having aides blow smoke in his eyes. And Mikhail Tal developed such an intense stare that rivals claimed he was trying to hypnotize them.

During this process, you and your team will be subjected to extensive scrutiny. Every possible weak spot will be noted. But just as in chess, once they have evaluated their position, you may be surprised at the speed of the endgame.

The endgame generally involves very few players, with great range to move. This is when the most extreme demands may be made. Your team must show unanimity, because as long as the Russians believe they might extract another con-

Marketing Note

While city leaders in Moscow reported a push to eliminate banner advertisements by 2013 within the Garden Ring (a circular road around the center of Moscow), outdoor billboards still proliferate, as do hackers. One night in January 2010, a 27-foot by 18-foot (9-meter by 6-meter) electronic billboard was hijacked in downtown Moscow. For two minutes, a pornographic video flashed on one of Moscow's busiest roads. The culprit was eventually caught. Be aware of the technical capabilities of Russian hackers, and insist upon strong security measures for any electronically based marketing campaigns your firm may develop. Electronic banner ads, billboards, and cell phone apps can all be subject to sabotage.

cession, the deal will not close. When the Russian negotiators have decided there are no further constructive moves, you may receive sudden notice that the contract has signed. Unexpectedly announcing their acceptance of the deal is another way the Russians exhibit control.

LANGUAGE

Cyrillic script (used in the Russian alphabet) was purportedly created by two saints in the ninth century: Saint Cyril, and his brother Saint Methodius. Over the centuries, the alphabet has been modified from its original 43 letters to its current 33. This is still considerably more than the 26 letters used in English, which makes using Twitter more difficult in Russian.

Here are a few phrases that may help you in Russia. These phrases are excerpted from the digital *Kiss, Bow, or Shake Hands* product (www.kissboworshakehands.com). A variety of free Russian language programs are also offered through the BBC (http://www.bbc.co.uk/languages).

ENGLISH	RUSSIAN (PRONUNCIATION GUIDE)
Hello.	zdrAstvuytye
Good morning.	dObraye Utra
Good-bye.	da svidAniya
Excuse me.	izvinItye
Good afternoon.	dObri dYEn
Good evening.	dObri vYEchir
Please.	pazhAlusta
How are things?	kAk dilA
Thank you.	spasIba
Fine, thanks.	kharashO spasIba
Yes, please.	dA pazhAlusta
No, thank you.	nYEt spasIba
Pleased to meet you.	Ochin priYAtna
I don't speak Russian.	Ya nYE gavarYU pa rUski
What is your name?	kAk vAs zavUt
Do you speak English?	vY gavarItye pa anglIski
My name is . . .	minYA zavUt
What is it called in Russian?	kAk pa-rUski
Where is . . . ?	gdYE
How much is it?	skOlka stOyit
Slower, please.	mYEdliniye pazhAlusta
I don't understand.	YA nYE panimAyu
I would like . . .	mnYE khatYElas bY
. . . a glass of wine.	bakAl vinA
. . . a bottle of beer.	butYlku pIva
. . . a bottle of wine.	butYlku vinA
. . . a cup of coffee.	chAshku kOfye

WOW FACTOR!

While initial meetings are generally formal, after hours Russians' sense of humor is legendary. Do not be surprised if they joke with you. In January 2011, Russian Prime Minister Vladimir Putin told a (typically long) joke on television. RIA Novosti has the clip. The joke went something like this:

An American spy comes to Lubyanka. He is asked, "Who do you spy for?" He says, "I am an American spy and want to turn myself in." "Go to room five," he is told. He goes. "Do you have a gun?" the US spy is asked. "Yes, I do," he answers. "Then you have to go to room seven," a Russian official tells him. He goes to room seven and says, "I am an American spy, and I have a gun." He is told to go to room ten. There he is asked, "Are you carrying communication equipment?" "Yes, I am." "Then you have to go to room number twenty." He goes there. "I am an American spy, and I have a gun and a communication system, and I want to give myself up!" Finally, the US spy is asked, "US spy, do you have a mission?" "Yes, I do," says the spy. "Then go carry it out and stop bothering people at work!"

Putin's joke was followed a brief comment that while this inefficient manner is how things have been done for decades, if not for centuries, Russia now has a chance to change these practices.

SAUDI ARABIA

Conventional long form: Kingdom of Saudi Arabia

Local long form: Al Mamlakah al Arabiyah as Suudiyah

Local short form: Al Arabiyah as Suudiyah

Population: 26,131,703, including 5,576,076 nonnationals (2011 estimate)

Median age: 25.3 years

Age structure: (2011 estimates)
    0–14 years: 29.4%
    15–64 years: 67.6%
    65 years and over: 3%

GDP per capita (PPP): $24,200 (2010 estimate in US dollars)

Suffrage: Males, 21 years old; however, no date for national elections has ever been set

Legal drinking age: None, because alcohol is prohibited to all

Cultural Note

There is a saying in the Arabic world: *You cannot clap with one hand.* Remember this precept during your negotiations. To achieve results, you should seriously consider every participant's offer, have room for concessions, and be prepared to reach a consensus somewhere in the middle.

ICEBREAKERS

BRILLIANT!

1. Learn the traditional greeting in Arabic. The first phrase is generally *Assalamu a'alaikum*, which means "peace be upon you." The correct response is *Wa alaikum assalam.*

   After the introductions, you might inquire about how your prospect started in the industry and became successful. This may lead to many related topics of travel, education, and family.

2. Saudi Arabia's national football (soccer) team is a popular topic. It first qualified for the World Cup in 1994, when the World Cup was hosted by the United States, and it is now one of Asia's most successful teams. Nicknames for the team include *Al-Sogour* (the Falcons), *Al-Akhdar* (the Green), or "the Green Falcons." Be certain not to repeat the faux pas (under Boorish point #2) that has occurred with soccer balls and the Saudi flag.

BOORISH

1. Religion is not an appropriate topic for conversation, unless it relates directly to the work at hand. Do your research before your arrival, since the fundamentalist Wahabi branch of Sunni Islam in Saudi Arabia delineates specific guidelines for proper behavior. However, you should not spend time asking your prospect about appropriate conduct while in the Kingdom.

2. Be exceedingly careful about the use of Saudi Arabia's flag. The Arabic text on the flag is the *Shahada*, the sacred testament of faith, which is translated as "There is no God but Allah, and Muhammad is his messenger." The name of Allah is considered sacrosanct by Muslims. Therefore, the flag must be handled carefully and is never flown at half-mast. Since Arabic reads from right to left, the flag is always hoisted so that the flagpole is to the right of the flag.

Unfortunately, there have been multiple instances when the flag of Saudi Arabia has been placed on promotional items, sports equipment, or literally hung above beer kegs at ill-advised college events. Since the Saudi Arabian football team's first World Cup, its flag has appeared multiple times on a facet of soccer balls (along with the flags of other participating nations). Not only is it blasphemy to put the name of Allah on a product, but a product that one kicks with the foot is an even greater insult. (The foot is considered unclean in the Middle East.) One regrettable incident of this nature occurred in 2007 when the US military dropped soccer balls from a helicopter in Afghanistan. The balls displayed the flags of World Cup participants—including Saudi Arabia—on them. The gifts were intended for local Afghan children, but the air drop resulted in a demonstration by Afghanis, who took umbrage at the insult to Islam. A spokeswoman for US forces in Afghanistan expressed regret over the incident and mentioned the efforts they were making to work together with local leaders, elders, and mullahs to show respect for their culture.

WHAT TIME SHOULD I ARRIVE?

As a foreigner, you are expected to be prompt. However, punctuality is not a traditional virtue in the Kingdom. Your counterpart may be late or might not even show up at all. Punctuality may not be a virtue in Saudi Arabia, but patience surely is.

WORKWEEK

Friday is the Muslim holy day; no business is conducted. Most people do not work on Thursday either. Thus, the workweek runs from Saturday through Wednesday, but many firms may be open at least a half day on Thursday.

Saudi officials traditionally worked six hours per day. While this has changed, mornings are usually best for appointments, since companies may close for several hours in the afternoon (which may involve the noon prayer). Confirm appointments, because schedules and business hours may vary in different parts of the Kingdom.

Some Saudi businesspeople work well after dark. Do not be surprised if you receive a request for a late-evening appointment.

Normally, employers offer a minimum of 23 paid vacation days, plus various additional paid holidays—including Eid al-Fitr (the Feast of the Breaking of the Fast, which follows Ramadan) and Eid al-Adha (the Festival of the Sacrifice). The Embassy of Saudi Arabia lists official holidays at www.saudi embassy.net.

HOW CLOSE SHOULD I STAND?

Approximately 1 foot apart. Men will stand closer to other men than to women. The important thing to remember is that you should not back away. If you do, your Saudi counterpart will probably adjust the distance again to restore the "proper" balance.

DO I KISS, BOW, OR SHAKE HANDS?

GREETINGS VARY

Since several styles of greeting are currently in use in Saudi Arabia, it is safest to wait for your counterpart to initiate the greeting, especially at a first meeting.

Cultural Note

The three holiest cities in Islam are Mecca, Medina, and Jerusalem. The first two of them are in Saudi Arabia. This geographical fact elevates the importance of Saudi Arabia within the Muslim world, or *ummah*. While you are in Saudi Arabia, never forget that you are on holy ground. Mecca is the holiest city and is the destination of every Muslim who wishes to complete a Hajj, the pilgrimage that is one of the five pillars of Islam.

To Muslims, the most important title of the king of Saudi Arabia is Custodian of the Two Holy Mosques. The Two Holy Mosques are Masjid al-Haram in Mecca and Masjid al-Nabawi in Medina.

To protect this holy land from non-Muslims, Saudi Arabia only allows Muslims to enter the country without a sponsor. If you are a non-Muslim businessperson, you may not enter Saudi Arabia without being sponsored by a Saudi national. Of greater concern to some is the fact that, once in, you may not leave Saudi Arabia without your sponsor's permission. There have been occasional incidents in which, because of a business disagreement, a foreign executive has been detained.

Westernized Saudi men shake hands with other men.

One traditional Saudi greeting between men involves each grasping the other's right hand, and placing the left hand on the other's right shoulder. Then they exchange kisses on each cheek.

Some Saudi men will shake hands with Western women, although this violates observant Muslim traditions. Also, remember that there are roaming religious police, called the Mutaween, in Saudi Arabia. Even a Saudi male who is willing to shake hands with a woman in private may not do so in public view of the Mutaween. If your Saudi contact puts his hand on his chest, rather than shaking your hand, do not take offense. The gesture may mean that he or she is an observant Muslim and prefers no physical contact with the opposite sex.

Cultural Note

Do not get down to business too quickly. Saudi conversations traditionally begin with long inquiries into your journey, your health, and your family. Saudis enjoy humor. Do not be surprised if they joke with you. Avoid being overly sensitive; Saudis do not respect someone who overreacts to being teased. Sports and cars are good topics of conversation. Besides football (soccer), popular sports include car, horse, and camel racing; hunting; and falconry. Be aware that betting is prohibited.

Traditionally, Saudi women do not have any physical contact with any males to whom they are not related. In fact, if you encounter a veiled woman with a Saudi man, it is not traditional for him to introduce her.

BUSINESS CARDS

- There is no Saudi tradition involving the exchange of business cards. However, treat all business cards with respect.
- Remember to present your card with your right hand.
- Your cards should be formatted in advance with Arabic on one side and your country's language on the other.
- Pork and pig products are prohibited under Islam. Do not keep your cards in a pigskin card case or wallet.
- If your cards are in your wallet, do not keep your wallet in your back trouser pocket.

THREE TIPS FOR SELLING IN SAUDI ARABIA

1. **Respect Saudi Prohibitions and Customs**
2. **Establish Personal Relationships**
3. **Understand Arabic Hyperbole**

1. RESPECT SAUDI PROHIBITIONS AND CUSTOMS

If you come from a country with an egalitarian culture (such as Sweden, Australia, or the United States), you may disagree with the Saudi practice of hiring foreign workers to do all the physical labor in Saudi Arabia. But Saudis demand respect, and any real or perceived slight against a Saudi will ruin your chances of doing business there.

Violating Saudi customs can also spoil any chance of success. The fact that you cannot enter Saudi Arabia without a native sponsor should be enough to alert you that you should do things the Saudi way. You can be deported for seemingly minor violations, such as being caught with alcohol or pornography. If this happens, you bring shame upon your company and your Saudi sponsor.

Here are some guidelines for Saudi norms of behavior:

■ Do not bring up the subject of women unless your Saudi counterpart does so first.

■ Do not even inquire as to the health of a Saudi's wife or daughter.

■ Men and women who are not married or related should not be seen together alone in public. Make every effort to avoid being alone with a person of the opposite sex (unless you are related or married). France's president, Nicolas Sarkozy, fell afoul of this protocol when he planned to bring his fiancée, Carla Bruni, with him to the Kingdom in 2008. Saudi officials expressed their dismay to US diplomats in Riyadh, and Bruni's trip was canceled.

■ Watch for elevators that may be segregated by gender in some buildings.

■ Be certain not to depict a man and woman alone together in any of your advertisements or general documentation.

■ Abide by modest standards of dress. Remember, not only must most of the skin be covered, but clothes should not be too tight. Never wear anything revealing.

■ If non-Muslim women wish to show respect for Saudi customs, they may wear an *abayah* (a black, robe-like cloak). But it is not advisable for a man to try to dress like a Saudi, unless your Saudi contact approves of it. Wearing a *thobe* (generally a white floor-length tunic) is not appreciated, as it may imply that you are trying to impersonate a Saudi. (As in other Muslim countries, citizens have more rights than visitors.)

- Use your right hand whenever possible. As is the tradition throughout much of the region, in both Muslim and non-Muslim countries, the left hand is considered unclean. Never eat with your left hand. No one is left-handed in Saudi Arabia; children who display left-handedness are retrained to use their right.

- Consider your feet unclean. Do not touch anyone with your foot, and do not show the sole of your feet to anyone. (Men must be careful when they cross their legs not to show the sole of their shoe.)

- If you wear a crucifix or Star of David, you may want place it on the inside of your clothing. Displaying one around your neck will generate unwanted attention and possible controversy—the antithesis of your sales goal.

- It is also forbidden to celebrate non-Muslim religious ceremonies. Do not look for a Christian church in Saudi Arabia; there aren't any.

- Observe silence during prayer times. Public activity (especially eating and drinking) should cease during prayers. If you are walking, do not cross between people who are praying and Mecca (in other words, do not cross the line of the direction in which they are praying).

- During the holy month of Ramadan, when observant Muslims do not eat, drink, or smoke during the daylight hours, avoid eating, drinking, or smoking in front of fasting Muslims. (This does not mean that you cannot go to a restaurant during the day.)

2. ESTABLISH PERSONAL RELATIONSHIPS

As in other countries, business relationships in Saudi Arabia are not between a Saudi and your company; they are between a Saudi and you. This is why lengthy small talk is never wasted. It is part of establishing your personal relationship with your client.

Cultural Note

Saudi holidays are marked by the Muslim calendar, which is shorter than the Western (Gregorian) calendar. Muslims use a lunar calendar of 354 days called the Hijrah. As a result, according to the Western calendar, Muslim holidays advance by about 11 days per year. Paperwork for Saudi businessmen should carry two sets of dates: the Western-designated C.E. (for Common Era) and Muslim dates, designated H., for Hijrah.

French leader Nicolas Sarkozy's first two visits to Saudi Arabia were disappointingly brief in the eyes of the Saudis. Many foreign leaders look forward to staying at King Abdullah's royal ranch in Jenadryyah. The king loves Arabian horses and is the founder of an equestrian club in Riyadh. During his third visit, President Sarkozy finally spent the night at King Abdullah's ranch, which is a normal stage in developing solid relations with the ruler and his family.

Companies often make the mistake of switching their representative in Saudi Arabia. Whether it is simply company policy to give employees experience in different parts of the world or impatience with an apparent lack of progress, it is not a wise decision. Each new representative has to start almost from the beginning, creating his or her own personal relationship with Saudi prospects.

Kim Willing, director of international sales for a medical instrumentation firm, described the process of working with Saudis and leaders of the other five members of the Cooperation Council for the Arab States of the Gulf (Bahrain, Kuwait, Qatar, Oman, and the United Arab Emirates).

The Council distributes a list of products it wishes to purchase for its government hospitals, and you must then send a sample of every product for evaluation. Be incredibly tenacious, because Council evaluations can take years. (In our case, we sent our products over for 10 years!) Consistency is vital, because once they do award a contract, Council mem-

Cultural Note

Besides knowing about Mecca and Medina, you should be familiar with the three other major cities in Saudi Arabia. Riyadh, the capital, has almost as many people as the other four cities combined. The second most populous is Jeddah, a seaport on the Red Sea. And Ad Damman (or Dammam) is the main seaport on the Arabian Gulf. Be sure to refer to this body of water as the Arabian Gulf while visiting Saudi Arabia—not the Persian Gulf!

bers are loyal. If they trust that you will be reliable, they will be, too.

When you are establishing business relationships, keep in mind that nepotism is accepted in Saudi Arabia. Not only do you have to outdo general competitors, you also have to convince your Saudi client that you are a better choice than a relative, or a friend of a relative.

3. UNDERSTAND ARABIC HYPERBOLE

Compared with other linguistic traditions, Arabic is a language of hyperbole. Superlatives—the best as well as the worst—are commonly used.

Saving face is all-important to a Saudi. It is much easier to express an insincere yes than a blunt no. If a Saudi becomes evasive, it may be another way of graciously saying no. You are expected to be able to tell the difference between a face-saving, polite yes and an actual yes. How do you tell the difference? The sincere yes will be followed up by action: paperwork, an appointment with a lawyer, a request for technical information, or something similar.

However, in Arab tradition, a verbal agreement is considered just as binding as a written one. Once a sincere yes is given, you can be confident that the deal is done.

If difficulties arise, never confront a Saudi personally. Always use an intermediary to deliver bad news, just as the

Sales Note

Expect that closing a deal in Saudi Arabia will take three or four times as long as it would in northern Europe.

Where you may need the most patience is in a traditional-style presentation. In most Western countries, you get to do a focused, linear sales pitch. That may happen in Saudi Arabia if your prospect is a foreign manager (often a Lebanese). However, a traditional meeting will not proceed in that manner. Here are some characteristics of a conventional Arabic meeting:

- You may not be alone with the Saudi decision maker. Friends and relatives may constantly come in and out, taking the focus away from you.
- Expect your sales presentation to be interrupted several times. In addition, you may be asked to go back to the beginning when someone new arrives.
- It is possible that you may never be certain who is really in charge. The true decision maker may be an elderly Saudi who watches but never speaks to you.

Saudis used US diplomats to tell the president of France he shouldn't bring his fiancée to visit.

If you do hear a Saudi make a negative statement, it may be a highly charged, emotional comment. Negative Arabic statements can sound dire, insulting, and exaggerated to Western ears, but they are generally not meant literally.

LANGUAGE

Arabic is the official language of the Kingdom of Saudi Arabia and of the other 21 countries that make up the Arab League. However, there are many variants of Arabic.

The Holy Qur'an (or Koran) was written in a form of Arabic called Classical Arabic. This formal, written form is used in religious ceremonies and by scholars, and is somewhat complex.

The version that is most commonly used in the media, by public speakers, and in schools is Modern Standard Arabic (MSA). All Arab speakers can communicate through MSA, even if their local dialects are mutually unintelligible, as are Algerian (or Northern African) and Iraqi (or Levant Region) Arabic. If you hire a local representative in Saudi Arabia, make sure he speaks the type of Gulf Arabic that will make your clients feel comfortable. The dialect of Arabic that a person speaks reveals his or her origins.

Arabic speakers greet one another by saying, "Peace be upon you." Here are the various singular and plural, masculine and feminine conjugations of that greeting. You will not generally hear the last vowel pronounced.

As-Salāmu `alayk(a).	Masculine, singular
As-Salāmu `alayk(i).	Feminine, singular
As-Salāmu `alayk(umā).	Plural for two people, any gender
As-Salāmu `alayk(unna).	Feminine plural, to a group of three or more
As-Salāmu `alayk(umu).	Plural, to a group of three or more, where one or more is male

And here is the template of the correct response. It, too, varies according to how many people you are addressing and their gender:

Wa `alayk(. . .) s-salām.

Following are a few more phrases that may help you in Saudi Arabia. Also, a variety of free Arabic language programs are offered through the BBC at http://www.bbc.co.uk/languages.

ENGLISH	ARABIC TRANSLITERATION
Hello.	marhaban
Good-bye.	ila al'likaa'
See you later.	ma'a salaama

ENGLISH	ARABIC TRANSLITERATION
Please.	min fadlak
Thank you.	shukran
You're welcome.	a'afwan
Yes.	na'am
No.	la'a
How are you?	kaifa haluka
I'm fine, thank you.	bi-khayr, shukran
Pleased to meet you.	tasharrafna
I'm sorry.	ana a'asef
Excuse me.	laa mu'aakhadha
My name is . . .	ana ismee
I don't understand.	lam af'ham

WOW FACTOR!

All graphics must adhere to the Muslim sense of modesty. Images of people should show as little skin as possible. Foreign magazines are censored in Saudi Arabia; pages showing too much skin are removed or blacked out. Since certain animals are taboo to eat or considered unclean, they should not be the central focus of an advertisement. These animals include pigs and dogs.

Remember that Arabic is read from right to left. This is the opposite of English and most modern European languages, which are read left to right. The front cover of an English book, magazine, or prospectus is the back cover of an Arabic one. Even if your sales material is in English, keep in mind that, out of habit, the first thing a Saudi may look at is the back of your publication. Never invest all your design dollars on the front of your annual report—or book jacket—and ignore the back cover; it should be attractive, too.

Moreover, there have been several incidents in which an innocuous English phrase or graphic, when viewed from right to left, is interpreted as an insulting phrase in Arabic. One

famous example is the Nike Air-B-Que sneaker: the unfortunate logo sewn on the back resembled Arabic script with the
name of Allah in it. Thousands of sneakers had to be recalled.

Another design error occurred when a pharmaceutical firm
released a print ad for an antidepressant. On the left side, the
ad depicted a sad individual suffering from depression. The
drug was in the center, and on the right side was another
photo of the same individual, much relieved after taking the
medication. It looks like a logical ad—if you read from left
to right. But if you speak Arabic (or Hebrew), the ad looks
as though a perfectly happy man took your product and then
became distressed.

All of your material, including brochures and advertisements, should be vetted by a native speaker of Arabic before
being used in Saudi Arabia.

SOUTH AFRICA

Conventional long form: Republic of South Africa

Abbreviation: RSA

Population: 49,004,031 (2011 estimate)

Median age: 25 years

Age structure: (2011 estimates)
　　0–14 years: 28.5%
　　15–64 years: 65.8%
　　65 years and over: 5.7%

GDP per capita (PPP): $10,700 (2010 estimate in US dollars)

Suffrage: 18 years old; universal

Legal drinking age: 18 years old

Advertising Note

> If you talk to a man in a language he understands, that goes to his head. If you talk to him in his language, that goes to his heart.
>
> —Nelson Mandela,
> former president of South Africa

For advertisers, there is always a question of which South African language to choose for their advertisements. There are 11 official languages; the most widely spoken is Zulu (or isiZulu). The others, from largest number of speakers to fewest, include isiXhosa, Afrikaans, Sepedi (Northern Sotho), English, Setswana, Sesotho (Southern Sotho), Xitsonga, isiNdebele, Tshivenda, and siSwati.

The answer to your language selection depends largely upon your target market. If you want to reach the most generic, economically powerful demographics, you advertise primarily in English and secondarily in Afrikaans. English is not even in the top three most commonly spoken languages at home, but it is the primary language used in the media and government. However, native African markets buy goods and services as well, and South Africa is a gateway to many other countries in Africa.

Since more people in South Africa speak Zulu and Xhosa than Afrikaans and English, you might consider learning a few phrases, along with how to make the intriguing click that is in many Zulu words. Indigenous South Africans are very proud of their languages, enjoy hearing them used in person, and are delighted to see them in marketing materials. No matter what language you use in your advertisements, they should be highly engaging visually and use explanatory graphics to bridge the gaps among the many different languages spoken in South Africa.

ICEBREAKERS

BRILLIANT!

1. South Africans often describe themselves as "sports mad." This characteristic was bolstered by the 2010 FIFA World Cup soccer championship, which resulted in more than $2 billion in infrastructural improvements. Be sure to know

Cultural Note

South Africa's spirits are a point of national pride and have won major awards. In 2010 a South African brandy, the Laborie Alambic, was voted as the best in the world by the 2010 International Wine and Spirits Competition in London.

While wines from South Africa have received more coverage since the end of apartheid, some vineyards on the southwestern tip of the cape have been in production for hundreds of years. Constantia and Stellenbosch are the two oldest wine regions. Others, including the Franschhoek and Paarl vineyards, now produce some of the most famous varietals. Chenin blanc (or Steen as it is locally known) has traditionally been South Africa's most popular white wine, but their sauvignon blanc and chardonnays are now gaining accolades. Notable South African reds include Pinotage (historically the signature wine of South Africa), Shiraz, and cabernet sauvignon (cabernets have been both highly recommended and panned over the past few years, but production is outpacing Pinotage).

Become familiar with some South African wines before your trip; the topic may be of interest at business meals or *braais* (barbecues). And if time allows, take a tour of several estates that offer wine tastings paired with South African cheeses, olives, and chocolate.

who won! (Spain beat the Netherlands, 1–0.) When visiting South Africa, you should be able to talk intelligently about a variety of sports. Soccer (football) is the most popular sport, but many more are of interest—from rugby, to tennis, to golf, to virtually any outdoor activity. Plan to visit outdoor South African attractions such as Kruger National Park.

2. Recognize that the term *Rainbow Nation* refers to postapartheid South Africa. The term is credited to Archbishop Desmond Tutu in 1994 and was popularized by the country's first black president, Nelson Mandela. The term acknowledges South Africa's multicultural identity. The rainbow is also a symbol of hope among some of the indig-

Advertising Note

Music is an important aspect of South African culture. All European and North American musical genres, from classical to rap, are represented in South Africa. Jazz proved especially popular with the black community—so much so that it diversified into three sub-genres, called township jazz, black jazz, and marabi. Indigenous music is often used as an accompaniment to advertisements. Kwaito, a dance music often described as South African hip-hop, also has been successfully employed in advertisements.

And, of course, don't forget the South African horn called the vuvuzela, which became famous during the 2010 World Cup. This instrument is so popular there is even an app to play the sound on your iPhone. Although it is possible to make melodious notes on a vuvuzela, most vuvuzela-playing fans at sporting events don't see that as a priority.

enous cultures (although some recognize five colors in the rainbow, not the seven colors identified in the West). Since the term was coined, it has been used in many contexts, including advertising.

BOORISH

1. Most people are aware of the racial issues of South Africa's past, but you should not dwell on them. Diversity is now commonplace, and thanks partially to the government's Black Economic Empowerment (BEE) program, black South African executives now have positions in every major firm.

   Of course, politics can be a similarly incendiary topic. Avoid it; there will rarely be complete agreement in a room with more than two people.

2. Do not assume that South African accomplishments are confined to sports and spirits. The first successful heart transplant was performed by Dr. Christiaan Barnard in

Cape Town in 1967. And two South Africans have won the Nobel Prize in Literature: Nadine Gordimer in 1991 and J. M. Coetzee in 2003.

WHAT TIME SHOULD I ARRIVE?

As a foreigner, you are expected to be on time. Small companies tend to be more relaxed about punctuality than larger companies. In addition, attitudes toward time vary between ethnic groups. However, businesspeople of all ethnicities are generally prompt.

Michael Cordier, vice president of Fiizika, noted that small businesses in South Africa tend to be highly flexible about scheduling meetings, even at the last minute. And among those firms, your word is your honor. Never endanger your reputation with an inflated claim; reliability is vital to your success.

WORKWEEK

South African businesses usually follow the British model, with a workweek that begins on Monday and ends on Friday. The difference is that the workday often starts at 7:30 A.M. with a breakfast meeting. Lunch may start at 12:30 P.M., and dinner at 7:00 or 7:30 P.M.

Since the sun rises at 6:00 A.M. and sets by 6:00 P.M., many appointments (including breakfast, lunch, and dinner) run at hours more similar to those in the United States than in Europe or Latin America. For those who commute from Pretoria to Johannesburg, traffic jams can start as early as 6:00 A.M.!

South Africans' love of outdoor trips encourages people to take three-day weekends. You have your best chance of catching people at work on Tuesday, Wednesday, and Thursday.

Cultural Note

Like many countries, South Africa has to contend with an illegal-drug problem. Since street drugs have multiple nicknames, advertisers must make sure they do not inadvertently choose a product that sounds like a street drug. Examples are *tik* (crystal meth), *unga* (cheap heroin), *dagga* (cannabis), and *whoonga/wunga* (an addictive drug mixing several ingredients, including the anti-AIDS drug Stocrin, which the government provides to approximately one million of its citizens).

Compensated vacation days can vary in different industries and parts of South Africa, but they generally start at two weeks annually and can often go to three weeks. In 2011, South Africa observed 14 holidays, which may not all be included in a salary package.

HOW CLOSE SHOULD I STAND?

Distance varies by culture. Among black Africans, a comfortable distance may be as close as 8 inches. Anglo businesspeople generally stand up to 3 feet apart.

DO I KISS, BOW, OR SHAKE HANDS?

SHAKE HANDS

The short, powerful handshake between men has become standard in South African business circles. Even South Africans with different ethnic traditions often shake hands with foreigners. Direct eye contact and a smile usually accompany the handshake.

Greetings with black South Africans tend to be very warm. Often, your right hand will be grasped and then covered in a

Cultural Note

White South Africans are divided into English speakers and Afrikaans speakers. Historically, many of the Boers (Afrikaans for "farmers") moved north in the 1830s and 1840s. This event, remembered as the Great Trek, was intended to find good farmland free from the political domination of the English speakers. (At the time, South Africa was a colony of the United Kingdom.) Of course, good land is usually already occupied, and the Boers had to fight the Zulu people for the land.

While there has been a considerable amount of unification since then, there are still some characteristics that distinguish the north and south. Afrikaans speakers remain more religious and conservative than most English speakers. Consequently, the country's north remains more conservative. Businesspeople dress more formally in the north. Should you be invited to a *braai* by Afrikaans speakers, expect there to be a prayer before the meal begins. Beer tends to be preferred to wine.

In the south, especially the coastal regions, people tend to be more relaxed. Dress codes are more informal. The coast is South Africa's primary wine-growing region, and wine is preferred to beer.

friendly manner with the left hand. This handshake is a pleasant surprise to many international executives.

Black South African men may not offer to shake hands with females. But if the handshake is initiated by the woman, they will reciprocate. If a nonwhite South African elects not to shake your hand, do not take it as an insult; assume that he or she is observing the tradition of his or her ethnic group. Keep your hands at your side and nod your head—that is all that is required.

Men and women do not usually greet with a kiss or hug in a business setting, unless they are good friends. Kisses are more common in social settings.

BUSINESS CARDS

- There is no South African tradition involving the exchange of business cards. However, you should treat all business cards with respect.
- Remember to present your card with your right hand.
- Since English is the major language used in South African business, your cards should be formatted in advance with English on one side.
- South Africa's many minorities include South Asians, who may be Hindus or Muslims. Many Hindus are vegetarians, and pig products are prohibited to observant Muslims. If you expect to do business among this ethnic group, do not keep your cards in an animal-skin card case or wallet.
- If your cards are in your wallet, do not keep your wallet in your back trouser pocket.

THREE TIPS FOR SELLING IN SOUTH AFRICA

1. **No Country for Introverts**
2. **International Prestige**
3. **46664**

1. NO COUNTRY FOR INTROVERTS

South Africans are extraordinarily friendly. They quickly invite foreigners to their homes for a *braai* (barbecue). And they expect foreigners to be open and friendly as well. However, be aware that South Africans do not generally talk over each other, so never interrupt when someone is talking.

Many South Africans host a *braai* several times a week. These events are usually very informal. When you become friends, you are usually welcome to stop by uninvited. However, it is considered courteous to phone the hostess and ask if you can bring anything. (A *braai* in which each guest brings a food item is sometimes called a "bring and *braai*.") *Braaivleis* (grilled meats) are always accompanied by a porridge called *pap* (similar to polenta).

The *braai* is so popular among South Africans of all ethnicities that the tradition is celebrated on Heritage Day, September 24. This National *Braai* Day is promoted under the name Braai4Heritage.

The *braai* often appears in South African advertisements. In the 1970s, General Motors used a jingle that celebrated "*Braaivleis*, rugby, sunny skies, and Chevrolet."

(By the way, if you encounter something called monkey-gland sauce at a *braai* or restaurant, don't worry; there is no monkey in it. Its major ingredients are garlic, onion, tomatoes, and ginger.)

If you are uncomfortable socializing in informal settings, South Africa is not the country for you. Men will be expected to talk enthusiastically about sports (preferably about a sport played in South Africa; being a fan of baseball or ice hockey isn't terribly useful). Both sexes are expected to enjoy the outdoors and to visit South Africa's parks.

For foreign women, being comfortable with sports and the outdoors may make socializing easier. There are relatively few female senior executives in South Africa, and foreign women who do business there may find the environment a bit challenging.

2. INTERNATIONAL PRESTIGE

Under apartheid, South Africa endured decades of international sanctions and boycotts. This made foreign businesspeople a rare commodity in South Africa. If a foreign executive did come, it generated substantial interest.

Holding meetings with foreigners can still convey some prestige. Don't hesitate to ask for an interview with anyone you want to see. Contact your embassy's international trade center to arrange appointments for you before your trip. Generally, you may need several weeks to set up meetings with senior executives at multinationals.

One drawback to the prestige associated with being a multinational executive in South Africa is that businesspeople may agree to meet with you even if they have no intention of working with you. There is simply a cachet involved in a schedule of meetings with foreign executives.

3. 46664

The numbers 46664 carry weight in South Africa. They were former-president Nelson Mandela's prison numbers. He was jailed for 27 years by the apartheid regime and was released on February 11, 1990. The numeric indicated he was prisoner number 466 and had been imprisoned in 1964.

Nelson Mandela decided to use the numbers of his internment as a symbol for his fight against HIV/AIDS. (He lost one of his sons to AIDS-related causes.) His charity, 46664 (see www.46664.com), has become an icon to communicate his belief that all people are equal human beings, and individuals infected with HIV/AIDS deserve the same rights to live and be treated with dignity.

More people are living with HIV/AIDS in South Africa than anywhere else on earth. More than 5 million individuals are infected, and the country's life expectancy has dropped to under 50 years old. In 2009 approximately 310,000 South Africans died of AIDS. However, AIDS is not the leading cause of death in South Africa; tuberculosis (TB) is. Many people contract both diseases because of their weakened immune systems. Despite accounting for less than 1 percent of the world's inhabitants, South Africa has 28 percent of the people who live with both TB and HIV.

If you are considering how to allocate your South African advertising and convention dollars, make sure you use embassy contacts to get references for reputable local advertising agencies, and follow through in all your normal venues. But simultaneously explore other options to sponsor the fight against HIV/AIDS and tuberculosis, and to care for its victims. This will give back more than good public relations.

Additionally, South Africa puts on more than 1,000 conferences and exhibitions a year. If your firm will participate

Cultural Note

South Africans are fans of innovative designs. Attendees at the 2010 FIFA World Cup were able to drink Castle Lager in a novel way: out of a "Can of the Year" award winner. The entire top of the can was designed to be easily removed, effectively turning the can into a cup. This large-event design eliminated the need to pour the beer from the can into a plastic cup, cutting down on serving time and waste.

in these world-class meetings, consider adding a truly unique side tour. Volunteer with a well-organized charity, like Habitat for Humanity. That organization has built several thousand houses in South Africa and intends to build dozens of new homes for children, many of whom have been orphaned by the AIDS epidemic. Contact http://www.habitat.org for information on how to place your firm on higher ground in South Africa.

LANGUAGE

As mentioned in the beginning of the chapter, there are multiple languages in South Africa. Here are a few words in Afrikaans, followed by a few in Zulu to start your conversations.

ENGLISH	AFRIKAANS
Hello.	*Hallo.*
Good morning.	*Goeiemôre.*
Good evening.	*Goeienaand.*
Thank you.	*Dankie.*
You're welcome.	*Nie te dankie.*
Good-bye.	*Totsiens.*
Please.	*Asseblief.*

ENGLISH	AFRIKAANS
Excuse me.	*Verskoon my.*
Excuse me! (when passing a person)	*Ekskuus!*

ENGLISH	ZULU
Hello / Good morning / Good evening.	*Sawubona.* (singular) / *Sanibona.* (plural)
Please.	*Ngiyacela.*
Thank you.	*Ngiyabonga.*
You're welcome.	*Kulungile.*
Yes.	*Yebo.*
No.	*Cha.*
Excuse me.	*Uxolo.*
Good-bye. (to one who stays)	*Sala kahle.* (singular) / *Salani kahle.* (plural)
Good-bye. (to one who leaves)	*Hamba kahle.* (singular) / *Hambani kahle.* (plural)
Good-bye for now.	*Sobonana.*

WOW FACTOR!

Advertising in South Africa is very visual. This is due to the multitude of languages in South Africa, as well as the disparity in educational levels. Therefore, as much as possible, try to tell the entire story graphically.

As in many countries, humor in advertising sells very well. Of course, it can be difficult to find something that all of South Africa's many cultures will laugh at (and not be offended by). Animals are often a good choice. A good example is the highly successful Buddy the Boxer campaign for Toyota from Draftfcb South Africa. This series of ads featured a live dog that spoke via computer animation.

SOUTH KOREA

Conventional long form: Republic of Korea

Local long form: Daehan-min'guk*

Local short form: Han'guk

Abbreviation: ROK

Population: 48,754,657 (2011 estimate)

Median age: 38.4 years

Age structure: (2011 estimates)
    0–14 years: 15.7%
    15–64 years: 72.9%
    65 years and over: 11.4%

GDP per capita (PPP): $30,200 (2010 estimate in US dollars)

Suffrage: 19 years old; universal

Legal drinking age: 19 years old

*South Korea recently adopted changes to its official spelling of Korean words. This is reflected in the change from *Taehan-min'guk* to *Daehan-min'guk*, as well as the change from *Kam-sa-ham-nida* to *Gam-sa-ham-nida*.

Advertising Note

Every December, Korean companies traditionally give out calendars and diaries to clients. Many are high-quality products, such as wall calendars featuring Korean artwork on heavy paper. Often, Koreans get more complimentary wall calendars, desk calendars, pocket calendars/diaries/organizers than they can use, and the extra ones get thrown out. Unless you have an amazingly unique idea for a calendar, it's best to stay out of this overcrowded niche.

ICEBREAKERS

BRILLIANT!

1. Korean is considered an extremely difficult language for Westerners to learn. Foreigners are not expected to master it, but Koreans will appreciate your attempt to learn a few simple phrases. A list of general phrases is at the end of this chapter.

   Korean uses a unique alphabet, called Hangeul (or Hangul), which was created in 1443 C.E. Koreans consider Hangeul "the most scientific writing system in the world." It has only 24 letters, compared with the thousands of characters in Chinese and Japanese writing systems. (The limited number of letters makes Hangeul well adapted to computer keyboards.) Furthermore, unlike the letters in other alphabets, some Hangeul letters represent the position of the tongue and mouth when the letter is spoken.

   Koreans are so proud of their alphabet that they celebrate it with an official holiday. October 9 is Hangul Day in South Korea; in North Korea, it is observed on January 15.

2. Ask about South Korea's Economic Miracle, as well as the sacrifices that Koreans endured to make such progress. At the end of World War II, South Korea was an impov-

erished, Third World nation. The Japanese had occupied Korea for decades during the war; they built some factories in the north, but used the south primarily as an agricultural supplier. Today, South Korea boasts the world's 15th largest economy. Demonstrate that you are interested in South Korea's achievements and the work it takes to keep them (but be aware of mentioning a US-supported dictatorship that did not end, in many Koreans' viewpoint, until the free election of President Roh Tae Woo in 1987).

BOORISH

1. Don't talk about yourself as an independent entity. Hubris about your own accomplishments will not impress Koreans. Everyone needs to be part of a group. There is no doubt that the only way you obtained your appointment with a senior Korean executive was through a personal introduction. Cold calling is not common in South Korea, and businesspeople use intermediaries to help them make appointments. One common way of finding a link is through alumni contacts at one of the well-known universities in South Korea, including Seoul National University, Yonsei University, Korea University, or Ehwa Women's University.

   The sensibilities of what is best for the group extend from the introduction to the close. Never try to close a deal based upon how it may benefit one person, one department, or sometimes even one company. Work backwards: explain how this product or service would benefit South Korea, then the company, then the group. Most South Koreans are very patriotic, and contracts that contribute to the success of *oo-ri-na-ra* (our country) will resonate with them.

2. Don't complain about being jostled on crowded Korean streets. Just accept it, and learn how to say "I'm sorry" in Korean. *Mianhamnida* (pronounced *mee-an hum-needa*) will be a very useful phrase for you in many situations.

Cultural Note

South Koreans have a very strong work ethic. A 2008 report by the Organization for Economic Cooperation and Development stated that an average South Korean employee works 2,357 hours a year. That is a higher average than any other member of the OECD. (The 34 member countries do not include Brazil, Russia, India, or China.)

In the past, Korean success was usually compared with Japanese success. Today, some Korean firms have matched and even exceeded Japanese firms on the global market. South Koreans are highly incented to stay competitive with Chinese interests as well.

Among the challenges South Korea faces is a declining birthrate. As a result, there have been several regulatory changes to the laws barring foreign workers. There is now a sizable foreign workforce in South Korea, primarily to fill low-wage, manual-labor positions (jobs that the increasingly well-educated Koreans tend to avoid). However, there are also an increasing number of high-wage, non-manual foreign workers as well.

WHAT TIME SHOULD I ARRIVE?

As a foreigner, you are expected to be on time for both business and social events. But do not be distressed if your Korean counterpart is late.

Do not get down to business too quickly. Koreans may ask you questions that seem somewhat intrusive, such as how old you are (age is still respected in Korea) or if you have any children. These questions help them to place you in their hierarchy. If you do not want to answer a question that you think seems too intrusive, evade it by changing the subject as gracefully as possible.

Good topics of conversation include Korea's cultural heritage, the Hangeul alphabet, kites (very popular in Korea), and food. Sports—particularly golf and figure-skating—may be a

Cultural Note

Despite government antismoking campaigns, cigarette smoking is ubiquitous in South Korea. Koreans who do not start smoking as teenagers often acquire the habit when they enter the military. (South Korea has universal military conscription for men.) However, certain large private and public buildings strictly forbid smoking, and the increasing price of cigarettes is expected to become a substantial deterrent.

Smoking is sometimes seen as an integral trait of the aggressive male character. Macho film stars and politicians usually smoke. It is estimated that half of Korean men smoke. Korean women smoke less than men, and rarely do so in public.

good topic of conversation with some Koreans. Seoul hosted the Summer Olympics in 1988, and South Korean athletes have won many medals in archery and speed skating.

WORKWEEK

As previously mentioned in the cultural note, South Koreans work long hours. The pressure to work hard starts in the school systems; students attend extra "cram" schools so they can score well on college entrance exams and be admitted to a top university. (The top three are often called SKY universities—for Seoul National University, Korea University, and Yonsei University.) A good education is supremely important to South Koreans and is considered the prerequisite for a successful career, a strong professional network, and a good marriage. Parents sacrifice heavily to ensure their children receive the best education possible. Some fathers even send their children and wives to live in the United Kingdom, United States, Australia, or New Zealand, so they can speak English like natives. These families are called "wild geese," because the

Cultural Note

Koreans are avid multitaskers; they are used to doing several things at once. (Cultural anthropologists may refer to this as *polychronic*.) Foreigners from extremely linear cultures, where activities are sequential, can have trouble in Korea, and vice versa. In *Riding the Waves of Culture: Understanding Diversity in Global Business* (p. 127), Fons Trompenaars and Charles Hampden-Turner described a Korean manager who visited his boss in the Netherlands for the first time and expressed his disappointment in the meeting:

> He (the Dutch boss) was on the phone when I entered his office, and as I came in he raised his left hand slightly at me. Then he rudely continued his conversation as if I were not even in the room with him. Only after he had finished his conversation five minutes later did he get up and greet me with an enthusiastic, but insincere, "Kim, happy to see you!" I just could not believe it.

If the Korean manager were meeting an important colleague for the first time, he would have interrupted his phone call for at least a moment to rise and greet the visitor.

South Korea is said to be the most wired nation in the world. The mobile-phone penetration rate is greater than 100 percent, and South Koreans' Internet usage puts some other G20s to shame. If you want to reach a Korean executive, text him or her. The executive will continuously juggle multiple tasks while simultaneously texting or surfing the Net.

fathers stay behind in Korea to supply the income and, hopefully, visit their families in the summer.

Business hours are generally from 8:30 A.M. to 5:00 or 6:00 P.M., Monday through Friday (although many people stay later). Many businesses keep Saturday hours as well, but usually only until noon or 1:00 P.M. The best times for business meetings are 10:00 to 11:00 A.M. and 2:00 to 3:00 P.M.

South Koreans generally receive two weeks of paid vacation annually. In 2011, the government listed 15 holidays.

HOW CLOSE SHOULD I STAND?

Approximately 3 feet apart. Basically, you stand far enough apart to allow ample room for both parties to bow.

DO I KISS, BOW, OR SHAKE HANDS?

SHAKE HANDS OR BOW

South Koreans bow to each other. If you come from a culture where bowing is the traditional greeting, feel free to do so. However, South Koreans have come to accept a handshake as customary with Western executives. They may follow a handshake with a bow.

Good friends (of the same sex) may hold hands. However, that is the only physical contact you are likely to see in public. Public displays of affection between the sexes are frowned upon. In general, it is best to refrain from touching your Korean contacts.

BUSINESS CARDS

- The exchange of business cards is a formal event. Remember to treat all business cards with respect.
- As in any culture influenced by Confucianism, hierarchy is very important in South Korea. Your business card and job title are important indicators of your rank in that hierarchy.
- Present your card with your right hand. To convey respect, you may support your right wrist with your left hand.
- Offering or accepting a card with both hands is another way to show respect.
- Your cards should be translated into Korean on one side. Your native language may be on the back. Present your card with the Korean side showing.
- If your cards are in your wallet, do not keep your wallet in your back trouser pocket.

Cultural Note

Disputes—and occasional gunfire—routinely break out between North and South Korea. How dangerous is doing business in South Korea? Since North Korea cannot even feed its people, the country tends to threaten violence—perhaps by invasion, perhaps through use of its small nuclear arsenal—on its neighboring country. To make North Korea back down, South Korea and its allies give the North what it needs (usually increased food aid).

Most experts maintain that China, North Korea's only ally, will not allow a major war to break out. Such a war would disrupt the South Korean economy, and South Korea is China's third-largest trading partner. China does not want the North Korean government to collapse—if only because that would send hundreds of thousands of hungry North Koreans across the border into China, looking for better living conditions.

What should you do? First off, don't panic every time there is a crisis. As long as it doesn't last more than a week or so, supply chain disruptions should be minimal. However, once you become known in South Korea, be sure your company's computer network is as secure as possible. It is believed that in July 2009, North Korea launched a massive cyber attack against the South Korean government, businesses, and foreign companies that do business in South Korea.

THREE TIPS FOR SELLING IN SOUTH KOREA

1. Celebrities
2. *Kibun*
3. Entertainment: Karaoke, Room Salons, and Golf

1. CELEBRITIES

South Korea is as starstruck as many other wired countries, and celebrity advertisements are big business. However, there are more products than celebrities in South Korea. If "one star = one product" is your goal, you are better off picking a pop idol from outside South Korea.

For example, one of South Korea's most popular movie stars, Jang Dong-kun, appears in advertisements for Nintendo, SK Telecom, Hite beer, Samsung digital cameras, and Chung Jung-won food products.

Since they are advertising so many products, Korean celebrities often cannot show up at corporate events. Consequently, some Korean firms use famous personalities from Hollywood or the United Kingdom. Recent choices included model Kate Moss and actor Pierce Brosnan.

2. KIBUN

There are many pitfalls to establishing your product or service in South Korea. For one thing, almost any product or service you can offer will have a local competitor. If there isn't one, there will be: Korean entrepreneurs are always looking for something new.

To be successful, you need to divine and develop the right *kibun*. The Korean concept of *kibun* can be translated as a "feeling" or "mood." It's the emotional appeal of a product.

External to Korea, South Koreans have a reputation as being careful, deliberate consumers who use logic to make buying decisions and do not need instant gratification. However, many South Korean advertisers believe logic is not enough. They maintain that sales and branding are best achieved through *kibun*, the feelings consumers have for the product or service, not the reasoning behind it.

Kibun is also the solid connection, or the chemistry between you and your Korean business partners. Just as your advertisements need emotional appeal, you must develop the right *kibun* with your Korean associates. If you present an inflexible attitude about your product or price, all the discounts and service options you may muster will not help. There are many subtleties during negotiations, and you should be flexible and humble enough to build rapport and adapt to your prospect's requests. You need the instincts to read situations and the capability to say the right thing at the right time. In South Korea, this sensitivity is called *nunchi*.

Cultural Note

Korean contracts may not mimic the rigor that is normally found in more litigious Western environments. Contracts may be more of a consensus statement than a detailed list of protections against liability. Broad views and flexible options work better in South Korea's consensus-based culture.

3. ENTERTAINMENT: KARAOKE, ROOM SALONS, AND GOLF

South Koreans work hard. If you have an opportunity to participate in a social event during the minimal hours they do not work, accept the invitation. Social events are integral to building friendships and trust, and there are a variety of options for an evening gathering, usually starting with a *norae bang* (karaoke) bar.

The fact that Koreans consider drinking alcohol part of the social process can be helpful in a *norae bang*. It can also help you cultivate an appreciation of Soju beer or other local beverages. Do not refill your own drink; another member of your party pours it for you. And when someone in your party finishes a drink, feel free to fill his or her glass. (Use both hands to pour; this shows respect.) Never let a senior executive pour his or her own drink.

After a drink, be game enough to sing a song or two. There will be a selection of popular music videos, some of which will be in English. Try your best; your efforts will be appreciated.

Before traveling to any international location, make sure you alert your hosts and counterparts to any issues you may have with particular foods, alcohol, dancing, singing, or other types of activities.

The CEO of a multinational firm took his first major trip to Asia in 2007 and had an unfortunate experience.

Cultural Note

In many Asian cultures, open displays of emotion are rare. In most of Asia, if a manager angrily rebukes an employee in public, both the employee and the manager have been shamed. However, Koreans are much more prone to show their emotions in public. Expect to see both positive and negative feelings on display.

This can be a problem for Koreans in other Asian countries. For example, there are many factories in Vietnam that are owned and managed by Koreans. Statistics indicate that Vietnamese factory workers are more likely to go on strike at Korean-owned factories than at factories owned by most other Asian nationalities. Observers believe this is because Korean managers are more likely to rebuke Vietnamese employees in public, which is a serious breach of etiquette in Vietnam.

His potential distributors were very honored that he would be visiting and planned multiple activities for his stay. The initial event had to be impressive, so they escorted him to an exclusive "room salon." But when he entered the venue, he looked around and refused to sit down at the place of honor. Instead of bonding with his associates over a carefully planned, expensive evening, he bowed out. They had no idea that as a profound Southern Baptist, he did not drink alcohol, sing, dance, or (in his view) consort with young hostesses. The gentleman knew his Bible cover to cover and would not consider partaking in that sort of amusement. His abrupt departure left all the associates, from both the United States and Asia, extremely embarrassed. The agenda for the rest of the trip suffered as well. If the parties involved had all talked prior to his visit, he would have just brought his Callaways, and all would have been well.

Before any trip abroad, be certain to review your personal predilections, interests, and any restrictions based on religious beliefs or medical conditions with your contacts. If you do not

Cultural Note

Y. E. Yang (male winner of the 2009 PGA Championship), K. J. Choi, Se Ri Pak, Grace Park, and Michele Wei are names that every Korean golfer knows. Since the government of South Korea stopped discouraging golf as an elitist pastime, Korean golfers (particularly women) have come roaring onto the world circuit. Some parents withdraw their daughters from regular schools and can pay $5,000 a month for golf academies, tutors, and travel, hoping to get them into the Korean LPGA. The sacrifices that families incur for these pursuits are enormous and result in extremely intense competition. Parents are not as zealous about putting their sons in the game—perhaps because the requirement that all males serve in the military for two years is a fatal interruption of training. But many male executives look forward to their golf outings and will appreciate your interest in the game.

drink alcohol, can only eat certain foods, or don't want to sing or participate in other forms of entertainment, let your associates know those details before your trip. The wisest course of action is to inquire what the entertainment options are and communicate a list of activities you would appreciate. You can always visit sites of interest like the Changduk Palace's "Secret Garden" in Seoul, the National Museum, or the Jongmyo Shrine. Also, ask where the best locations are to close and celebrate a deal; in South Korea, it may be at a golf resort.

LANGUAGE

Here are a few phrases that may help you in South Korea. Also, a list of online Korean language programs is available at the Omniglot website, http://www.omniglot.com/writing/korean.htm.

Cultural Note

As in some other Asian cultures, an infant is considered to be one year old when he or she is born. Laws pertaining to age are based on the first of the year. For example, the drinking age in South Korea is 19, so a teenager in Korea can drink on January 1 of the year he or she turns 19.

ENGLISH	KOREAN
Hello. / Good morning. / Good afternoon. / Good evening.	An-nyeong-ha-se-yo.
Good night.	An-nyeong-hi ju-mu-se-yo.
Good-bye.	An-nyeong-hi ga-se-yo.
Please.	Bu-ta-kye-yo.
Thank you.	Gam-sa-ham-ni-da.
Excuse me.	Shil-lye-ham-ni-da.
How are you?	Eo-tteo-se-yo?
Yes, please.	Ne, bu-ta-gi-e-yo.
Fine, thanks.	Ne gwaen-cha-na-yo.
No, thank you.	A-ni-yo. Gwen-cha-na-yo.
I don't speak Korean.	Na-neun hang-gung-mal mo-tae-yo.
Pleased to meet you.	Man-na-seo ban-ga-wo-yo.
Do you speak English?	Yeong-eo hal-jjul a-se-yo?
What is your name?	I-reu-mi mwo-e-y?
My name is . . .	Nae-i-reu-meun . . .
What is it called in Korean?	Hang-gung-mal-lo meo-e-yo?
Where is . . . ?	. . . eo-di-e i-sseo-yo?
Is it nearby?	Ga-kka-I i-sseo-yo?
How much is it?	Eol-ma-e-yo?
Could you repeat that?	Da-shi mal-hae-ju-se-yo?

ENGLISH	KOREAN
Could you say it more slowly?	*Deo cheon-cheon-hi mal-ha?*
Sorry, I don't understand.	*Mi-an-ha-ji-man mo-da-ra-deu.*
Help!	*Do-wa ju-se-yo!*
I would like . . .	*. . . jom ju-se-yo.*
. . . a beer.	*Mek-jju han-byeong . . .*
. . . a glass of wine.	*Wa-in han-jan . . .*
. . . a coffee.	*Keo-pi han-jan . . .*
. . . a cup of tea.	*Cha han-jan . . .*
. . . mineral water.	*Mi-ne-ral mul . . .*
I'm . . .	*Na-neun . . . wa-sseo-yo.*
. . . from the United States.	*. . . mi-guk-seo . . .*
. . . from Canada.	*. . . ka-na-da-seo . . .*
. . . from England.	*. . . yeong-guk-e-seo . . .*
. . . from Australia.	*. . . ho-ju-e-seo . . .*
Cheers!	*Wi-ha-yeo!*
Bottoms up!	*Geon-be!*

WOW FACTOR!

A well-known South Korean attorney was posed a question about what to do at business dinners in Asia if you do not drink alcohol. Can you refuse your host's offer to have some wine? Can you just drink water, soda, or tea? Acknowledging that this is a common dilemma, not just in Korea, but for many people in many cultures, he suggested the following approach:

Even if you do not normally drink alcohol, it can be helpful if you agree to have a glass of wine with dinner, if only for the toasts. Of course, if you drain your glass, your neighbors will fill it up for you again. In fact, they will likely feel obligated to do so. But if you absolutely cannot drink any more, it is better to leave a good amount in your glass. If they offer to fill your glass again, and thereby suggest that you consume more of the alcohol, you can thank your hosts for the excellent wine, and politely mention that you've probably had enough for now. Your Korean hosts will not force you to drink, and they will not be offended as long as you seem appreciative of their cordiality and cheerfully participate in the conversations. Toasting with a glass of water or soda is another option, but it might be less awkward to receive the first glass of wine, drink as much as you like or can (even a sip), and then enjoy your meal and company!

TURKEY

Conventional long form: Republic of Turkey

Local long form: Türkiye Cumhuriyeti

Local short form: Türkiye

Population: 78,785,548 (2011 estimate)

Median age: 28.5 years

Age structure: (2011 estimate)
    0–14 years: 26.6%
    15–64 years: 67.1%
    65 years and over: 6.3%

GDP per capita (PPP): $12,300 (2010 estimate in US dollars)

Suffrage: 18 years old; universal

Legal drinking age: 18 years old

Cultural Note

Personal introductions are the most effective way to meet decision makers in Turkey. Embassies, law firms, accounting firms, and chambers of commerce can advise you about your industry and help you contact and recruit the potential representative and/or distributor you will need in Turkey.

Choose your representative carefully before you have any real exposure to your industry. The person you select will define your entrance into the market, and the market in Istanbul is currently booming. *Forbes* magazine recently reported that Istanbul had 28 billionaires, close behind the 32 in London.

ICEBREAKERS

BRILLIANT!

1. Family is exceedingly important in Turkey—and is often a good topic of conversation. If your prospect has children, he or she will probably enjoy talking about them.
2. In Istanbul, be familiar with some of the more significant cultural sites, such as the Topkapi Palace, Hagia Sophia, and the Blue Mosque. Sports are also a good topic for conversation, since many Turks are avid sports fans. Football (soccer) is by far the most popular sport. Basketball and volleyball are also popular, and in the Olympics, Turkish weightlifters have won several gold medals. Motor sports and sailing have been increasing in popularity.

BOORISH

1. While you are showing your appreciation for the local heritage and history, make sure you are expressing appreciation for *Turkish* heritage and history—not relics from the Roman or Byzantine eras. Remember that the Turks conquered a territory that had been occupied for thousands of years. Unless your contact has a financial interest in tour-

Cultural Note

The Turkish national sport is called *yağlı güreş* (oiled wrestling)—so called because the wrestlers grease themselves with olive oil to make it difficult for an opponent to grasp them. *Yağlı güreş* has been an established sport since Ottoman times.

ism, the average Turkish businessperson may view Roman or Byzantine ruins with ambivalence.

Of course, Turks are unhappy that foreigners have made off with their Roman and Byzantine artifacts (just as the Greeks resent the fact that the British hold the Elgin Marbles). If you are discussing Turkish achievements that you admire, be sure you start with those of Kemal Atatürk, Turkey's first president and the founder of the modern Turkish state.

2. If you are old enough to remember the Cold War, you'll recall a time when Turkey was a staunch ally of the United States. Relations between Turkey and its old allies—the United States and Israel—are currently in flux. Turkey objected to the US-led war in Iraq (which is one of the eight countries that Turkey borders), and refused to allow the use of its bases or airports. Turkish relations with Israel deteriorated in June 2010, when the Israeli Navy stopped a flotilla of ships that intended to deliver aid to the Palestinians. During the interdiction, nine Turkish nationals were killed. The deaths of the nine Turks caused widespread protest against Israel throughout Turkey.

This doesn't mean that, if you are from the United States of America or Israel, you won't be able to do business in Turkey. But don't bring up the subject of Turkish relations with your home country. (Some Turks may also resent the German and French governments' reluctance to admit Turkey to the European Union.)

Cultural Note

Turks smoke. Some 25 percent of the population are smokers. According to the World Health Organization (WHO), Turkey is one of the 10 nations that account for two-thirds of the world's tobacco consumption. In an effort to combat this, the Turkish government put an indoor-smoking ban into law in July 2009. The Turkish Health Ministry is also conducting a vigorous anti-smoking advertising campaign, primarily using banners and public events like marches to raise awareness.

WHAT TIME SHOULD I ARRIVE?

As a foreigner, you are expected to be on time. Although punctuality is not a traditional virtue in Turkey, many Turkish businesspeople are prompt. Others may be late, and the general excuse is the traffic. In large Turkish cities, especially Istanbul and Ankara, traffic jams are dreadful and frequent. Give yourself plenty of travel time.

WORKWEEK

Unlike most countries with Muslim majorities, Turkey is officially secular, so the workweek runs from Monday through Friday (or Saturday for retail). Observant Muslims will attend mosques on Fridays at noon, and appointments may be somewhat difficult to schedule on Friday afternoons.

Senior executives may arrive later in the morning—somewhere around 9:00 A.M. Morning appointments should be scheduled around 10:00 or 11:00 A.M.

Most corporate environments provide two weeks of paid vacation annually. In addition, there were 16 holidays in 2011 in Turkey, which include Seker Bayrami (Eid al-Fitr) and Kur-

Cultural Note

> Turks may write the date in an unusual way: they include the day of the week in the middle of the date. They usually write the day first, then the month, then the day of the week, and finally the year. For example, December 3, 2015, is written as 3.12.Thursday.15 (periods are used rather than commas).

ban Bayrami (Eid al-Adha). Some holidays might not be paid, but are observed. During the summer months, many private and public offices around the Aegean and Mediterranean coasts may close earlier—or have no afternoon hours at all.

Every year, on November 10 at 9:05 A.M., the entire population of Turkey observes a moment of silence in remembrance of the founder of modern Turkey, Kemal Atatürk, who passed away at that time in 1938. Failing to observe this silence is a serious insult.

HOW CLOSE SHOULD I STAND?

Approximately 1½ feet apart. Remember that while Turkey has a secular government, its population is predominantly Muslim. Men and women may opt not to stand as close to each other as they would with their own gender.

DO I KISS, BOW, OR SHAKE HANDS?

SHAKE HANDS

Turkish men usually shake hands with other men. The handshake is firm, brief, and accompanied by direct eye contact. Two-handed shakes are not uncommon. Handshakes are traditional at the beginning of a meeting, but not at the end.

Cultural Note

Foreign graphic designers often erroneously decorate books, magazines, articles, or other materials about Turkey with images that reflect a totally different Middle Eastern or Islamic country. Here are some guidelines:

- Turkish men do not wear the tasseled pillbox hat called a fez. As part of the country's modernization program, wearing a fez was outlawed in the 1920s.
- Turkish businessmen usually dress conservatively, like many Europeans. However, during the hot summer months, they may remove their jackets and ties.
- Turkish women in urban areas dress much like women in most European countries. Some wear a headscarf, some do not. Women going to Turkish universities are *prohibited* from wearing a headscarf. Even in conservative rural areas, Turkish women rarely wear the wrap-around garment called a chador.
- Of course, when entering a mosque, you need suitable attire: long sleeves, long pants or skirt, headscarves (for women), and no shoes (you leave them at the door).

If you are greeting a number of men, shake hands with the eldest first. Elders are highly respected in Turkey.

Turkish businessmen will usually shake hands with women, although this violates strict Muslim norms. Male visitors may wait to see if a Turkish woman extends her hand. If so, definitely shake hands with her. Businesswomen shake hands with other businesswomen.

Close friends in Turkey may greet each other with a kiss on both cheeks. However, it will take a considerable amount of time for a foreigner to reach this level of familiarity.

Since most foreign executives are not familiar with the Turkish language, your attempt to speak a few words will definitely make a good impression. There are a variety of video lessons on the Web. One provided through a youth organiza-

Cultural Note

As in many countries, television in Turkey tends to reflect the positions of the media magnates who own the stations. The same announcers who calmly read the news may segue into a political tirade that is startling in its vehemence.

tion called solarnet is at http://www.solarnet.tv/forum/index .php?topic=21277.0.

BUSINESS CARDS

- There is no Turkish tradition involving the exchange of business cards. However, treat all cards with respect.
- If possible, present your card with both hands. If you can only use one hand (say, because you are holding your brief-case), be sure to use your right hand.
- Bring a substantial number of cards. When you go to an office, you will leave one card with the receptionist and others for the executives you meet.
- Your cards should be translated into Turkish on one side.
- If your cards are in your wallet, do not keep your wallet in your back trouser pocket.
- You may not get a card in return on your first visit. A Turkish businessperson may not give you a card until he is convinced that he wants to be in business with you.

THREE TIPS FOR SELLING IN TURKEY

1. **Secularized Islamic Nation**
2. **Relationships and Patience**
3. **Presentations**

1. SECULARIZED ISLAMIC NATION

Turkey is not like most of its neighbors in the Muslim world. It is a parliamentary democracy, not a dictatorship, and the government is fiercely secular.

Turkey has no official religion, but 90 percent of the population is Sunni Muslim—many of whom are part of a nonorthodox sect called Alevi. While every Turk is basically familiar with the precepts of Islam, they do not read Arabic, and they have passed legislation to ensure gender equality. However, your Turkish associates will probably observe Islamic holidays like Ramadan, which may affect their work schedules on Fridays.

For the foreign businessperson, this means that you are going to a country where alcohol is freely available and enjoyed by many Muslim Turks. Dining, drinking *Raki* (an anise-flavored national spirit locally called "lion's milk"), and listening to traditional music are common practice in *meyhanes*—the Turkish equivalent of taverns.

Unlike in Saudi Arabia or the United Arab Emirates, advertisements in Turkey can include pictures of a man and woman alone. For example, Turkey's Culture and Tourism Office has promoted its beach resorts with photos of women in bikinis and men in swim trunks.

The Turks are proud of their country—and they have every right to be. It is a region of the world with an immense (some say 8,000-year-old) history. Turkey's many ancient shrines bring to light the diverse civilizations and belief systems that have existed and now coexist in Turkey.

But this pride means that real or imagined slights against Turkish honor can have disastrous implications. Honor is so important that it is a crime to slur Turkey; conviction is punishable by a jail sentence. The Nobel Prize–winning Turkish author, Orhan Pamuk, has been charged with insulting Turkishness. So has Turkey's current most-popular female author, Elif Shafak. Her offense was writing about the Armenian

Advertising Note

Outdoor advertising is alive and well in Turkey. Istanbul has the full range of outdoor ads, from bus shelters to advertising pillars to electronic billboards.

Television advertising is still the most popular investment, followed by newspapers and the Internet. However, Internet and smartphone ads are expected to outpace newspaper advertising dollars in the near future.

genocide and Turkey's refusal to recognize its culpability. (In both cases, the prosecutions were eventually dropped.)

Be certain that your marketing materials are vetted by in-country experts.

2. RELATIONSHIPS AND PATIENCE

As in many countries, business relationships are not between Turks and companies. They are between Turks and the people who work for the companies. This is why an investment in face-to-face visits and conversation is never wasted; it is part of establishing your personal relationship with your client.

Once you have made contact, do not expect anything of substance to happen during the first meeting—perhaps the first several meetings. All meetings in Turkey tend to be leisurely, starting with small talk and cups of tea. (Aromatic Turkish coffee tends to be served at the end of a meeting. Don't drain your cup: there are coffee grounds at the bottom.) Avoid the temptation to get down to business too quickly.

Turkish businesspeople cannot be rushed. Decisions will be made on their own time, which is probably slower than in your native country. However, Turkey is a dynamic country with an average age of 28. As younger Turks come into positions of power, the pace of decision making is increasing.

Cultural Note

The most expensive—and popular—Turkish movie ever made was called *Valley of the Wolves—Iraq*. The villains of the movie are US troops. The film fictionalizes several actual incidents that occurred in Western-occupied Iraq and Afghanistan. The cast includes some US actors: Billy Zane plays a ruthless, crazed Christian US commander; Gary Busey plays a Jewish physician who harvests the organs from Arab victims and sells them to wealthy Westerners. Despite the fact that the film's dialogue was in Turkish rather than Arabic, this movie was very popular throughout the Arab world.

During your first meetings, you may be vetted by junior executives before you get to sit down with the senior decision makers. (Since many businesses are family enterprises, everyone you deal with may be related.) If the relationship shows promise, you will be invited to lunches or dinners in restaurants. The host always pays. You should reciprocate by hosting a dinner of your own in a restaurant. Some business-people recommend telling the restaurant maitre d' that he is to accept payment only from you—otherwise, your Turkish guest may pay for a dinner *you* host!

Eventually, you may be invited to dinner or a party at your host's home. Gift giving is not a large part of doing business in Turkey, but you should bring a gift of pastries or other sweets when you are invited into a home. Do not bring alcohol unless you are absolutely sure it is acceptable: a Turk who drinks alcohol in restaurants may nonetheless observe the Muslim prohibition on alcohol at home.

Be certain that your firm understands how vital it is to keep the relationships constant with your Turkish clients. If your company makes the mistake of switching its salesperson or local representative towards the end of the sales cycle, it will probably lose the sale.

Cultural Note

Be sure to give your interpreter any specific vocabulary—or jargon—used in your industry far ahead of time. A month is not too soon. You will want to review the interpreter's comprehension of your materials several days before your visit. Never use one interpreter for more than two hours straight; it is cognitively draining to interpret high-level discussions. Mistakes can be made when interpreters get weary. If you have two interpreters, you can have them spell each other every few hours. After the event is over, meet with them again to review the results and resolve any questions.

3. PRESENTATIONS

You will probably not be invited to give a sales demonstration or presentation until you have established a relationship. Effective presentations in Turkey should have strong visual appeal. Sharp graphics should be accompanied by models if possible. Use a variety of techniques: everything from three-dimensional demonstrations to avatars on a big screen that your prospect can control can be helpful. Of course interactive video discussions and tweets with your headquarters can build credibility as well.

Your oral presentation should also be exciting. If you are speaking in your native language and it is not English, German, French, or Turkish, make sure you have an excellent interpreter (see Cultural Note on interpreters above). Your written and digital materials must be sharp as well. Having them translated into fluent Turkish is an asset.

Turks tend to be comfortable multitasking. Do not become distracted if they seem to be doing other things during your presentation, or if people keep coming in and out of the room. They also may ask you to repeat your presentation for a senior executive who was not initially present. That is a good sign: your new audience may be the ultimate decision maker.

LANGUAGE

Here are a few phrases that may help you in Turkey:

ENGLISH	TURKISH
Hello.	*Merhaba.*
Good-bye.	*Hoşça kal. / Güle güle.*
Yes.	*Evet.*
No.	*Hayir.*
Please.	*Lütfen.*
Thank you.	*Teşekkür ederim.*
Excuse me.	*Efendim.*
Sorry.	*Pardon.*

WOW FACTOR!

Although Ankara has been the capital of Turkey since 1923, Istanbul has a far larger population (approximately 12.5 million in 2011). Istanbul is also Turkey's economic and industrial center. Since Istanbul absorbed the district to the south (Asian) side of the Bosporus, it became the only city on earth that spans two continents: Europe and Asia. About 30 percent of the city's population lives on the Asian side, and approximately 2.5 million people commute across the Bosporus every day.

UNITED ARAB EMIRATES

Conventional long form: United Arab Emirates

Local long form: Al Imarat al Arabiyah al Muttahidah

Former: Trucial Oman, Trucial States

Abbreviation: UAE

Population: 5,148,664 (2011 estimate)

Median age: 30.2 years

Age structure: (2011 estimate)
    0–14 years: 20.4%
    15–64 years: 78.7% (In this age group, 73.9% of the
        population is nonnational.)
    65 years and over: 0.9%

GDP per capita (PPP): $40,200 (2010 estimate in US dollars)

Suffrage: None (The government is appointed by the emirs.)

Legal drinking age: Citizens may not drink; non-Muslim foreigners
may drink at designated locations if they are at least 21 years
old.

Cultural Note

The global recession hit the emirates, especially Dubai, hard. In late 2009, Dubai had to be bailed out (with approximately US $20 billion) by its fellow emirate, Abu Dhabi (which has most of the UAE's oil reserves). So why would you want to do business in the United Arab Emirates?

The obvious answer is that the United Arab Emirates is the most welcoming nation to foreigners on the Arabian Peninsula. In contrast, Saudi Arabia bars entry to its country unless you are sponsored by a Saudi national or you are a Muslim. The United Arab Emirates, in contrast, invites foreigners as workers, investors, salespeople, and even tourists.

The United Arab Emirates has numerous free-trade zones in which you can set up your business. As of this writing, these zones offer the following benefits:

■ No personal UAE income tax and no corporate UAE taxes for 15 years
■ 100 percent foreign ownership of your business (no local partner required)
■ 100 percent exemption from UAE import and export taxes
■ 100 percent repatriation of capital and profits

Arguably, the United Arab Emirates offers the most generous deals for foreign businesses in the entire Cooperation Council for the Arab States of the Gulf (which also includes Bahrain, Kuwait, Qatar, Oman, and Saudi Arabia). Be aware, though, that if you visit a dealer or distributor, you will probably meet with a Lebanese or Indian manager. There are far more foreigner managers than native Emiratis in private industry. However, if your appointment is in the public sector (in government), you will most probably meet with an Emirati.

ICEBREAKERS

BRILLIANT!

1. Become familiar with some of the many architectural accomplishments and luxurious accommodations in the United Arab Emirates. Emiratis are happy to talk about

their country. Ask about the impressive Palm Jumeirah (an artificial archipelago created in Dubai), and make a few gracious comments about the beautiful Burj Al Arab (the sail-shaped hotel) or Burj Khalifa (the tallest tower in the world). The Sheikh Zayed Mosque in Abu Dhabi also is an exceptional topic for study and discussion. Like the Vatican in Rome, there is a code for appropriate attire and behavior in this grand mosque of Abu Dhabi. When visiting the Sheikh Zayed Mosque or any other mosque, you must abide by the following rules of proper conduct:

■ Wear modest, conservative, loose-fitting clothing, including long sleeves and long (ankle-length) skirts and trousers.
■ Do not wear any transparent (see-through) clothing.
■ Neither men nor women should wear shorts.
■ Do not wear any tight clothing, swimwear, or beachwear.
■ Remove your shoes before entering the mosque.
■ Headscarves for women are mandatory.
■ Intimate behavior (such as holding hands or kissing) is not acceptable in a Muslim place of worship.
■ Out of respect for worshipers, visitors are usually asked to stay within specific areas of mosques.
■ Smoking and food are not permitted in the mosque area.
■ Never place anything on top of a Qur'an or handle a Qur'an in a careless fashion in a mosque (or in any other Muslim community).

Listing these regulations for appropriate behavior inside of mosques may seem a bit extreme to include in a chapter about the United Arab Emirates—which is a very business-like, open-minded Muslim country. However, if you are at least familiar with formal Islamic protocol, it may save you and your firm from an inadvertent religious faux pas in person, or in print, at a later date.

2. Many Emiratis are well traveled and have studied in top universities in Europe or the United States. Inquiring about their educational experiences and the countries where they studied is a good way to share viewpoints.

BOORISH

1. Leave the political discussions at home. Most Emiratis do not consider politics a fascinating topic of conversation.
2. Never ask about the female members of a Muslim's family. Male Emiratis will not appreciate your interest in their wives or daughters. If they talk about their families, it may be in a general way, and only after they get to know you.

WHAT TIME SHOULD I ARRIVE?

As a foreigner, you are expected to be prompt. However, punctuality is not a traditional virtue in the United Arab Emirates. If your contacts are Indian or Lebanese, they may be on time.

Patience is your best friend when doing business in the United Arab Emirates. If your Emirati counterpart is late, whether to an appointment or with a contract, never take umbrage. Emiratis did not grow up in a country where "time is money." In general, no business is addressed in your initial meeting—it can be spent entirely on small talk. You are establishing a relationship, and hopefully you will obtain your prospect's personal cell phone number. This is far better than an e-mail address, since many Emiratis do not respond to e-mails. E-mails can be viewed as laborious, whereas a phone call or a text is far more personal and efficient.

Observant Muslims pray five times a day in the direction of Mecca. The five prayer times are:

Fajr (dawn)
Dhuhr (midday)
Asr (afternoon)

Cultural Note

Unlike many countries on the Arabian Peninsula, the United Arab Emirates is a tourist as well as a business or religious destination. While the UAE welcomes foreigners and allows them to dress as they please inside UAE resorts, everyone is expected to dress modestly in public.

Maghrib (sunset)
Isha (evening)

The exact times of each prayer, the direction of Mecca, special holiday information, and nearby mosques are available on smartphone apps and websites including Islamic Finder (www.islamicfinder.org). Even if you are not meeting with a Muslim contact, you should be sensitive to these events. If you are going to be with observant Emiratis, plan your agendas around prayers if possible.

In the United Arab Emirates, as in many parts of the Arabian Gulf, you may hear the muezzins (chosen Muslims who lead the call to prayer) up in the minarets.

WORKWEEK

There is some flexibility in the UAE workweek. Most businesses are open five days a week, from Sunday to Thursday (which is different than in Saudi Arabia), but some environments will be open six days a week, with Saturday hours as well. The UAE's free-trade zones may have different hours than other parts of the country.

Many offices in Dubai will close around 1:00 P.M. and then reopen from 4:00 P.M. to 7:00 P.M. This helps people avoid working during the hottest part of the day. Office hours may be significantly shorter during the month of Ramadan.

Cultural Note

Arabic is read from right to left, so the layout and design of your materials may be reversed. Invest extra effort in the back cover of your annual reports and marketing materials. The first thing your contacts see should be impressive.

Everyone in the United Arab Emirates observes the two most important holidays:

- Eid al-Fitr: The festival of breaking fast, a three-day feast celebrating the end of fasting during the month of Ramadan.
- Eid al-Adha: The feast of the sacrifice, a three-day festival that takes place after Muslims have completed a Hajj, a pilgrimage to Mecca.

No business will be conducted during these holidays.

Paid vacation days can extend to 30 days, which can be augmented by paid holidays. There were 13 holidays in 2011.

HOW CLOSE SHOULD I STAND?

Approximately 1 to 1½ feet apart. Your Emirati counterpart may not stand quite as close as other citizens from the Arabian Gulf would.

The United Arab Emirates hosts so many conferences and exhibitions that thousands of executives from all over the world are in the UAE, every day. Emiratis are constantly acclimated to various cultural orientations and accept different communication styles. However, if your Emirati contact stands quite close to you, always stay in place, even if you are not used to the proximity. If you back up, it may insult your UAE associate—who may unconsciously restore the "proper" distance between you anyway. Emiratis are exceedingly hospitable, and chatting close together is normal.

DO I KISS, BOW, OR SHAKE HANDS?

GREETINGS VARY

Since several styles of greeting are currently in use in the United Arab Emirates, it is safest to wait for your Emirati counterpart to initiate the greeting, especially at a first meeting.

Westernized Emirati men shake hands with other men. Many Emirati men will shake hands with Western women, although strictly observant Muslims may not. Similarly, some Emirati women will not shake hands with foreign men or women. However, most businesswomen shake hands.

Traditionally, Emirati women do not have any physical contact with any males to whom they are not related. In fact, if you encounter a veiled woman with an Emirati man, it is not traditional to introduce her.

In a traditional Emirati greeting between men, each grasps the other's right hand and places his left hand on the other's right shoulder. Then they exchange kisses on each cheek. They may even touch noses.

BUSINESS CARDS

- There is no Emirati tradition involving the exchange of business cards. However, treat all business cards with respect.
- Pork and pig products are prohibited under Islam. Do not keep your cards in a pigskin card case or wallet.
- If your cards are in your wallet, do not keep your wallet in your back trouser pocket.
- Have your card formatted in advance with Arabic on one side, to show respect for the culture.

THREE TIPS FOR SELLING IN THE UNITED ARAB EMIRATES

1. **Conferences, Exhibitions, and Collateral**
2. **The Seven Emirates**
3. **Negotiating**

1. CONFERENCES, EXHIBITIONS, AND COLLATERAL

The United Arab Emirates presents an amazing number of conferences, exhibitions, and trade shows throughout the year. In fact, more than half the covered exhibition space in the entire Gulf Cooperation Council is in the UAE. These events are not limited to the industries one associates with oil-rich maritime nations, such as the oil industry, automobiles, and yachting. There are conferences and trade shows of every description, from fashion to hunting to high technology. Chances are good that there is one for your industry or service. In addition, the United Arab Emirates hosts its own Grand Prix and the Dubai World Cup (the world's richest horse race). Make your reservations for these events six months to a year in advance, and avoid the chaos of a last-minute search for hotel space.

There are no labor unions in the United Arab Emirates; if you prefer, you can set up your own exhibit. If you need help, be sure to contract with a service, since the exhibit halls generally do not provide any on-site labor. You are generally permitted to serve tea, coffee, and some snacks in your booth, but (of course) alcohol is prohibited. Smoking is not permitted either, but you may see ashtrays in various locations.

Be familiar with top-drawer accommodations (even if you do not stay there), such as the Burj Al Arab, billed as the most luxurious hotel in the world.

The collateral you develop for your conference marketing and advertising in the United Arab Emirates can be challenging. Certain images are not permissible through sharia law. For example, it is not appropriate to depict a man and a woman alone in an ad. The use of certain animals, like pigs and dogs, also is not advisable either. Since the Qur'an prohib-

Cultural Note

Native Emiratis are the minority in the United Arab Emirates. Most of the other residents are guest workers from the entire Muslim world, especially India, Pakistan, Bangladesh, and Sri Lanka. UAE citizenship is closely guarded, and it is illegal for a foreigner to impersonate a UAE citizen.

Emiratis are well aware that they are greatly outnumbered by foreigners in their own country. Naturally, it is a sensitive subject to them, and not to be broached by outsiders.

Also, while many Emiratis seem to take a liberal view of Islam, remember that the United Arab Emirates is full of foreign Muslims. For example, even if your Emirati contact drinks alcohol or violates the Ramadan fast, this doesn't mean that you can do so in front of other Muslims with impunity.

If you do drink alcohol in a major hotel, do not leave the premises if you overindulge. You can be arrested for being drunk in a pubic venue, and driving under the influence is a serious issue. If you are involved in an accident while drunk, you will be in for a long, critical bout of trouble.

its the consumption of alcohol and pork, the following food items may be considered unappealing in any conference marketing materials or advertisements:

- Bacon, pepperoni, sausage, or hot dogs made from pork
- Food ingredients that obviously contain alcohol—for example, Dijon mustard
- Certain seafood, including lobster, shrimp, and catfish, which may be considered objectionable because they are scavengers (there is some variation in the interpretation of scavengers)

Be certain to vet your drafts for ad campaigns and conference materials with an in-country agency before you go to production. Additionally, there are organizations such as the Council for American-Islamic Relations (CAIR) that have downloadable publications on Islamic religious practices.

One innovative tactic used by an art show in the UAE was to symbolize women and men through the use of smaller and larger objects—in black and white. Black symbolized the *abaya*, the enigmatic flowing black gown worn by women. White symbolized the *kandura*, or dishdasha, the white robe worn by men. Black and white artists' paintbrushes, vases, and flashlights were placed side by side, and people in the UAE understood the imagery right away. Of course, while Emiratis comprehended the analogies, foreigners had a harder time recognizing the symbolism or appreciating the clever design.

2. THE SEVEN EMIRATES

The United Arab Emirates is made up of seven individual emirates. What is an emirate, and how long has the United Arab Emirates existed? You may appreciate the unique business environment if you are familiar with the history of this relatively new nation.

Archaeological evidence indicates that the periphery of the Arabian Peninsula was occupied by at least 2000 B.C.E. What is now the United Arab Emirates would have been settled around this time.

Islam arrived on the coast of Arabia around 630 C.E. and quickly became the dominant religion. The residents of the coast lived via trade, fishing, pearl diving, herding and small-scale farming, or piracy. Aside from the nominal rulers of the region, little changed for hundreds of years.

Led by the Portuguese, Western traders began to arrive in the 16th century. Around the same time, the Ottoman Turks became the predominant power in the Middle East, and the nominal overlords of the Arabian coast. Ruling through local sheiks and emirs, the Ottomans remained in control until the end of the First World War.

By the 18th century, the British had become the strongest Western power in the Arabian Gulf. Their primary interest in the emirates was the suppression of piracy, which threatened the trade routes to British India. The British defeated the Qawasin pirates in 1819. This led to the decline of the al-Qawasin dynasty, which ruled the emirate of Ash-Shariqa (now known as Sharjah). In their absence, the Banu Yas con-federation, whose leaders were based in Abu Dhabi, became the primary local power.

The United Kingdom was the dominant power in the Arabian Gulf after the Ottoman defeat in World War I. Oil exploration had begun in the 1930s but did not result in valu-able finds until 1962. As the British Empire contracted, the British announced in 1968 that they would withdraw their forces from the Arabian Gulf by the end of 1971. At that point, preparations began for the Trucial States to become self-governing.

Negotiations were slow and difficult. In the end, Bahrain and Qatar decided not to join the new United Arab Emirates. Six emirates—Abu Dhabi, Dubai, Sharjah, Fujairah, Ajman, and Umm al-Qaiwain—united to form the United Arab Emir-ates in 1971. A seventh emirate, Ra's al-Khaimah, joined in 1972.

Rising oil prices in the 1970s brought prosperity to the United Arab Emirates. The oil boom fostered massive con-struction and attracted thousands of foreign workers.

Politically, the United Arab Emirates tends to be pro-Western, although Israel remains a point of contention. The UAE contributed troops to liberate Kuwait in 1990 and sent peacekeepers to Kosovo in 1999. Currently, UAE investment is helping to rebuild Iraq.

3. NEGOTIATING

The emirates were originally trading outposts, and Emiratis pride themselves on their negotiating skills. Expect them to use multiple tactics to get their way, and remember that Ara-bic is a language of hyperbole. An Emirati may have a very emotional response to an issue. But dire forecasts are not nec-essarily permanent, so maintain a calm and agreeable view-point. Better deals are often requested at the last minute, even after a verbal agreement has been reached. This can be a traditional bargaining maneuver.

One common negotiating tactic is for an Emirati to ask what would be the discounted unit price for your product if he ordered a large quantity. Be advised that once you admit that

Cultural Note

Sports and cars (particularly luxury sports cars) are good topics of conversation. Dubai is the sports capital of the Middle East and hosts many spectacular events. Soccer (football), horse and camel racing, hunting, and falconry are the traditional Emirati sports, but individual sports preferences vary. A well-traveled Emirati may be a fan of a sport that is unusual in a desert country—such as grand prix racing, golf, or ice hockey.

you can provide your product at a lower cost, that cost will be the price the Emirati demands, even for a small quantity.

If an Emirati becomes evasive regarding a deal, it may simply be because he does not wish to embarrass you by saying no. You should be prepared to sacrifice some part of your deal for no other reason than to keep your Emirati's reputation and pride intact. Even if your proposal is ultimately rejected, you may be given the impression that it is being seriously considered. This is their way of making sure you are not publically embarrassed.

LANGUAGE

Arabic is the official language of the United Arab Emirates and of the other 21 countries that make up the Arab League. However, English is considered the language of business and is widely spoken. Almost all road signs are in both English and Arabic. Native Emiratis speak the Gulf dialect of Arabic, but the United Arab Emirates attracts workers from all over the Arab world, so many variants of Arabic can be heard, as well as other languages.

Arabic speakers greet one another by saying, "Peace be upon you." Here are the various singular and plural, masculine and feminine conjugations of that greeting. You will not generally hear the last vowel pronounced.

As-Salāmu `alayk(a).   Masculine, singular
As-Salāmu `alayk(i).   Feminine, singular
As-Salāmu `alayk(umā).   Plural for two people, any gender
As-Salāmu `alayk(unna).   Feminine plural, to a group of three or more
As-Salāmu `alayk(umu).   Plural, to a group of three or more, where one or more is male

And here is the template of the correct response. It, too, varies according to how many people you are addressing and their gender:

Wa `alayk(. . .) s-salām.

Following are a few more phrases that may help you in the United Arab Emirates. Also, a variety of free Arabic language programs are offered through the BBC at http://www.bbc .co.uk/languages.

ENGLISH	ARABIC TRANSLITERATION
Hello.	marhaban
Good-bye.	ila al'likaa'
See you later.	ma'a salaama
Please.	min fadlak
Thank you.	shukran
You're welcome.	a'afwan
Yes.	na'am
No.	la'a
How are you?	kaifa haluka
I'm fine, thank you.	bi-khayr, shukran
Pleased to meet you.	tasharrafna
I'm sorry.	ana a'asef
Excuse me.	laa mu'aakhadha
My name is . . .	ana ismee
I don't understand.	lam af'ham

WOW FACTOR!

Learning as much as you can about the UAE government and some characteristics of the seven emirates will help you comprehend the sales process and show respect for their united nation. The United Arab Emirates is a federation with specified powers delegated to the UAE federal government; other powers are allocated to the member emirates.

The head of government of the UAE is the prime minister, who has traditionally also held the post of vice president. The head of state is the president. There is a Council of Ministers appointed by the president. In theory, the president also appoints the prime minister.

The leaders of the seven emirates make up the Federal Supreme Council (FSC). The seven members of the FSC elect the president and vice president. The president and vice president serve for five-year terms; there are no term limits. The citizens of the UAE do not vote.

Here is a list of the seven constituent members of the United Arab Emirates and some of their characteristics:

Abu Dhabi	The capital; largest; has most of the oil
Ajman	Smallest emirate; highly developed
Dubai	Hotels, development, and tourism; the most trade zones
Fujairah	Almost entirely mountainous
Ra's al-Khaimah	Joined the United Arab Emirates a year after the others
Sharjah	Has most of the manufacturing; currently the most observant Muslim emirate (no alcohol)
Umm al-Qaiwain	Least populous emirate

The UAE tourist bureau has further information and links to governmental sites at www.uaeinteract.com.

UNITED KINGDOM

Conventional long form: United Kingdom of Great Britain and Northern Ireland (Great Britain includes England, Scotland, and Wales)

Conventional short form: United Kingdom

Abbreviation: UK

Population: 62,698,362 (2011 estimate)

Median age: 40 years

Age structure: (2011 estimates)
  0–14 years: 17.3%
  15–64 years: 66.2%
  65 years and over: 16.5%

GDP per capita (PPP): $35,100 (2010 estimate in US dollars)

Suffrage: 18 years old; universal

Legal drinking age: 18 years old

Advertising Note

Londoners, particularly the young, tend to have a rebellious edge, which extends to their sense of humor. If your ad is going to stand out, it should be direct, show some resistance to authority, and be funny.

ICEBREAKERS

BRILLIANT!*

1. Since meetings generally start soon after your arrival, you will not have much time to be brilliant. Expect a bit of informal talk about the weather, the route you took to your meeting, or the day's headlines.

2. If there is time to chat, you might like to talk about sports. Brush up on your football (soccer) or rugby, and ask, "What team do you support?" Be careful not to position yourself as a supporter of a rival club. There are currently 14 professional football teams just in London, and everyone has a favorite.

BOORISH

1. Never call someone from Scotland, Wales, or Northern Ireland "British" or "English." Use the correct terminology for each of the four countries of the United Kingdom. Each country has its own culture, language, and identity. Most citizens of the United Kingdom do not consider themselves European either, even though they are members of the European Union.

*Throughout the book, we have borrowed the British one-liner *Brilliant!* The words *brilliant* and *boorish* headline each Icebreaker section for a reason. They are quintessential crisp British responses. The close of a conversation may be as simple as "Brilliant, right?"

Cultural Note

> Above the London Stock Exchange hangs a sign with the Latin words *Dictum Meum Partum* (My Word Is My Bond). While this may sound archaic and naïve in the 21st century, there are still businesspeople in the United Kingdom who close deals based upon their word, not a contract. If there is a contract, it is generally rather rigorous, and, once signed, nonnegotiable.

2. Avoid interrogating your prospect with intrusive questions about where he or she lives, his or her hobbies, or anything of a potentially personal nature. Privacy is valued, and most executives don't appreciate an inquisition. Also refrain from the inane sales technique of repeating the other person's name over and over during a conversation. (For example: "That's an excellent question, Alex!") You may be viewed as patronizing or dim.

WHAT TIME SHOULD I ARRIVE?

Arrive promptly! Being late is not amusing. Your prospect will still meet with you, but you will have started off on the wrong foot. Everyone knows about London traffic, so unless you were with the queen, there is no excuse.

WORKWEEK

Monday through Friday is the normal workweek. Business hours vary, but retail establishments often close at 6:00 P.M. Meetings generally run an hour or less.

Although quite a few pubs have folded, many people still find time to go out after work for a round or two.

Cultural Note

The history of packaged, branded goods essentially began in England, as early as the year 1600. These products were not foodstuffs; they were what we would call patent medicines. At first, the labels were simply posters, folded and wrapped around the bottles or boxes. Over the years, successful purveyors developed branding techniques: colorful labels, claims of efficacy by experts, endorsements by royalty, and warnings not to accept imitations. They even sold products in distinctive containers; Turlington's Original Balsam was sold in a pear-shaped bottle.

Entrepreneurs in other countries copied the success of British nostrums. A druggist in Williamsburg, Virginia (USA), ordered some 1,700 bottles and labels for Stoughton's Drops in 1754. He did not, evidently, order the patent medicine itself. No doubt he filled the bottles with a mixture of his own devising. It would take some years before patents provided protection for manufacturers within a country, and even longer to protect intellectual property between nations.

Since the history of selling packaged, branded goods began with the industrial revolution in England, the British have seen it all. Make sure your product is expertly packaged.

Most companies offer 20 days' paid vacation and approximately 8 paid holidays a year. In 2011 there were 15 total holidays listed for the United Kingdom.

HOW CLOSE SHOULD I STAND?

Ample personal space is customary. Give your counterpart at least 2 feet during the first introduction. You will be able to tell if the proximity is wrong: your prospect will look vaguely uncomfortable and step back.

Sales Note

Although a great deal of business is conducted in Cardiff (Wales), Belfast (Northern Ireland), and Edinburgh (Scotland), London is still unique as the powerhouse for the majority of commerce in the United Kingdom. It is true that London's high rents and dense population are driving more firms to relocate to the "provinces." But London remains the hub for many business and cultural endeavors.

London is not a homogeneous city. It boasts a vast spectrum of ethnicities. Diversity is common in marketing and sales collateral and in the workforce. Be ready to meet with executives of Indian, Asian, African, or Hispanic descent, all speaking the Queen's English.

DO I KISS, BOW, OR SHAKE HANDS?

SHAKE HANDS

Give a brief, decisive handshake, accompanied by a short, steady gaze. Do not dawdle over the handshake, and do not gape at your prospect during the entire meeting. Eye contact is sporadic in most of the United Kingdom.

BUSINESS CARDS

- Have your business cards printed on good stock.
- The higher the executive (or politician), the less likely it is that he or she will have a card.
- The exchange of cards often takes place near the close of the meeting.

Cultural Note

As in the United States, the British are often comfortable with a win-win strategy in negotiations. Highlighting the benefits of the agreement for both firms is logical and may move the contract up faster to the final decision makers. This can be particularly important if a board of directors is involved.

THREE TIPS FOR SELLING IN THE UNITED KINGDOM

1. Brevity and Briefs
2. British Reserve
3. The Passing of Posh?

1. BREVITY AND BRIEFS

Scientific facts are irrefutable evidence to the English, the Scots, the Welsh, and the Irish (well, perhaps not the Irish). Prepare a brief for your first meeting, and make sure it is filled with objective data. Keep your presentation as clear and concise as possible. Being overly enthusiastic or interjecting your opinions, feelings, and ideologies into the presentation will not add to your credibility. Your most persuasive tool is a concrete fact. If you are being too melodramatic, your British associates may lean back and cross their arms. This is not a good sign: boredom or disbelief has set in. If all goes well, you can show some emotion after the meeting; preferably after you leave.

2. BRITISH RESERVE

Privacy is not just a personal predilection in the United Kingdom. Information is a currency unto itself. Trying to pry financial details from an English or Welsh executive is tough enough, but an Irishman or a Scot?

Your best option may be to build some rapport through patience and by sharing a bit about your finances. For example, Tony Macaluso, a Palm Beach real estate broker, described his first two trade missions to London this way:

Frankly, they really did not result in any cooperative listings between the two countries. It wasn't until our third trade mission that I finally asked the British estate agents what percentage or what price it would take for us to work together on some international transactions. I believe they were taken aback, but then they asked how we normally handle the fees. I said that I understood there were many differences in the sales process (Google "Gazumping" in the United Kingdom), but when the paperwork was signed, we normally split the 5 percent or 6 percent commission equally. Their jaws dropped! That is when they revealed that British estate transactions only provided the agent with 1 percent or 2 percent. So 3 percent of a sale was a raise! After that third trade mission, there were a substantial number of Florida properties that went to UK buyers.

Also be aware that the British can sometimes deliver serious instructions in such a gracious manner that you may not realize the task is critical and time-sensitive.

3. THE PASSING OF POSH?

The United Kingdom is a nation of many different languages and accents. Besides English (which is probably the most influential export in history), the United Kingdom officially recognizes a variety of minority or regional languages. These include Welsh, Scots, Ulster Scots, Scottish Gaelic, Irish Gaelic, and Cornish. Among all these languages, every region and every class has its own distinct way of speaking.

Since the start of broadcasting in the United Kingdom, the standard for speakers on air has been what was called Received Pronunciation (RP). UK citizens who do not speak RP may refer to it as "posh." RP became the upper-class standard around 1800. It was considered the "proper" way to speak, and it divided the educated and upper class from the rest of the country.

Today, however, you can hear other accents on British broadcasting. The BBC even hired a news anchorman with a Welsh accent! The United Kingdom also has politicians who

Cultural Note

Marketing executives are generally very familiar with the major newspapers and media outlets in the United Kingdom, many of which are owned by the controversial Rupert Murdoch. However, there is a venerable UK-based weekly international-affairs magazine that is sometimes overlooked by global marketing and sales managers. *The Economist*, which has been published since 1843, covers international affairs, news, and topical issues with a uniquely dry, witty voice. While *Economist* advertisements (and subscriptions) can be pricey, it is an exceedingly helpful resource for sales executives who need to have a deeper look at global politics and economics.

speak with regional accents: former prime minister Gordon Brown has a Scottish accent.

The sales profession has always used whatever accent seemed to best appeal to its audience. An expensive product may call for a posh accent, or one might go another way, especially if the ad is comedic. The important point is not to assume that every product or service has to be sold with a RP accent. A recent study of British call centers found that the most popular accents were those of Edinburgh and Yorkshire. It could be that British callers found those accents comforting—or the data could show that the majority of call centers are located in Edinburgh and Yorkshire.

LANGUAGE

Many people know the popular quote by George Bernard Shaw: "England and America are two countries separated by a common language." And everyone knows that the same word in English can have widely different meanings between the United Kingdom and the United States.

We have written about this before but thought it would be helpful to include words related to a specific topic this time—driving. We hope you'll be "chuffed to bits" or "dead chuffed" (really delighted) by these examples and their various meanings in the United Kingdom and the United States.

ENGLISH WORD	UNITED KINGDOM (COMMON MEANING)	UNITED STATES (COMMON MEANING)
aerial	antenna on your car	midair or airborne
amber	yellow (on a traffic light)	fossilized tree resin (or the color yellow)
bonnet	hood of the car	fashionable hat in the 1800s
boot	trunk of the car	footwear
cat's eyes	road reflectors	feline ocular organs
central reservation	median strip	hotel switchboard(?) (no equivalent)
diversion	detour	entertainment
double yellow lines	no parking zone	no passing zone
full stop	period (the punctuation mark)	what you do at a red light or a stop sign
jam sandwich	police car	PBJ without the PB
panda	police car	an adorable ursidae
juggernaut	large lorry (truck)	18 wheeler
manual	stick shift	stick shift, or a book of instructions
muffler	scarf	silencer for a car
silencer	muffler	attachment to the muzzle of a gun
slip road	entry or exit ramp	(no equivalent)
spanner	wrench	(no equivalent)
ticking over	idling (car)	(no equivalent)
windscreen	windshield	(no equivalent)
wing	fender	part of a bird or plane

WOW FACTOR!

There is an aphorism that illustrates the differences between the citizens of the United Kingdom and of the United States: "Americans think that 100 years is old; Britons think that 100 miles is far." Possessing even a general knowledge of the history and culture of Great Britain will improve your chances of making a good impression, particularly if you learn about events before the Victorian era, which ended in 1901.

Not only are Londoners conversant in history, geography, and politics, they are also often exceedingly well read. Remember that England is still Shakespeare's "blessed plot." Of course, the Scots, the Welsh, and the Irish all have wondrous writers, from Scotland's national bard, Robert Burns to the Welshman Dylan Thomas to Ireland's four Nobel Laureates in Literature: William Butler Yeats, George Bernard Shaw, Samuel Beckett, and Seamus Heaney. If you wish to discuss literature, try to commit to memory a few quotes from one of Great Britain's literary icons:

> This royal throne of kings, this sceptered isle,
> This earth of majesty, this seat of Mars,
> This other Eden, demi-paradise,
> This fortress built by Nature for herself
> Against infection and the hand of war,
> This happy breed of men, this little world,
> This precious stone set in the silver sea,
> Which serves it in the office of a wall
> Or as a moat defensive to a house,
> Against the envy of less happier lands,
> This blessed plot, this earth, this realm, this England.
>
> —William Shakespeare (1564–1616),
> *King Richard II*, act 2, scene 1

UNITED STATES
OF AMERICA

Conventional long form: United States of America

Conventional short form: United States

Abbreviation: US or USA

Population: 313,232,044 (2011 estimate)

Median age: 36.9 years

Age structure: (2011 estimates)
0–14 years: 20.1%
15–64 years: 66.8%
65 years and over: 13.1%

GDP per capita (PPP): $47,400 (2010 estimate)

Suffrage: 18 years old; universal

Legal drinking age: Varies by state, but the federal government mandates that 21 years of age is the minimum age to purchase or publicly possess alcohol

Cultural Note

The United States of America breaks records—from scientific and technological discoveries to bailouts of entire industries. It is a country of superlatives, and virtually every multinational corporation in the world does business there.

The United States is not only a magnet for global business ventures, but also attracts enormous numbers of immigrants each year (1,046,539 in 2008). This vast array of ethnicities gives the nation a highly diverse labor pool, and is projected to make Anglo males a minority in the workplace by 2020.

To understand the United States of America, it helps if you read the Oath of Allegiance. This oath is recited by every new US citizen:

I hereby declare, on oath, that I absolutely and entirely renounce and abjure all allegiance and fidelity to any foreign prince, potentate, state, or sovereignty of whom or which I have heretofore been a subject or citizen; that I will support and defend the Constitution and laws of the United States of America against all enemies, foreign and domestic; that I will bear true faith and allegiance to the same; that I will bear arms on behalf of the United States when required by the law; that I will perform noncombatant service in the Armed Forces of the United States when required by the law; that I will perform work of national importance under civilian direction when required by the law; and that I take this obligation freely without any mental reservation or purpose of evasion; so help me God.

The extraordinary aspect of this oath is that, with prior permission, the US Citizenship and Immigration Services will sometimes allow individuals to omit the following phrase: "that I will bear arms on behalf of the United States when required by law; that I will perform noncombatant service in the Armed Forces of the United States when required by law." It is also possible to receive permission to refrain from speaking the final phrase "so help me God." In other words, individual rights start at the inception of one's US citizenship.

ICEBREAKERS

BRILLIANT!

1. In social situations, the most common icebreaker is "What do you do?" or, if you are in Washington, D.C., "Where are you from?" (Few politically related professionals who work in the District of Columbia are originally from the area.)

   At a normal business appointment, you would already know your contact's title, company responsibilities, and why you are both there. In the limited time you may have before the meeting starts, you may hear generic questions, such as "How are you?" "How was your trip?" and "Did you have any trouble finding us?" None of this takes more than five minutes. The East and West Coasts (particularly New York City and Los Angeles) are known for fast-paced meetings that get right down to business.

   While the high-tech, financial, and pharmaceutical industries are known for their rapid fire communications, other vertical markets have highly structured, time-sensitive cultures as well. Wal-Mart is known for their brief, rigorously businesslike meetings between buyers and vendors. Appointments are held in nondescript "pitch" rooms, never private offices. Personnel among buyers may change very often, so that vendors cannot build up a strong relationship with any one buyer. And if Wal-Mart buyers are not interested in any portion of your presentation, they will let you know immediately.

2. In the central and southern parts of the country, people may not get down to business as quickly. Conversations may start with inquiries into your background, what you know about the area, etc. Longer conversations can include work-related stories, the newest technological gadgets, sports, music, books, movies, the weather, travel, hobbies, and good places to eat. Be aware that common hobbies in southern states may include hunting (with guns or bows and arrows) and fishing.

Cultural Note

Workdays are long. During the winter months, senior executives may start and end their days in the dark. High-level executives may rise before 6:00 A.M. to exercise, help take children to school, and commute to the office by 7:30 or 8:00 A.M. Extensive personal and business obligations mandate tightly managed schedules. Meetings can start as early as 7:30 A.M. and can be followed by many more appointments throughout the day. Additionally, priorities constantly shift: be flexible if you have to wait through an important phone call or e-mail.

When you arrive, be prepared for your meeting with a concise agenda (which you have in both print and digital format), have backup data available to support your proposal, and be prepared to answer a flurry of questions within the prescribed time. Get to the point fast, and have a good close.

You should be ready with questions about the firm, its goals, and perhaps the decor of the office. If photos are on display, you may make a gracious comment about them. But be careful not to get too inquisitive about personal matters (see Boorish point #1)

BOORISH

1. Don't immediately ask about personal matters. If your US prospect brings up the topic of her or his family—or makes inquiries about yours—then it is perfectly fine to share your personal stories. But executives who evade questions about their private lives should not be pressed for any information. If they do not volunteer any data, do not pursue it.

2. Sensitive topics to avoid may include religion, politics, sex, dieting (many people in the United States are overweight), smoking (it is generally banned), and age. The US culture is youth oriented, and discussions of age may make older executives somewhat uncomfortable.

WHAT TIME SHOULD I ARRIVE?

Time is money in the United States. Saving, spending, and wasting time are all common descriptive phrases in time management. While various areas of the country—particularly the Deep South—are more relaxed about schedules, businesspeople are all expected to be prompt for appointments. Most appointments are scheduled within a finite time frame, such as 10:00 A.M. to 10:30 A.M. Vendors should never cancel face-to-face appointments.

Once the conversation turns to business, make every second count. The faster you get to the point, the more you acknowledge that your prospect's time is valuable.

Purchasing decisions can be made rapidly, sometimes during the first meeting. The decision may be followed up with a contract or, if you are fortunate, with a simple purchase order.

There is a short-term orientation in the United States. Contracts often range between one and three years, with clauses for termination with cause. Finance divisions may require short-term contracts so it is easier to amortize the projects for tax purposes. Certain industries, like high-tech and pharmaceuticals, may be accustomed to short-term deals because their vertical markets are extremely dynamic.

WORKWEEK

The standard workweek is 40 hours, but many people work in excess of that figure. Businesses hours can vary by industry, but if you call your contacts after 9:00 A.M. or before 5:00 P.M., you can usually reach them (or their voice mail). Many executives respond to text messages and e-mails after normal working hours.

Many stores and some banks are open seven days a week. Convenience stores (usually selling gas, coffee, and snacks) are open 24 hours a day.

The United States has no federal laws that mandate paid vacation days, but they are considered a normal part of a benefits package. Two weeks is a reasonable standard, but vacation days may be accrued based upon years of service or one's title within the organization. In some situations, paid vacation days can range from one week to one month. There are typically 10 or 11 holidays each year—which are generally part of the compensation plan.

HOW CLOSE SHOULD I STAND?

Approximately 2 feet apart. This can vary depending upon the height of the people involved, their arms' length, and their ethnicity. Generally, people favor more distance during an initial greeting and may back away after the handshake. Never try to close up the distance with a US executive.

DO I KISS, BOW, OR SHAKE HANDS?

GREETINGS VARY

A firm grip has long been an indicator of strength of character in the United States, but styles of handclasps can vary based upon the ethnicity or gender of the person you are greeting. You may receive a gentle grasp from an Asian executive in San Francisco or a "fingertip grip" from a southern female in Savannah, Georgia. But traditionally, a strong, brief handshake with direct eye contact will give a positive first impression to your US prospect.

Your first name is more important than your last name in the United States. Many people introduce themselves with just a first name or a nickname, and they will expect the same from you.

Titles are rarely used, unless you are speaking to a physician, a judge (in a courtroom setting), someone in law enforce-

Cultural Note

Do not be surprised to see very young-looking executives in positions of substantial responsibility. Young managers in senior positions are often quite capable and exceedingly competitive. Alternatively, they may be youthful looking because of surgical interventions.

ment, a member of the military, or a politician (e.g., a senator or governor).

BUSINESS CARDS

- The exchange of business cards is informal. Depending upon the industry, a card may include a photo of the person—even holding a family pet (generally a dog or cat).
- Business cards are usually presented with one hand and may be distributed like a deck of cards—slid one-by-one across a table toward all seated parties.
- A business card may be considered a miniature note card. US executives are known for writing extra data on business cards (for example, details about how they should follow up with you).
- At conventions, every card you hand out at a booth will probably be scanned into a database for future reference and sometimes for an opportunity to win a promotional item at the conference. You may also see individuals scan your business card into their personal smartphones (there is an app for that).
- Your card may also be placed in a wallet, which may go into a male executive's back pants pocket. None of this is considered insulting.

THREE TIPS FOR SELLING IN THE UNITED STATES

1. Innovation
2. Litigation
3. Admission

1. INNOVATION

A multitude of books, buzzwords, and entire firms in the United States are dedicated to innovation, change management, creative inspiration, futurism, potential visualization, paradigm shifts, tectonic shifts, thought leadership, and thinking out of the box. So-called cutting-edge technology and next-big-thing candidates were passé buzzwords even while book proposals based upon those titles were being submitted to publishers.

Research and development is huge in US firms, and educational institutions teach abstract, creative thought processes in all grade levels. The large pool of research money attracts sophisticated talent and innovators to the United States and helps business stay highly dynamic. Internet access will be ubiquitous soon and has sped up innovation, particularly among entrepreneurs eager to promote their new concepts and products globally. While it is true that religious sensibilities or ethical viewpoints can slow down or even preclude certain fields of study (e.g., stem cell research or animal testing), in general, advanced research is highly encouraged.

Prospects may welcome an opportunity to be an alpha- or beta-test site for your newest technological developments. The strong sense of competition in many industries motivates them to gain an edge by evaluating the latest products.

Since many Americans are used to fast-paced environments, entrepreneurs of all ages are taking advantage of the democratizing nature of the Internet to start businesses. Many sharp ideas that are tested online end up co-opted by larger corporations, which have also learned to monitor everything from social networks to digital university research sites for the next big thing.

The negative aspect of innovation in the United States is that every product has a limited shelf life, and every service is soon forgotten. The catchphrase "What have you done for me lately?" demonstrates the ephemeral nature of success and the constant pressure to consistently produce exceptional achievements to stay in the market.

2. LITIGATION

The United States of America is the most litigious society in the world. Lawsuits can be filed for frivolous claims—or for enormous injustices. Virtually any US citizen has the right to walk into a courthouse and file a claim against a company, family member, or a stranger on the street.

Concrete evidence of your claims is very important. Never bluff. Your presentations should be filled with scientific evidence about your product and its features. Every claim you make, from your sources of research to your client list, must be corroborated. Among the three variables (feelings, faith, and facts) that people consider as evidence, your US clients will always opt for factual, measurable data.

Although people in the United States do value relationships, the only variable that matters in the final stages of a decision-making process is the evidence: Is your product superior? Is the price better? Will the product maintenance be sufficient? Quantitative data not only will be important in a decision-making process, but will also be vital if you consider the potential of having to produce evidence later in a legal proceeding.

Keep thorough records of every meeting and promised delivery dates. In many transactions, lawyers are brought in early. In-house counsel can be involved from the negotiating stage through the final contract close. As a result, many contracts become incredibly unwieldy in the United States. Obtuse, dense writing seems to proliferate, and trying to change even standard, boilerplate clauses can delay your contracts by weeks. Ask to review a standard contract early in the process, so you can pass it along to your firm's counsel. It may save you some time later.

Cultural Note

Competition, whether personal, professional, or national, is a primary motivator in the United States. One of your primary sales strategies should be to consider: *How can my product give a client or customer an advantage over their competition and make them more successful?* Even competing with other countries is a strong national motivator—e.g., John F. Kennedy's "first man on the moon" speech after Sputnik.

Whether your prospect is a sole proprietor of a small business or the CEO of a Fortune 50 multinational—be sure to understand how they compete with others in the marketplace. Demonstrating how your product's technological features, lower price point, or service options will help them surpass their competition will be a strong motivating force for buying your product.

Here is one caveat about the litigious business environment and the affection Americans have for humor. Many people in the United States enjoy jokes at work, and personal tastes can vary from broad comedy (slapstick) to puns. Do not be surprised if US executives start meetings or presentations with a joke. But be careful not to tell jokes that are personally insulting or demeaning to any gender or ethnicity. Equal Employment Opportunity and anti-discrimination laws prohibit many behaviors in the workplace. You will not see the humor if you are brought up on charges of discrimination for telling an ill-advised joke.

3. ADMISSION

The United States is an egalitarian culture. Not only is everyone equal, but if you wish to become a citizen, you must renounce any hereditary titles or positions of nobility you may have at your Oath of Allegiance ceremony.

This democratic, classless society ensures that you have potential admission to every consumer in the country. You have as much right to try and market your services to total strangers as do Ford, Allstate, or JCPenney. Private solicitors still call residences at dinnertime (even though they are not supposed to), vendors still stick marketing flyers under windshield wipers, and everyone receives e-mail offers for secret funds from long-lost relatives.

The trick is to understand how to approach people correctly in the United States, since everyone either is a prospect or can lead you to a prospect. There are entire tomes that support the "number theory" of prospecting, which involves placing a certain amount of initial cold calls to generate qualified leads, which ultimately results in closes. This numeric winnowing process applies to everything from identifying sales prospects to recruiting candidates for exceedingly expensive universities. And currently, online social networks are dramatically influencing and expanding lead opportunities.

Additionally, marketing and advertising are huge in the United States; some estimates say $10 billion is spent annually on marketing focus groups alone. A relatively new field called neuromarketing concentrates on making those marketing research dollars more effective by empirically measuring biological and psychological responses through brain mapping, eye tracking, and other neuroscientific tools. (See David Brooks's article, "The Young and the Neuro," published in the *New York Times*.) This field of cognitive neurology is attracting many young researchers who apply studies of the brain and the senses to measure true consumer reactions to products and marketing. Cognitive neurology is also corroborating many aspects of the field of cultural anthropology. People from different cultures actually do absorb, process, and act upon information differently.

After you have completed your marketing analytics and have targeted the appropriate prospects, pick up the phone. Many US executives are accessible, have received cold calls, and (if you have an engaging reason for contacting them) will generally listen.

Of course, the easiest means of reaching your prospect is through an established contact. This can occur through professional or personal acquaintances, quasi-social professional networks like LinkedIn, or more traditional means—conferences, trade fairs, or the seat next to you on an airplane.

LANGUAGE

The linguistic differences and dialects in the United States are well researched. There are a variety of books like *American English: Dialects and Variation (Language in Society)* by Walt Wolfram and Natalie Schilling-Estes that delve into the speech disparities across the country.

Despite all the ethnicities, languages, and cultures represented in the United States, there is a perception that "time is money," and therefore there is a predilection for brief conversations, short meetings, and concise e-mails or texts in many industries. Managers may give succinct instructions to their staff at early morning meetings and will not expect or appreciate long rambling discussions or explanations before the work gets started. Learn to speak in sound bites.

WOW FACTOR!

In some countries, businesspeople assume that every time they close a deal, they win and their counterpart loses. However, in the United States, most executives look for the "win-win deal." This optimistic theory maintains that both parties in a negotiation can get what they want. Here are some guidelines for a win-win scenario in the United States:

- Imagine that every negotiation is a partnership.
- Find common goals with your prospect.
- Ask questions, never make demands, and listen to the prospect's priorities.
- During final negotiations, never let a contract hinge on one point of contention.

Cultural Note

PepsiCo kicked off a promotion for its Amp Energy energy drinks with an iPhone app called "Amp Up Before You Score." The app segregated women into 24 categories—sorority girls, foreign-exchange students, etc.—and then provided users with a pickup line for each type of woman. The app then encouraged users to brag about their triumphs on Twitter and Facebook. It was a monumentally stupid, misogynistic idea, designed to appeal to young heterosexual males. Besides alienating a good number of potential female consumers of the Amp Energy drink, it generated bad publicity for PepsiCo. After about two months, PepsiCo removed the app and apologized. The company's Twitter statement read, "Our app tried 2 show the humorous lengths guys go 2 pick up women. We apologize if it's in bad taste & appreciate your feedback. #pepsifail."

As we noted in the section on litigation, be extremely careful about prompting US consumers to participate in an event that may be discriminatory or fodder for ridicule. US customers often verbalize their views about products and services online, and a certain percentage of them can be "trolls" (Internet slang for people who post unpleasant, provocative comments in online communities). If your ad is insulting enough to anyone in the United States, you should expect a torrent of negative feedback—and not just from the trolls.

A single issue may stop the entire process because it generates a win-lose scenario. If the prospect says that price is the final sticking point, add another factor like delivery time, warranties, or some other variable to the mix. Try to get back to common multiple goals, and work together to achieve them.

APPENDIX A

INTERNATIONAL DINING, DRINKING, AND DELICACIES

Global sales and marketing involves meals. Hopefully, you will be dining with your international prospects from the initial sales call through to the contract's close. Therefore it is wise to learn about particular customs they may observe around mealtime. You can be sure they will be observing your mannerisms at the table. Understanding how to manage an important meal is indicative of your capability to manage an important contract. Some dining tips have already been included in several chapters (for example, Malbec, beef, and *mate* in Argentina and toasting in South Korea), but we would like to expand that data here. Also look for our Global Dining, Drinking, and Dealmaking blog at www.kissboworshake hands.com.

We present this information in the form of a quiz. Try answering each of the questions, and then check your knowledge on dining etiquette around the world. Enjoy!

DINING QUIZ

1. Diners in France, Italy, and many other European countries dine Continental style: the fork stays in one's left hand. It is never switched back and forth between left and right hands. As a polite diner in Paris, your fork is in your left hand, tines down, but getting the vegetables up onto the back of the fork and making them stay there

until they reach your mouth is difficult. **True** or **False**: It is totally acceptable to turn your fork over, tines up, to eat.

ANSWER: False. How you wield a fork is important. While your fork is in your left hand, never turn it around like a shovel and load it up with food. That juxtaposition of good and bad manners will definitely get noticed in France. Try practicing this before your big business meal in Madrid, Milan, or Marseille: spear a bit of food onto the end of the fork, tines down, then push more food up on top of that with your knife. If you simply cannot manage it, eat US-style. But try not to wave your utensils around as you swap them back and forth. And keep your elbows in, with your arms and hands horizontal to the table.

2. Which of the following table mannerisms is NOT rude at a restaurant?

   A. Unfurling your napkin with a "fwap" and draping it over your lap
   B. Tasting your food as soon as it is served
   C. Setting your cell phone on the table alongside your place setting
   D. Leaving a napkin on the floor if you accidently drop it.

   ANSWER: D. If you drop a napkin (or a utensil), leave it on the floor, and quietly ask the wait staff for a new one.
   The other responses are incorrect because:

   A. Your napkin is not a towel, and you are not in a locker room. Place it, still semi-folded, unobtrusively upon your lap.
   B. Do not begin until everyone is served and the host invites you to eat.
   C. Do not put any personal items, including your cell phone, on the table.

3. You can silently communicate information to the wait staff with the position of your utensils. **True** or **False**: When you are finished with your meal, line your knife and fork up together on your plate, with the tips at ten o'clock and the ends at four o'clock.

   ANSWER: True. The manner in which you set your utensils on your plate indicates to the wait staff whether you are finished. If you are not finished, cross your knife and fork on your plate in an X formation.

4. At dinner, your bread plate will be on your left. **True** or **False**: If someone uses yours by mistake, take the one to your right.

   ANSWER: False. Never replicate an error by taking your neighbor's bread plate. If someone annexes your plate, and you would like bread, just balance it on the edge of your dinner plate.

   When you eat bread and butter, break your bread into manageable pieces (nothing larger than a few bites). Take a pat or two of butter from the butter serving dish, put it on your bread plate, and butter the piece you are about to consume. Do not take butter from the butter dish and slather it directly onto your bread. It is not your private butter dish.

5. **True** or **False**: When you are not using your utensils (fork, knife, or chopsticks), you should lean them off the edge of the plate, onto the table.

   ANSWER: False. Never let your utensils touch the table once you begin to eat. This goes for Western cutlery and is similar with chopsticks. For Western cutlery, balance the utensils completely on the plate when you put them down. Never hook or balance them off the edge of the plate, onto the table. For chopsticks, balance them either on a chopstick rest or on your plate, side by side. Never separate them and set them on either side of your plate, as if they are a knife and fork. Never set them down on the table, and never cross your chopsticks in an X formation.

6. Different varieties of chopsticks can be found in South Korea, China, Japan, Taiwan, and other parts of Asia. They may be wooden or metal, angular or smooth, connected at the base or wrapped in a beautiful packet, made in different sizes, etc. Which of the following behaviors with chopsticks is appropriate?

A. Passing or receiving food between your chopsticks and another diner's chopsticks

B. Gesturing, tapping, or spearing food with your chopsticks

C. Sticking your chopsticks straight up in your rice bowl

D. Repeatedly rubbing the large ends of your wooden chopsticks together after you've split them apart

E. Turning your chopsticks around and using the large end to serve yourself from communal plates

ANSWER: E. If you are serving yourself from a communal plate or bowl, and there are serving chopsticks on the large plate, use them. If there are none, turn your chopsticks around, and use the larger end to transfer food onto your plate.

Why are the other responses wrong?

A. Traditionally, there is only one time when two people hold a single item with their chopsticks. It is at a funeral, when relatives may pass the remaining bones of cremated ancestors to each other with chopsticks.

B. Do not wave chopsticks about or point them at people or food. Spearing food with the end of your chopstick is inappropriate as well.

C. This visual reminds many Asians of the joss incense sticks used during ceremonies for those who have passed, or the chopsticks placed in bowls of rice for ancestors.

D. If you rub the chopsticks together too much, you are implying that you think they are cheap and might give you splinters.

7. You are suffering from a miserable cold but must attend a business dinner in Tokyo. **True** or **False**: It is appropriate to use a handkerchief as discreetly as possible during your meal.

   ANSWER: False. You should never blow your nose at the dinner table. Excuse yourself politely, and take care of it in the rest room. And never use a handkerchief. The Japanese find the custom of preserving mucus in a carefully folded handkerchief to be grotesque. Use tissues.

8. Soy sauce is a strong condiment and should never be poured directly over your rice. **True** or **False**: You should dip the rice side of your sushi in your little bowl of soy sauce, perhaps mixed with wasabi.

   ANSWER: False. If you dip the rice side in, you may leave some soaked rice in the dipping bowl, which can look crude. Turn the sushi over, and dip the fish side in the soy sauce/wasabi mixture. Sometimes Japanese diners use their fingers to eat sushi. Emulate whatever your Japanese associates do.

9. Before you begin to eat, you may hear various expressions in different countries. Match the saying with the country.

   A. *Bon appétit!*　　**1.** Japan
   B. *Itadakimasu!*　　**2.** Spain
   C. Dig in!　　　　　**3.** France
   D. *Buen provecho!*　**4.** Texas

   ANSWERS: A. 3; B. 1; C. 4; D. 2

10. Which of the following behaviors is NOT *mal élevé* (ill mannered) in France?

   A. Excusing yourself to visit the restroom during dinner
   B. Asking whom one voted for in the last election
   C. Feeding your dog from the chair next to you in a restaurant

   ANSWER: C. Dogs are welcome in many French establishments.

11. Your final interview in Milan is conducted over lunch. As sophisticated as you are, you commit a few dining faux pas. Which of the following is NOT a faux pas?

   A. Leaving a trail of lipstick on the crystal
   B. Cutting your pasta with your knife
   C. Folding your salad with your knife, instead of cutting it
   D. Using the fork above your plate for salad

   ANSWER: C. Never cut your salad with a knife and fork. And if you see a fork and spoon above your plate, they are for dessert and coffee.

12. In what order do the seven courses in a Parisian restaurant arrive?

   A. Soup, salad, meat or fowl, sorbet, fish, dessert, coffee
   B. Soup, fish, sorbet, meat or fowl, salad, dessert, coffee

   ANSWER: B. Salad is served toward the end of the meal, which is why the little salad fork is nearer the plate in a formal Continental place setting. (With utensils, you start on the outside and work your way in.) Dessert may include a cheese plate, with or without fruit.

13. A plate of cheese is often served toward the end of a formal French dinner. Invariably, it will include a wedge of Brie. **True** or **False**: It is impolite to cut just the tip off of the Brie and put that on your plate.

ANSWER: True. Never cut the tip off Brie cheese. Cut it as though it were a slice of pie. If you serve yourself just the tip, you would be taking the largest portion of the center part of the cheese, leaving other diners more of the rind. If you cut slender wedges, everyone has a balanced amount of cheese and rind.

> *Comment voulez-vous gouverner un pays qui a deux cent quarante-six variétés de fromage?*
>
> How can you govern a country which has two hundred and forty-six varieties of cheese?
>
> —Charles de Gaulle, president of France,
> *Les Mots du Général,* 1962

14. **True** or **False**: If you are pouring wine, use your right hand.

ANSWER: True. Using your left hand to pour wine is offensive in enough countries (including Argentina and South Korea) that it is far wiser to simply use your right hand. Also remember that the left hand is considered unclean in most of the Mideast, Africa, and the Indian subcontinent.

15. Match the toast with the country.

A. Germany		**1.** *Sláinte!*
B. Japan		**2.** *Prosit!*
C. Ireland		**3.** *Kampai!*
D. Mexico		**4.** *Cin cin!*
E. Italy		**5.** *Salud!*

ANSWERS: A. 2; B. 3; C. 1; D. 5; E. 4

16. **True** or **False**: *Cin cin* (pronounced chin-chin) is also an appropriate toast in China.

ANSWER: False. It sounds like a Chinese word used to describe a small boy's male appendage.

17. Match the taste treat with its country.

A. Kidney pie	**1.** China
B. Haggis (sheep entrails)	**2.** Saudi Arabia
C. Grasshoppers	**3.** France
D. Sheep's head	**4.** Scotland
E. Scorpions	**5.** Mexico
F. Escargot	**6.** Indonesia
G. Durian	**7.** England

ANSWERS: A. 7; B. 4; C. 5; D. 2; E. 1; F. 3; G. 6

18. Match the taboo with the country.

A. Saudi Arabia	**1.** Hands in your lap
B. United States	**2.** Pork
C. India	**3.** Dog
D. France	**4.** Beef
E. Spain	**5.** Dinner before 8:00 P.M.

ANSWERS: A. 2; B. 3; C. 4; D. 1 (in France, keep your hands resting on the edge of the table, not in your lap); E. 5

19. **True** or **False**: In many Asian, Arabic, and African homes, you may be invited to sit on the floor to eat.

ANSWER: True. For example, if you are invited to a Saudi's home, you may sit upon cushions on the floor to eat. Be sure to only use your right hand, and do not expect constant conversation during the meal.

20. Seating arrangements are strict in some countries. **True or False**: As in North America, an honored guest in China sits to the right of the host.

   ANSWER: False. The honored guest would sit directly across from the host. The least important people sit next to the host, and the second and third most important guests sit to the right and left of the guest of honor.

   We look forward to hearing your experiences with dining, drinking, and delicacies as well! Please visit www.kissbowor shakehands.com for further quizzes, contests, and our international dining blog.

APPENDIX B

DANGEROUS DIVERSIONS AND RELIABLE TRADE RESOURCES

International trade is so complicated that even experienced managers can get caught in global scams. Despite your product being sold and the buyer's check clearing, you may be amazed at what can go wrong. Joanna Savvides, the former president of the World Trade Center of Greater Philadelphia, has seen a multitude of dubious practices. She offered this anecdote on one hazard involving "diverters."

Pricing is always a sensitive issue—but in international markets, it is critical to establish careful, secure guidelines to protect your products.

Multinational firms often sell their products to their own subsidiaries in different countries. This is done via the "transfer price method," which is based on cost and a small margin (3 to 5 percent). The subsidiary then fulfills orders for that region of the world. Sales managers on both sides need to be very careful to assure that their product is not being "sold" at an unusually low export price.

A problem with a transfer occurred when the UK subsidiary of a major food manufacturer in the United States received an exceptionally large purchase order from Afghanistan. The size of the order (several 40-foot containers) was attractive, but the buyer insisted on a very low price for the "poor people of Afghanistan who like US products!"

A substantial discount was agreed upon, and the product was delivered by the US plant to Newark, New Jersey, for shipment directly to Afghanistan.

The UK office was able to sell at such a low fee because of its transfer pricing from the parent company. Unfortunately, the product never made it to Afghanistan. Indeed, the buyer never intended to ship it to Afghanistan. The "diverters" who placed the bogus order absconded with the shipment at the port of Newark and redirected the delivery to discount chain stores in the southern part of the United States!

Subsequently, the director of international sales received a highly agitated call from the Southern US region's sales director. "You're killing us down here!" he complained. "Why are you dumping product at huge discounts in our region?"

The international director at the US headquarters tracked the shipment (or lack thereof) and traced the trail to Florida. The Afghan buyer was working for a diverter in Miami!

At the same time, the international director contacted other export managers in the food industry and found that many of them had similar situations at the same time. Ultimately, the authorities were contacted, and an entire criminal ring was exposed. Several convictions resulted.

Overall, enabling diversions via low pricing is a bad strategy. The margin is made by a third party instead of any division of the company. Diverted product may end up in markets where there is no distribution or marketing preparation and eventually can harm the brand in that specific market. Always know your customers and your distributors. If you ever have any doubt as to the destination of the goods, sell it CIF (cost, insurance, and freight)—in other words, delivered to the intended destination. This will avoid surprises and prohibit unscrupulous individuals from escaping with your goods and your profits!

If you are considering trading in new markets, a multitude of resources can help you develop a solid global export plan. Always begin with the deepest, free sources: governmental agencies. Every nation in this book has an international trade department, which exists to promote trade with the country and increase exports. It is incredibly easy to type "export" and the name of your own country into an Internet search engine and then follow the leads. For example, when you enter "export UK" into a Google search, the results show an excellent series of links, starting with the UK Trade and Investment website (http://www.ukti.gov.uk) and the British Chambers of Commerce global trade site (http://www.britishchambers.org.uk).

In the United States, the International Trade Administration's Export.gov website (http://www.export.gov) provides a portal to all export-related assistance and market information offered by the federal government. It provides trade leads, free export counseling, help with the export process, and more.

The next US site you should research is a Department of Commerce website called BuyUSA.gov (http://www.buyusa.gov). Here is a bit of data culled directly from the site:

> BuyUSA.gov is the US Commercial Service site, which is the trade promotion unit of the International Trade Administration. The US Commercial Service is a global network of 1,800 trade professionals located in more than 250 cities worldwide, dedicated to assisting US exporters and supporting US business interests abroad. In the United States, the US Commercial Service operates an extensive network of Export Assistance Centers that offer companies easy access and efficient response to exporting and international trade inquiries. Overseas, the Commercial Service is present in nearly 80 countries, representing more than 95 percent of the world market for US exports.

You can find more specific assistance in each country as well. For example, the US Commercial Service in Argentina (CSA) is co-located with the US Embassy in Argentina. Its mission is to create jobs in the United States by advancing commercial opportunities in Argentina and assisting firms to export US products and services. CSA has developed many services designed specifically to assist companies to do business in Argentina.

Additionally, you will want to reference the US Department of State's resources (http://www.state.gov). The State Department disseminates background notes, a directory of Key Officers of Foreign Service posts, and daily press briefings.

For security information, monitor the Bureau of Consular Affairs travel information at http://www.travel.state.gov, which offers travel warnings and Consular Affairs publications containing information on obtaining passports and planning a safe trip. Also, the Overseas Security Advisory Council's website (http://www.osac.gov) provides security information and regional news relevant to US companies working abroad.

The website of the US Centers for Disease Control and Prevention (http://www.cdc.gov) gives the most recent health advisories, immunization recommendations or requirements, and advice on food and drinking-water safety for regions and countries.

In addition to the basic research that you can do on the Web, make sure you use existing relationships with your corporation's legal and accounting firms. They often have in-country representatives who can help you develop contacts, vet potential distributors, and set up appointments. And of course, utilize the World Trade Centers Association, chambers of commerce, and major associations in your industry segments—directories of all these are available on the Internet.

INDEX

ABOUT THE AUTHORS

Terri Morrison and **Wayne A. Conaway** are coauthors of nine books, including *Kiss, Bow, or Shake Hands: The Bestselling Guide to Doing Business in More than Sixty Countries* (a *Library Journal* Best Business Books winner with more than 275,000 copies sold), and *Dun & Bradstreet's Guide to Doing Business Around the World*.

Terri Morrison is president of Getting Through Customs, the developers of the *Kiss, Bow, or Shake Hands* digital product now offered through McGraw-Hill. She conducts seminars in intercultural communications, diversity, and globalization. Clients include AT&T, the American Bar Association, American Express, Boeing, Deloitte Touche Tohmatsu, E. I. du Pont de Nemours, Franklin Templeton Investments, IBM, Microsoft, NATO, the National Association of Realtors, and many universities.

Both Terri Morrison and Wayne A. Conaway have appeared repeatedly on National Public Radio, Public Radio International, and many other media.

Wayne A. Conaway has also written articles on a wide variety of subjects. He is currently the president of the Brandywine Valley Writers Group and vice president of the Main Line Writers Group. Both organizations support writers in the Philadelphia, Pennsylvania, area.

We welcome your feedback on this book and on all our materials, whether it supports or diverges from our data. If you would like further information on our books, seminars, or the digital *Kiss, Bow, or Shake Hands* product, feel free to contact Terri Morrison by e-mail (TerriMorrison@kissboworshakehands.com), by telephone (610-725-1040), or by visiting our website (www.kissboworshakehands.com).

Open **Markets**, Open **Borders**, Open **Minds** with Essential Knowledge for Doing Business with People from Around the Globe—**Kiss, Bow, or Shake Hands**

Do you know what drives the local economies in the BRIC countries?

In which countries does a "yes" answer actually mean no?

At what point at a meeting in China is it considered polite to start talking business?

Knowing the answers to these and other questions when doing business globally isn't just trivia; in today's fast-paced borderless economy, it's a necessity.

Kiss, Bow, or Shake Hands is the digital product for Doing Business Around the World with instant access and downloadable content on more than 70 countries, including:

- Country Background

- Business Practices and Protocols

- Cultural Notes and Key Phrases in Local Languages—with interactive Cultural IQ quizzes to help you memorize key facts.

Learn more at http://www.kissbowshakehands.com

For a free trial to see how Kiss, Bow, or Shake Hands can help your business do more business anywhere in the world, contact Chaun Hightower: **Chaunfayta_hightower@mcgraw-hill.com**